Claude Monet

1840–1926

Claude Monet

1840–1926

Charles F. Stuckey

With the assistance of Sophia Shaw

Thames and Hudson

The Art Institute of Chicago

Claude Monet: 1840–1926 was published in conjunction with the exhibition of the same title, organized by The Art Institute of Chicago and presented from July 22 through November 26, 1995.

The exhibition and catalogue were made possible by a grant from Ameritech.

Ameritech

The exhibition was supported by an indemnity from the Federal Council on the Arts and Humanities.

Copublished by The Art Institute of Chicago and Thames and Hudson

First published in hardcover in the United States of America in 1995 by Thames and Hudson Inc., 500 Fifth Avenue, New York, New York 10110

ISBN: 0-500-09246-X

Library of Congress Catalog Card Number: 94-61569

Catalogue text and photographs researched and developed by Nina Gordon and Sophia Shaw, Department of Twentieth-Century Painting and Sculpture
Exhibition checklist and photography assembled by Barbara Mirecki, Department of Twentieth-Century Painting and Sculpture

The Publications Department of The Art Institute of Chicago
Susan F. Rossen, Executive Director
Edited by Faith Brabenec Hart, Britt Salvesen, and Robert V. Sharp, Associate Director of Publications
Production supervised by Katherine Houck Fredrickson, Associate Director of Publications—Production
Designed by Ed Marquand with assistance from Tomarra LeRoy, Marquand Books, Inc., Seattle
Map designed by Vikki Leib

Printed and bound by CS Graphics, Singapore

Frontispiece: Pierre-Auguste Renoir, *Portrait of Claude Monet*, 1875. Oil on canvas; 85 × 60.5 cm, 33½ × 25⅝ in. Musée d'Orsay, Paris, Bequest of Mr. and Mrs. Raymond Koechlin, 1931 (RF 3666)

Contents

Sponsor's Foreword

A century ago, Claude Monet was in the midst of an artistic career that spanned more than sixty years, and the world continues to admire this brilliant artist for the exquisite body of work he produced and for his bold and innovative style. From another culture and another time, Monet communicates with us, sharing not only the images he saw, but also his impressions of continually changing natural light and movement.

Ameritech celebrates excellence in all facets of communication, so we are particularly pleased to underwrite The Art Institute of Chicago's extraordinary exhibition of Monet's work. Drawing first upon the many paintings by Monet in its own collection, including *On the Bank of the Seine, Bennecourt* and *The Beach at Sainte-Adresse,* the Art Institute has gathered more than 150 paintings from public and private collections throughout the world for the first such American exhibition in four decades—and, in fact, the largest Monet retrospective ever assembled.

Whether you call Chicago home, or are just visiting this great city, the men and women of Ameritech join me in welcoming you to this once-in-a-lifetime experience. We hope that you enjoy the exhibition and that you respond to Claude Monet's magnificent ability to communicate his artistic vision with each of us.

Richard C. Notebaert
Chairman and Chief Executive Officer
Ameritech

Foreword

The wealth of new information on Claude Monet that has been brought together in this catalogue has added an additional dimension to our present opportunity to realize the most comprehensive museum retrospective ever of this great artist's work. The exhibition brings together the finest examples from the full range of Monet's many subjects—extraordinary works from every period of his career—assembled through the generosity of over 100 public and private collections internationally. We are confident that even visitors who remember the Art Institute's 1975 exhibition "Paintings by Monet," or more recently, the exhibition "Monet in the '90s: The Series Paintings" will encounter fresh surprises and enrich their understanding of favorite works.

Naturally, considering the number of masterpieces that Monet painted in his long career, this exhibition is missing as many key works as it proudly contains. Most obviously, no museum retrospective can include the artist's crowning achievement, the ensemble of mural-scale paintings of water lilies that since 1927 have been glued to the walls of the Orangerie in Paris (at the request of Monet himself, who was fearful that they might be removed as taste in art changed). Although these canvases are by definition, then, untransportable, it may come as small consolation to Chicagoans that officials of the Art Institute journeyed to Giverny in 1920 to make a serious offer to buy these works, two years before Monet donated them to the French nation.

Several outstanding Monet paintings were unavailable because they have been donated to museums on condition that they never be lent. A similar policy has become necessary for a handful of Monet's paintings that have become icons for the museums that are fortunate to possess them—works such as *Impression, Sunrise,* perhaps the artist's single most famous work, now understandably treated as a permanent fixture of the Musée Marmottan in Paris. As testimony to Monet's technical skill, few of his paintings have deteriorated in physical condition to the point where shipment is exceptionally risky; yet among this handful are works that belong in an ideal retrospective: the decorative, mid-1870s *Luncheon in the Garden,*

which Gustave Caillebotte bequeathed to the French National Museums; the ultramodern *Poplars* painting left to the Metropolitan Museum of Art, New York, by the Havemeyers; and the large 1916 *Water Lilies* originally bought by Baron Matsukata and now at the National Museum of Western Art in Tokyo.

Such unavoidable omissions notwithstanding, this retrospective exhibition, and the catalogue that accompanies it, have been conceived to provoke a reconsideration of this important artist and to foster a renewed appreciation of his legacy. Intended as a basic reference book, the catalogue includes color reproductions of every work in the exhibition, as well as reproductions of Monet's best paintings unavailable for loan. The principal text consists of an extensive chronology designed to bring together in an accessible and much-needed format the greatest amount of information about one of the world's best-loved artists whose profound impact on art of this century is only now being fully understood.

James N. Wood
Director and President
The Art Institute of Chicago

Claude Monet: 1840–1926

Monet's Achievements

Monet was the leader in one of the most sweeping revolutions in the history of art: Impressionism. With Edouard Manet, Paul Cézanne, Edgar Degas, Berthe Morisot, Camille Pissarro, Pierre-Auguste Renoir, and Alfred Sisley, Monet made art address the previously unacknowledged, yet most commonplace, kind of visual experience: the glance. As it defines these artists' primary goal, the term "impression" signified the sensory information registered on the retina prior to cogitation of any sort (the eye, for example, sees tiny black spots before it recognizes them as faraway pedestrians). "When you go out to paint, try to forget what objects you have before you, a tree, a house, a field or whatever," Monet explained to an American neighbor in Giverny, "merely think here is a little square of blue, here an oblong of pink, here a streak of yellow, and paint it just as it looks to you, the exact color and shape, until it gives you your own naive impression of the scene before you."[1] He later claimed that he wished he might share the experience of a blind person suddenly granted the power of sight. On guard against the blinding habits of looking at things in preconceived ways, Monet studied and collected Japanese prints, made in innocence of the premises of Western pictorial traditions. For Monet and his colleagues, the basic truths of visual experience —here "a little square of blue . . . here a streak of yellow"— could be best recognized in the glance, even though its brief and fragmentary character was at odds with the accepted idea that great art address eternal truths. But representing the subject of this glance posed an impossible challenge for these artists, now forced to recognize the discrepancy between the instantaneous moment required for perception and the longer time necessary to record manually its contents in pictorial terms. While it extended the traditional norms of Realism in art, Impressionist truth became predicated on painting with unprecedented speed, using skipping, flickering brushstrokes that themselves revealed unexpected abstract rhythms and harmonies. At first debunked as childishly unskilled, the stenographic nature of Impressionist brushwork eventually gave license to new realms of automatic and purely abstract painting.

Starting as early as the mid-1880s, within a decade of the historic first group exhibition of the Impressionists in 1874, many ambitious young artists, including Paul Gauguin, Vincent van Gogh, and Georges Seurat, sought to escape what seemed to them to be thoughtlessly virtuoso "retinal painting" —descriptive of external facts but disregarding fundamental invisible realms of feelings and intuitions. Although Monet's works made after the mid-1880s, when more controversial avant-garde art had moved away from Impressionism, were praised extravagantly by critics and avidly sought after by turn-of-the-century collectors, they have not been included in the standard history of twentieth-century art, which traces a rapid succession of breakthrough modes. In recent years, scholars have too often dismissed Monet's widely reproduced works as luxury goods by a great artist who prostituted his integrity to the marketplace. At best, art historians have relegated the majority of Monet's mature paintings to a limbo for masterpieces made too late to matter much. They have preferred, instead, the late works of his friend Cézanne, complex diagrams of which have become paradigms for twentieth-century purists, as if such diagrams might not be just as easily superimposed on Monet's works, both early and late. Generally speaking, Monet's achievements beyond the mid-1880s have so far been counted in only two respects. First, historians of twentieth-century art have recognized that Monet's successful realization of painting and exhibiting works in series was an impetus for the later evolution of seriality as a standard mode of presenting many styles of art, from the color field paintings of Mark Rothko to the pop silkscreens of Andy Warhol to the minimalist sculpture of Donald Judd. Second, art historians have acknowledged that Monet's manner of sweeping brushwork, developed for his late mural paintings, was an important precedent for post-World War II abstract gestural painting by artists ranging from Jackson Pollock to Joan Mitchell.

When his life's work is considered from start to finish, Monet's output after the early 1880s emerges as far more than a lengthy coda to his pioneering activity of the 1870s. Although Monet did continue throughout his life to extend the premises of classic Impressionism that he had helped to invent, it seems more significant that he achieved two additional and no less important bodies of work, each of which rivals the best art made by younger painters belonging to first and second Post-Impressionist generations. Monet's richly painted works in series of the 1880s and 1890s, in which he treats the glance subject unhurriedly and in meditative detail, are as original, ambitious, and profound as anything he had attempted before. Now that the polemical dust of history has settled, his beloved post-1900 *Water Lilies* paintings should be acknowledged as daring and influential, on a par with the most highly acclaimed early masterpieces of Pablo Picasso and Henri Matisse.

Like so many twentieth-century artists who have stressed "nothing" as the ultimate theme, Monet conceived his primary subject as empty space. Beginning in the 1880s, Monet stressed that his greatest interest was to depict what he called the "envelope" of interactive colored light previously taken for granted by artists who focused on people and things. Stretching from near-at-hand to faraway, this transparent envelope was the most complex, poetic, and animating component of visual reality. When they are presented together, the paintings in Monet's famous series variations demonstrate that the color-flooded envelope constantly transforms how and thus what we see.

Ever more poetic and philosophical as he matured artistically, Monet used his unique understanding of the empty envelope as a vehicle to comment on the basic contingencies of all experience: space and time. Already in 1877, Monet had conceived his series of paintings of the Saint-Lazare train station in Paris (see cat. nos. 49–51) as references to these abstractions. Railroad travel put previous notions of time on a timetable, and it mechanically linked locales near and far with what was then astonishing speed and ease. Monet's Normandy coast paintings of the 1880s, which stress the manifest interactions of solar and tidal time, likewise transformed everyday Impressionist Realism into commentaries about the elemental verities of nature. In these works his subject is the full spectrum of time, observed as a succession of instantaneous truths of quickly moving light and water acting upon rocks and cliffs that were sculpted over centuries by relentless geological forces (see cat. nos. 63, 69–71, 79, 82–84). Like a manmade counterpart to such weathered cliffs, the façade of Rouen Cathedral—a monument to eternity as the bedrock of religious dogma—is the subject with which Monet made the scope of his meditations on time most explicit. In his *Rouen Cathedral* paintings (see cat. no. 105), Monet recorded the modern clock over the medieval structure's central portal (see fig. no. 61) as nothing more than a thick disc of color, suggesting the inadequacy of this device to assess the measureless majesty of time revealed in ever-changing individual perception.[2]

The term *féerique* (fairytale-like), denoting exotic fantasy when used to characterize literary works, entered Monet's vocabulary in 1884, when he began to specialize in paintings of uncommonly brilliant light, in which physical objects appear dematerialized into fantasies. These works extend the original goals of Impressionism from prosaic pictorial journalism to meditative nature poetry. While this change was immediately clear to most critics, modern art historians have tended to leave Monet's late works in the *féerique* mode (including his opulently colored London views so immediately influential for the young Fauve painters) out of their accounts of twentieth-century art history. As Monet perfected serial working methods in the 1880s and 1890s, his classic 1870s Impressionist mode of roughly stenographic brushwork became remarkably refined; his paintings evolved from quick observations into prolonged meditations, analogous to Marcel Proust's prose with its astounding slow-motion appreciations of fleeting, idle thoughts.

Monet's specialization in landscape has, perhaps, unfairly disqualified him from being called a twentieth-century master. By the end of the nineteenth century, it seemed to ambitious young painters that Monet and the Impressionists had effectively exhausted the possibilities of landscape painting. Consequently, landscape has usually been ignored as a category in histories of early twentieth-century art. Contemporaneous with Monet's Giverny works, Cézanne's 1906 *Bathers* compositions, on the contrary, are applauded by advocates of figure painting as the ultimate genre, since Cézanne's example pointed the way for Picasso and Matisse to link modern art with the figure paintings of Nicolas Poussin and the Old Masters. If one can set aside the prejudice in favor of figure painting, Monet's *Water Lilies* deserve to be recognized not merely as the culmination of nineteenth-century Impressionism, but also as revolutionary twentieth-century works, unsurpassed in their persistent and wide-ranging influence on the visual language of our century.[3]

Monet cropped the ostensible subject matter of these works to the smallest fragment of landscape ever used, effectively reducing landscape to the scale associated with still-life painting: his rare water plants play the role of bouquets, and the pond's surface acts as a tabletop. Rippled by breezes and the vibrating envelope of light, the pond's moving surface as represented by Monet is the subdued counterpart to the jagged rhythms invented at the same time by the Cubists and Futurists, who were intent on extending the discontinuous spatial indications in Cézanne's works. For spatial interpenetration, however, Monet's *Water Lilies* were arguably unprecedented when he painted them: superimposed on the mirror-like fragment of space under Monet's observation, the upside-down reflections of sky and treetops intrude distant space into nearby space, coalescing up and down, in front of and behind. As a

nineteenth-century painter, Monet had been obsessed with the parity between the world and its pictorial reflection on the surface of the Seine river; images incorporating both the riverbank and its upside-down reflection were among his hallmark compositions before 1900. Deciding, however, as he stared at his private water garden, that a reflection disconnected from its causal source would be a still richer subject, Monet made one of the most profound pictorial discoveries of the new century: the possibility that a single monochrome plane could evoke an inexhaustible field of all-encompassing space. In his *Water Lilies* paintings, Monet reduced conventional pictorial composition to modulated fields of only one or two tones each, creating all-green, all-blue, interlocking blue and green, and green and orange planes some fifty years before other painters equaled such daring. Decoratively accenting these flowing planes, the more or less uniformly shaped water lily blossoms introduce an irregular grid structure into twentieth-century painting. Taken separately or in tandem, the planar fields and the modularly arranged water lilies gave younger artists two new and seemingly inexhaustible pictorial modes. Monet's direct heirs, too often unacknowledged, include: Matisse, Sonia Delaunay, Robert Delaunay, Constantin Brancusi, Marcel Duchamp (yes, *The Large Glass*, with its "blossoming"), Jean Arp (the famous *Collage with Squares Arranged According to the Laws of Chance*), Piet Mondrian, Joan Miró (the so-called *Magnetic Field* paintings), Max Ernst (the *Shell-Flowers*), Yves Tanguy, Alexander Calder, Ellsworth Kelly, Yves Klein, and Robert Smithson. Monet may have been the greatest Impressionist, but looking at all his works, from his first to his last, it becomes clear that his contribution goes much further.

This Catalogue and the Monet Literature

More is known about Monet's life than about that of any other Impressionist artist. Only for Pissarro, Auguste Rodin, and van Gogh are anywhere near comparable records available. The present knowledge of Monet is the result of scholarly efforts during the last thirty years, most of all Daniel Wildenstein's model five-volume folio catalogue raisonné of Monet's roughly 2,000 surviving oil paintings and some 600 pencil notebook sketches, caricatures, and pastels. Wildenstein's publication also provides the definitive biography of Monet, incorporating an abundance of new documentary materials (none more important than some 3,000 letters written by Monet) and over

4,000 footnotes that acknowledge numerous previously published and unpublished commentaries about the artist, particularly rich in first-hand accounts by family members and close friends. An in-depth introduction and a basic reference resource for the general reader and specialist alike, *Claude Monet: 1840–1926* is intended before all else to be a reader's guide to Wildenstein's complex, expensive publication in French. As the Wildenstein volumes appeared, beginning in 1974, they inspired a new generation of Monet scholars, and we have tried to incorporate in this catalogue the full range of information included in numerous recent publications, many of them extensive studies of particular segments of his career.

A comprehensive chronology offered the best way to contribute meaningfully to the rich literature by organizing a wealth of information in a format that can be read from beginning to end or consulted for background material related to any particular question or issue. Like any form of historical writing, the chronology is an imperfect tool. First of all, a chronology is only a partial record, limited to documented events; events that were not recorded might be of equal or greater importance than the documented facts. For example, Sisley and Renoir were among Monet's closest associates, yet they play relatively minor roles in this chronology as compared to Pissarro or the politician Georges Clemenceau, who kept more records. Second, interrelated events as recorded in a chronology often occur as delayed reactions decades apart from each other, so that an incident in the 1860s might not make its full impact until the 1880s or later. Hopefully, the index to this catalogue will help readers to connect chronologically dispersed events.

With such limitations of the chronology in mind, the following introduction addresses several important issues for which documentation is slight. Indeed, the lack of documentation seems to have marginalized these very issues, as scholars inevitably concentrate on examining known historical events and documents rather than uncovering new information. Some isolated bits of documentation in the chronology (about Monet's relationship to Cézanne, for example, or the sorts of frames he used) call for elaboration, even if the only way beyond the limitations of the historical record is speculation. And the relative density of documentation for some years stimulates curiosity about years when less took place. Does the amount of available information indicate whether a particular period has greater or lesser significance, or is the amount of

information merely an accident of history? The lack of detailed information about Monet's artistic achievements after the classic years of Impressionism (1874 through 1886), for example, suggests that he spent the last half of his career in increasing isolation. Yet during these years he actually grew as a painter, his interests widened by contacts with progressive art journalists who supported a new generation of artists, both French and foreign. The following brief accounts of important unstudied topics should, therefore, provide counterweights to this catalogue's extensive chronology. Future Monet scholars can change and expand our understanding only by acknowledging the facts still off the record.

Monet and the Landscape Painting Revolution

Although by the end of his life Monet was determined to be represented in the Louvre as a figure painter, and although he took the greatest satisfaction in his paintings of Rouen Cathedral and London's Houses of Parliament, he was primarily a landscape painter, almost exclusively so after the early 1880s. Yet Monet studies often evaluate his achievements in terms of non-landscape issues, most of all Baudelaire's call for artists of the 1860s to paint the modern life around them. From such a point of view, Monet's mature landscapes without figures can seem ideologically vapid. Yet these same works, considered in relationship to the evolution of pure landscape painting, which underwent technological transformations around mid-century, extend important logistical and thematic notions of space (the "envelope") and time ("series"). Unfortunately, the history of landscape painting as a whole, and in particular the history of landscape painting in France in the nineteenth century, has gone relatively unstudied, though for understandable reasons: few sales records survive from the first half of the century, and the general titles under which landscapes were catalogued at contemporary art exhibitions has made it impossible in most cases to know what works were exhibited when. As a result, it has been the figure and history paintings of Eugéne Delacroix, Camille Corot, and Gustave Courbet—landscape artists Monet deeply admired—which have been most studied by scholars. Which landscapes the young Monet saw displayed publicly or privately are unknown, and even the Daubigny landscape that he briefly owned can no longer be identified. Lack of specific knowledge about French landscape painting around

1860 notwithstanding, examination of the topic is crucial to a fair appreciation of Monet's pre- and post-Impressionist works.

He was born Oscar-Claude Monet and signed himself "Oscar" until around 1864, judging from the few early works that survive. The shift to "Claude" may signal the artist's ambition to rival the most acclaimed of all French landscape painters, Claude Lorrain. This seventeenth-century master's realistic and poetic treatment of light guided the rise of modern landscape art in Great Britain a century later, which, after Waterloo, in turn inspired French painters to embrace the genre. Armed with lightweight materials, pads of paper, and pencils or watercolors, Claude and his followers, including J. M. W. Turner and John Constable, hiked the countryside to make detailed notes about natural motifs that they would later execute in oils in their indoor studios during the winter months when out-of-doors work was difficult. The practice of landscape painting changed dramatically around the time of Monet's birth, thanks in part to the proliferation of railroad connections enabling artists to reach favorite sites quickly. But more important was the manufacture of portable tin tubes for oil paints and the discovery of a wide range of new chemical pigments to package this way. As Renoir's son Jean pointed out, "[E]asily transportable paints in tubes . . . led us to paint directly from nature. Without tube paint there would have been no Cézanne, no Monet, no Sisley, no Pissarro, none of what the critics had to call Impressionism."[4]

Landscape painters, unlike figure painters, could avoid the considerable expenses involved in maintaining large studios, paying models, and renting or buying costumes. And landscape painters could also avoid the insulation from real life inherent in studio art. But making a living from landscape involved unprecedented logistical problems. Largely unknown to figure painters, the costs in time and money of transportation and lodging were overheads that nearly brought Monet to ruin during the 1860s, even though he was working at relatively inexpensive sites on modest-scale canvases (which he had to replicate and enlarge afterwards in the studio so that they could compete with non-landscape paintings submitted to the annual contemporary art Salons). Working in groups at colonies like Honfleur and Fontainebleau, landscape painters could share some of the costs, while providing moral support to one another. But sites around such colonies were soon too overworked to appeal to painters determined to stand apart from colleagues.

A day's work inevitably involved setting out early on foot, if possible carting paints, relatively small canvases, a large sunshade, and food. The time involved in getting to and from the site significantly shortened the workday of a landscape painter compared to that of one who worked in a studio. The weather was also a potential time waster: winds could blow canvases off easels and ruin works in progress, rain could halt work for days at a time, and sudden changes in light conditions could alter every color to be matched. Finally, there were pests, ranging from curious passersby to biting insects. Landscape painters of Monet's generation had to overcome such handicaps so that out-of-doors landscape painting could be as profitable on an hourly basis as conventional studio painting.

Roughly speaking, the tactical problem was to bring the studio along to the landscape or to bring the landscape to the threshold of the studio. By 1852 the Long Island painter William Sidney Mount had conceived a horse-drawn "artist waggon" with windows, investing $141.62 in such a vehicle in 1861. In France, the breakthrough came in 1857, when Daubigny built a studio boat and made it the subject of a portfolio of etchings in 1862. Although limited to riverscape painting, the studio boat solved every logistical problem, and Monet acquired his own version in 1872, painting it fairly often as a sort of self-portrait by proxy. Seldom considered in Monet studies, these Daubigny works introduced what would become Monet's most important compositional mode: landscape motifs observed in tandem with their reflections on the river's surface, an approach that provoked meditations about the relationship between the three-dimensional world and its two-dimensional image.

Meanwhile, Courbet, who transported supplies to his favorite landscape sites in his native Franche-Comté on a donkey that he called Gérôme in mockery of the acclaimed Salon painter, made plans in 1859 to buy adjoining plots in his hometown of Ornans so that he could plant different varieties of trees around a never-realized studio and thus make landscape paintings without leaving home. Notwithstanding its status as an independent work of art, Monet's elaborate garden at Giverny was a response to the tactical problems of landscape painting similar to that proposed by Courbet.

Courbet is central to the history of landscape painting. A self-promoting innovator, Courbet in the 1860s sought to carry artistic realism to its practical limits. He demonstrated that the landscape painting season could go year round to include snowscapes, if the painter were strong and fast. In addition, he confronted the most mercurial subjects possible, like skittish deer and crashing waves, in order to demonstrate his unprecedented speed of eye and hand. Courbet's single most important innovation was working in series. His 1865 campaign at Trouville on the Normandy coast resulted in around two dozen similar beachscapes, many exhibited together at a commercial gallery in Paris the following year. Guy de Maupassant saved precious information about Courbet's 1869 campaign at Etretat, where he had rented a beach house, the window of which overlooked the crashing surf.[5] Converting the limitations of a temporary studio space into an advantage, Courbet painted from his studio window a single view over and over, rather than using time and effort to seek out a variety of motifs.

Monet quickly responded to Courbet's innovations. For example, he employed Courbet's Etretat practice for his *Rouen Cathedral* paintings and his London series, made indoors while looking out a window. Although other would-be landscapists of the early 1880s, including Ernest-Ange Duez and William Merritt Chase, fashioned temporary shelters of netting or glass to work on beachscapes, Monet usually preferred the freedom to harvest many different motifs in his chosen away-from-home locales. To avoid wasting travel time on a single painting when working unsheltered, Monet modified the portable studio concept, leaving shelter behind but bringing along a studio stock of art supplies. Monet hired porters to transport groups of canvases to his chosen site and then to return them to his hotel with the paint still wet. To get the paintings back to Giverny and eventually to Paris for exhibition and sale, Monet had special slotted shipping crates made. Essential to Monet's landscape campaigns, these crates nevertheless imposed restrictions on the artist, since only certain standard-size canvases fit into them.[6]

With plentiful supplies handy, Monet could keep working even when light conditions changed, simply by replacing one work in progress on his easel with another. Instead of beginning a given work and carrying it through to completion, Monet began several works together and these evolved on subsequent days, so that little time was wasted waiting for certain light conditions to return. As a result of this serial painting practice, Monet not only saved the time he would have spent traveling to various remote sites, he also bought time for his portrayals of brief light effects. In theory, a given effect would recur on subsequent workdays. Such repeated opportunities to observe and record the same instantaneous light effect day after day, multiplied tenfold or more, extended the accuracy and subtlety of Impressionist out-of-doors painting. Moreover, Monet's pragmatic determination to reconsider an instantaneous perception as it recurred on subsequent days would lead him by the mid-1880s to develop concepts about time and visual sensation, moving his art beyond his initial Impressionist ideas.

Monet and Cézanne

There has been a considerable tendency throughout our century for art historians to study artists separately in monographs and retrospectives. These have provided valuable new material about the evolutionary development of single figures, but now the dialogues between artists need to be addressed. For example, one of the most intriguing gaps in our present record of Impressionism is the relationship between Monet, the most fully documented Impressionist, and Cézanne, the least documented one. When they met is not known; it was probably in the 1860s through Manet's eloquent advocate, Emile Zola, Cézanne's boyhood friend. The great Cézanne scholar John Rewald expressed surprise that it was Cézanne, rather than Renoir, who brought the collector Victor Chocquet to meet Monet in Argenteuil in 1876.[7] By then Monet may have already owned the first of around fifteen works by Cézanne that he would eventually collect, a small pastoral scene that appears to date from the early 1870s, which Monet accepted as partial payment from a dealer for a Bougival landscape (cat. no. 19). Otherwise, aside from their participation in the first Impressionist group shows, there are no verbal or visual records of exchange between the eventual giants of Impressionism until Christmastime 1883, when Renoir and Monet, during a brief trip to the Mediterranean, stopped to visit Cézanne at L'Estaque.

What was discussed at this summit meeting of avant-garde landscape painters is unknown, but the paintings that Monet started a few weeks later in Bordighera, Italy (see cat. no. 77) —some with views framed by interlocking trees looking out over rooftops to the water, others with simple rustic structures observed as geometric forms in lush garden landscapes, none with any figures—correspond more closely with Cézanne's work than with any of Monet's previous compositions. Since the dating of Cézanne's pictures during the late 1870s, 1880s, and 1890s can only be estimated from careful studies of his evolving style, whether or not the sudden change in Monet's works indicates a dramatic reaction to Cézanne's works at L'Estaque is far from certain. Ironically, recent scholars have categorized Monet's most Cézannesque Bordighera compositions as evidence of his blatant picture-postcard commercialism.

The question remains: who influenced whom? Did Cézanne ever see Monet's Bordighera paintings? Quite possibly. In July 1885, while many of these works were still in Giverny, Cézanne and his family visited the Renoirs at La Roche-Guyon. The visit was uncomfortable for Cézanne, who wrote to Zola asking for an invitation to nearby Medan. Awaiting an answer, the Cézannes left La Roche-Guyon and ended up staying for a week at a hotel in Vernon, across the Seine from Giverny. Presumably, Cézanne visited Monet at his new home and saw his recent works, including Normandy coastscapes, Bordighera landscapes, unresolved decorative still lifes related to a commission from the dealer Paul Durand-Ruel, and some paintings of haystacks in a neighboring field. Perhaps these last works elicited Cézanne's later comment: "[Monet] is a grand lord who treats himself to the haystacks that he likes. If he likes a little field he buys it. With a big flunky and some dogs that keep guard so that no one disturbs him. That's what I need."[8] Whatever the case, the many similarities in composition and coloring between Monet's paintings of the early 1880s and Cézanne's paintings of L'Estaque and Mont Sainte-Victoire (generally dated 1883–85 and 1885–87, respectively), should no longer be dismissed as coincidence.

Cézanne's documented direct contact with Monet from November 1894 to June 1895 apparently had enormous consequences for Cézanne. Monet had acquired a still life by Cézanne for his personal collection only months before Cézanne checked into the Hôtel Baudy in Giverny for the last three weeks of November. At the time, Monet was preoccupied with justifying the controversially high prices he demanded from dealers for his still-unexhibited *Rouen Cathedral* paintings. Perhaps to gain support for his stance, Monet invited his influential friends Clemenceau, Gustave Geffroy, Octave Mirbeau, and Rodin to Giverny for lunch on November 28. A secondary motive may have been to introduce these powerful figures to the visiting Cézanne, whose eccentric behavior that day (for example, falling on his knees before the decorated Rodin) has been often noted. In any event, the luncheon led to Cézanne's offering to paint a portrait of the critic Geffroy in his Belleville study, a project that required nearly daily

sessions from April to June the following year. Presumably, Monet and his art would have been an important topic of discussion between artist and sitter. This portrait project, having brought Cézanne to Paris, permitted him to visit Monet's large one-artist exhibition at Durand-Ruel's gallery, which included twenty *Rouen Cathedral* variations and six variations of snow-covered Mount Kolsaas, painted in emulation of Hiroshige during Monet's recent trip to Norway. The parallels between this series of mountaintop views and Cézanne's own late Mont Sainte-Victoire variations are self-evident. Less clear are the equally provocative parallels between Monet's all-foreground views of the stone facade of Rouen Cathedral and the all-foreground paintings and watercolors of rockfaces at the Bibemus quarry and at nearby Château Noir begun by Cézanne shortly afterward.

What direct or indirect role Monet played in arranging the historic first exhibition of Cézanne's works in November 1895 at the gallery of Ambroise Vollard, whom Cézanne did not yet know, has scarcely been considered.[9] As a collector of the so far neglected artist, however, Monet was a pioneer. He bought works at the first Vollard show and at regular intervals afterwards. Cézanne, though, was unable to afford a Monet, despite his expressed desire to own one. Monet's brisk and sophisticated style is inevitably considered as the antithesis of Cézanne's laboriously analytical one. Monet nevertheless deserves to be treated at length in the literature about Cézanne that has so far ignored him.

Monet and the Americans

The relentless nationalistic thinking structured into art museums and writing about art has inevitably marginalized the subject of Monet's interactions with foreign artists and collectors. Americans have been Monet-crazed for more than a century, but there is surprisingly little record of the huge role Americans played in Monet's career.[10] The near total absence of information about the Americans in Monet's life leaves a big blank in our picture of the otherwise well-documented artist.

When and how Monet met James McNeill Whistler, the first important American in his life, is unknown. They were both students of Charles Gleyre and both friends of Courbet. The similarity between Whistler's nearly impossible to date *Nocturnes* of the early 1870s and Monet's closely related *Impression, Sunrise* of around 1872 makes one wonder what ideas may have been exchanged between the two during Monet's wartime exile in London in 1870–71 or shortly afterwards when both artists were represented by Durand-Ruel, who showed the Frenchman's paintings in London and the American's in Paris. Monet's astounding idea, conceived in Montgeron in the Seine valley in late 1876, to devote a large decorative panel to white turkeys (cat. no. 46) seems irresistibly connected to Whistler's commission that same year in London to decorate a room with images of peacocks. Later, Whistler's London exhibitions installed in gallery spaces painted yellow and decorated with yellow furnishings might have inspired Monet to fashion an all-yellow dining room with yellow furnishings at Giverny.

In the late 1870s many other Americans began to enter the Monet story. Having been instrumental around 1877 in the first sale of work by Monet to an American collector, Mary Cassatt bought a work at the 1878 Ernest Hoschedé auction, less than a year before she joined the Impressionists in their fourth group show. These artists' active dialogue over decades has never been studied. Nor are we well informed about Monet's dialogue with John Singer Sargent, who, according to legend, introduced himself to Monet during the 1876 Impressionist exhibition and suddenly took up the new mode of painting. Only in 1885 does Sargent come downstage in the Monet drama. That year Sargent and Monet exhibited at the International Exhibition at the Georges Petit Gallery in Paris. Afterward, at Giverny, Sargent portrayed Monet at work on a painting of a haystack (fig. no. 46). By 1887 at the latest, Sargent, like Cassatt, began to collect and sell Monet works.

The year 1885 was a turning point in the story of Monet and the Americans. That summer, a man about whom nothing much is known, R. Austin Robertson, dined with Durand-Ruel in Paris.[11] Robertson represented a recently opened New York firm called the American Art Association, an entrepreneurial partnership that would revolutionize the international art market by bringing Impressionism to America, despite formidable U.S. customs duties then levied on imported works of art. Monet, who would benefit the most from the April 1886 New York group exhibition resulting from these 1885 negotiations, at first hated the prospect.

An inscription on a bird's egg collected by American painter Willard Metcalf indicates that he was in Giverny in May of that same crucial year, 1885. In 1887 Metcalf returned, with John Leslie Breck, William Blair Bruce, Louis Ritter, Theodore Robinson, Henry Fitch Taylor, and Theodore Wendel, to establish an English-speaking art colony at Monet's doorstep. Over the next several years, a growing group of Americans competed with Monet for the available landscape motifs in the neighborhood and greatly upset his household. "I could not make a study in the countryside without seeing myself surrounded by curious [Americans]. Easels and sun umbrellas sprouted around the garden like mushrooms. I was very annoyed and seriously thought about packing my bags [and leaving Giverny]," Monet wrote.[12] Monet's surviving output from the summers of 1887, 1888, and 1889 is negligible, consisting mainly of figure paintings for which the daughters of Alice Hoschedé (who would marry Monet in 1892) served as models. Although his own self-critical temperament—especially active as he ventured into what he conceived as an innovative hybrid figure-landscape mode—helps to explain the dramatic decrease in output, his need for privacy at work must also have been a big factor. Now more than ever, Monet was obliged to consider the creation of a garden that would function as a strictly private outdoor studio, and real (rather than painted) flowers presumably took up a great deal of his summers in the American-dominated late 1880s.

In early 1888 twenty-five-year-old Marthe Hoschedé fell into unrequited love with one of the "Yankees." By 1891 Monet had to ask two romantic-minded American painters to leave the village. One of these, Breck, had spent the summer on a series of fifteen *Wheatstacks* paintings remarkably similar in composition and concept to the group that Monet had just exhibited in Paris. In March 1892, when Suzanne Hoschedé announced her intention to marry Theodore Butler, Monet threatened to move away from Giverny. An enthusiast of the Nabis art of Edouard Vuillard, Pierre Bonnard, and others, Monet's stepson-in-law Butler presumably brought him into more active contact with 1890s decorative art, and the other Americans must have been sources of information about the volume and price levels of the American art market. Thus armed against manipulation by dealers, Monet expertly managed his own pricing and output and quickly made a personal fortune.

Sales to Americans boomed. James Fountain Sutton, a partner in the American Art Association that had co-sponsored the 1886 New York Impressionism exhibition, came to Giverny in July 1889, when the market for Monet works was especially active. Sutton's enormous support for Monet during the next dozen years is altogether unstudied. In 1893 Pissarro would claim that Sutton owned 120 Monet paintings, and in 1904 Boston collector Desmond Fitzgerald estimated that Sutton owned fifty. Not counting Durand-Ruel, no French collector loomed so large. Before the 1920s, only Ernest Hoschedé, Dr. Georges de Bellio, and Jean-Baptiste Faure owned thirty or more Monets (Faure owned around fifty; his support of Monet, like Sutton's, remains unstudied). Today, fewer than thirty works can be connected with Sutton. Perhaps U.S. customs duty records hold some of the answers to the gaps in provenance information.

Scarcely less significant, and as little documented, is the support of Bertha and Potter Palmer of Chicago, who bought thirty-three Monet works from Durand-Ruel alone between the summer of 1891 and the summer of 1893, apparently with some guidance by their equally little-documented art consultant, Sara Hallowell, who played an active role in exhibiting Impressionist art in Chicago in 1890 and again in 1893 as part of the World's Columbian Exposition. Why no works from the Palmer collection were included among the four Monets at that historic exhibition remains a mystery.

Decoration

Although Monet always used the term "decorations" when referring to the mural-scale *Water Lilies* paintings that obsessed him for the final twelve years of his career, the artist's role in the history of decorative painting is never addressed in monographic studies. Monet's final artistic testament, comparable in scope to the vast mural cycles associated with such acknowledged masters as Raphael, Tintoretto, and Peter Paul Rubens, ought to be understood as a delayed reaction to events separated by ten, twenty, or even fifty years from his final undertaking. Without a good history of late-nineteenth- and early twentieth-century French mural painting, however, the achievements of the greatest turn-of-the-century decorative artists, including Vuillard, Bonnard, Matisse, and Monet (all associated with the Bernheim-Jeune Gallery), will remain disconnected from the mainstream of modern art history.

Just before Monet left the Paris art world for military duty in Algeria in early 1861, he made a painting of his studio in which one wall is covered with a large decorative tapestry and the floor with a stylized flower-pattern carpet (fig. no. 3); these furnishings foreshadowed the artist's single-minded interest in decoration half a century later. Immediately after Monet's departure for Algeria, modern decorative painting

came of age in Paris. At the Salon, Pierre Puvis de Chavannes launched his career as a public muralist with enormous allegorical works, and in July 1861, Eugène Delacroix's last masterpieces, murals for a chapel in the church of Saint-Sulpice, were unveiled. As if to compete with the successes of these artists, by April 1862 Courbet expressed his ambition to make monumental modern-life paintings for such public buildings as churches and train stations.

Catching up with these events when he returned to Paris in late 1862, Monet soon undertook an unmarketable, architectural-scale (roughly 4 × 6 meters; 13 × 20 feet) modern-life painting, *Luncheon on the Grass* (cat. no. 5). Since this work was not finished in time for the 1866 Salon, it is not known whether Monet might have used the term "decoration" to describe it in the exhibition checklist. Likewise, it is unknown whether Monet would have applied the term to *Women in the Garden* (fig. no. 14), the Salon-scale (roughly 2.5 × 2 meters; 8 × 6½ feet) painting refused by the Salon selection jury the following year. No other works by any artist in the 1860s so closely prefigure the great 1890s architectural-scale projects of Maurice Denis and Vuillard.

After a lapse of ten years, Monet's ambitions as a decorative artist resurfaced at the Impressionist group exhibitions of 1876 and 1877. The earlier exhibition included a complex garden scene listed in the catalogue as *Decorative Panel*; and the next included a work listed as *The Turkeys (Unfinished Decoration)*, as well as the famous group of seven views of the Saint-Lazare train station in Paris, with which Monet initiated a hallmark mode of exhibiting decorative ensembles of similar paintings (cat. nos. 46 and 49–51). While *The Turkeys* (surely one of the first unfinished works ever exhibited) was commissioned by the Hoschedés as part of a dining-room ensemble, it nevertheless exemplifies a seldom-discussed effort around this time by Monet, Renoir, and Gustave Caillebotte to make large-scale works. These works have gone relatively unstudied, however, because they do not correspond with the notion of Impressionist paintings as portable, small-scale records of the first-hand observation of nature.

The ambition to work large at this time was probably related to the need for decorative art in the new public buildings being constructed to replace those destroyed during the Commune. Indeed, even Manet (who called Monet the "Raphael of water") was tempted by this opportunity, proposing in April 1879 to paint modern-life murals for the new Paris City Hall.

The following summer, Rodin was commissioned to make bronze doors *(The Gates of Hell)* for a proposed Museum of Decorative Arts. Such a museum, realized finally in 1895, had been the first priority of the Union Centrale des Beaux-Arts, organized in the 1860s to provide exhibition opportunities for artworks conceived as interior decor. By 1882 Antonin Proust, Manet's boyhood friend, had assumed leadership of the Union, which that spring held an important Salon of decorative art permitting painters to exhibit works too large for inclusion in the fine arts Salon. Among them were tapestries based on landscape paintings by recognized artists like Henri Joseph Harpignies, and a room ensemble of gray-toned landscape paintings by Jean-Charles Cazin, who would be a coexhibitor with Monet in 1885 at the Georges Petit Gallery. Such events, generally overlooked in Monet studies, nevertheless provide the essential context for the commission he received in May 1882 to paint three dozen still-life panels for the sitting-room doors in the residence of his dealer Paul Durand-Ruel (see fig. no. 42 and cat. nos. 75–77), and also for Monet's efforts in 1884 to develop some of his Bordighera paintings into decorations, one of which was destined for the new home of his Impressionist colleague Morisot (fig. no. 45). Renoir's May 1884 plans to organize a society of both fine and decorative artists likewise merits inclusion in the Monet story.

In the spring of 1890 at the first Salon of the Société Nationale des Beaux-Arts, decorative art objects were exhibited in tandem with paintings and sculpture.[13] The following year brought the first Nabis exhibitions, enthusiastically supported by Monet's critic friend Geffroy. Committed to decoration as a priority, the Nabis group also intrigued Monet's stepson-in-law, Theodore Butler, who participated in the last Nabis exhibitions in 1894. But despite such close interconnections with Monet, the cast of Nabis characters is usually omitted from Monet studies, as if he were immune to conceptual growth. Yet it is exactly during the early 1890s, when the *Wheatstacks, Poplars,* and *Rouen Cathedral* paintings were realized, that Monet (who purchased his Giverny home outright in late 1890) undertook his own interior decoration, by late 1893 choosing special colors for each room, the most often described being the yellow dining room à la Whistler. Also in the early 1890s, Monet's friend Caillebotte was decorating his own dining room doors with paintings of the rare orchids that grew in his greenhouse (fig. no. 64). Considering the widespread interest in decorative arts, it even seems appropriate to compare the crusted surfaces of Monet's early 1890s paintings, in particular those of *Rouen Cathedral,* to the thick, dripping, Japanese-style metallic glazes used by ceramist Ernest Chaplet.

In Paris the primacy of decoration reached its climax in late 1895 with the opening of Siegfried Bing's lavish Art Nouveau gallery, designed by Louis Bonnier (who in 1920–21 would collaborate with Monet on a never-realized building for his *Water Lilies* murals). Aside from showcasing Japanese and Western decorative arts of every sort, Bing provided artists such as Vuillard and Henri van de Velde with rooms in which to create total interior design environments. Never before had the art market offered readymade living rooms or dining rooms for sale, and this innovation should be understood as an early milestone in the history of today's installation art. Where Monet is concerned, it is intriguingly likely that by mid-1897 the mode of exhibition innovated by Bing directly inspired the artist to conceive and undertake an ensemble of decorative paintings of water lilies to be installed, wallpaperwise, almost at floor level, around a dining room.

Frames

One of the tragedies of modern art collecting is the widespread replacement of frames provided by artists. Although Impressionism gained enthusiastic recognition as a new style more quickly and widely than perhaps any other art mode ever, its supporters disliked and removed from the paintings their unconventional frames. Shockingly few Impressionist frames survive, even in such documentary forms as installation photographs or as background details in paintings of the homes of collectors. From written documents, however, it is well known that by 1877 Pissarro and Degas had begun to use white frames, and Cassatt, Cézanne, Seurat, Whistler, and van Gogh, among others, quickly followed the initiative with their own idiosyncratically simple frame types.[14] As far as is known, the artists' motives were economic as well as aesthetic. Starting in the 1870s, opportunities for artists to exhibit many works at once outside the Salons presented them with a considerable new overhead in framing expenses. Monet's pioneering efforts to exhibit closely related works (or series) together make the issue of frames particularly important and, in his case, especially poignant; one of Monet's last gestures was to hold up two fingers to indicate the width of the frames he wished for his final murals. Considering the responsibility that museums have for presenting works as the artist would have wished, the topic of Monet and frames, no matter how seemingly specialized, cannot be ignored in a museum-sponsored reference book like this one.

Less than two weeks after arriving in Bordighera in January 1884 to begin some three dozen lush Mediterranean landscapes, Monet decided to order gilded frames for the entire lot. These frames were to await his return to Giverny with the new paintings, even though nothing suggests that he yet had any exhibition plans for them. What these frames looked like is unknown.[15] The frame issue was also important for Monet's historic May 1891 Paris exhibition, which included fifteen very closely related *Wheatstacks* paintings. A few weeks before the exhibition opened, Monet wrote that two of the *Wheatstacks* would have white frames (the others presumably had gilded ones), an indication that framing was not used to establish some overall decorative harmony for the ensemble. When he exhibited fifteen *Poplars* paintings the following year, he ordered new frames, despite the similarity of formats to those of the *Wheatstacks*. Again, a few works in the series were framed differently from the others.[16] Letters relating to his 1895 Durand-Ruel exhibition (with three different series groups presented) reveal that Monet actually removed collectors' frames from works borrowed for the occasion, replacing them with his own frames, which he did not intend to sell (although he did accommodate four collectors who must have expressed a preference for the frames provided by the artist).[17] Presumably, Monet intended to reuse the fifty-one frames sent back to him after the closing of the exhibition.

The first visual document related to Monet's ideas about framing is a snapshot taken in July 1900 in his second studio at Giverny (fig. no. 78); several London paintings (both framed and unframed) appear in the foreground, and on the wall a framed 1898 painting of chrysanthemums that had been exhibited immediately on completion. The similarity between the 1898 and 1904 frames suggests that Monet was indeed by now reusing frames. The restrained, Louis XVI-style decorative moldings vary slightly from frame to frame. This consistency suggests that for his series paintings of a single motif with slight variations Monet did not use absolutely uniform frames, but instead chose frames of a given format with slightly different decorative carving. Snapshots taken several years later, prior to his *Water Lilies* exhibition (see fig. no. 89), indicate that Monet again used a variety of Louis XVI-style frames.[18] Letters relating to his 1902 and 1912 Bernheim-Jeune Gallery exhibitions and his 1904 Durand-Ruel Gallery exhibitions of London paintings make it clear that Monet's works were put on public view in frames that the artist provided and that were returned for possible reuse in subsequent exhibitions. Collectors who purchased the works during or after the exhibitions received them in frames provided by the dealers. Today not one Monet work is known to be in a frame that he provided.

The aim of this catalogue has always been to provide an essential companion to the life and works of Claude Monet. The purpose of this brief essay has been to address a group of particular subjects that remain unexplored or only partially examined. Modern viewers of Monet's paintings—even of the most familiar and often reproduced works—should gain from this book some fresh insights into Monet's extraordinary artistic achievement. Monet's own fondest wish was to share the experience of a blind person suddenly restored to sight, so that he could see the world anew. Readers of this catalogue—which documents the most comprehensive Monet exhibition yet attempted—would do well to share the artist's attitude. If it is important to know about Monet and his times to appreciate his art fully, it is no less important for us to put aside the historical perspectives that can blind us to what he really tried to do—to make us see in a way unknown before.

Notes

All works are fully listed in Works Cited (pages 267–70).

1. Perry, 120.

2. First observed (but not published) by Robert Knott at Wake Forest University. As Paul Hayes Tucker notes (Tucker 1989, 93), a study comparing Monet's concepts of time with the writings published by Henri Bergson during the late 1880s and 1890s could be as illuminating as George Heard Hamilton's extraordinary "Cézanne, Bergson, and the Image of Time" (see Hamilton 1956).

3. Not yet addressed in Monet studies is the fact that the water lilies theme was so widespread (in literature, allegorical painting, and most of all, the decorative arts) when Monet embraced it; therefore, his paintings amount to a rare case of innovation grounded in cliché. Monet's friend Octave Mirbeau spoofed the overuse of the subject of water lilies in art in an April 7, 1895 article in *Le Journal* ("Des Lys! Des Lys!"). Recently, Steven Levine surveys turn-of-the-century literature about the water lily theme (see Levine 1994).

4. Renoir, Jean, 87.

5. Herbert 1994, 68–71.

6. Given these practical limitations, it seems likely that all the unusually large works of away-from-home subjects were in fact made in Giverny based on standard-format versions of the motifs. Only by reverting to pre-Impressionist methods of replicating authentic out-of-doors works in the studio could Monet fulfill his lifelong ambition to make modern decorative paintings.

7. Rewald 1969, 39.

8. Gasquet, 149.

9. Doran, 5, 19.

10. There have been model studies on Monet and his first American collectors (see Selected Bibliography). And, during the last two decades, Chicago collector Ambassador Daniel J. Terra has worked tirelessly to publicize works painted by Americans at Giverny, supporting several valuable publications and establishing the Musée d'art Américain, *Giverny* in 1992.

11. P, I, 346.

12. Pays 1921.

13. Silverman, 208.

14. Martha Ward compiles information about frames and gallery installations of the period in "Impressionist Installations and Private Exhibitions" (see Ward).

15. In the background of an unfinished portrait of Monet in his Giverny studio painted in February 1885 by Swiss artist Charles Giron (W, II, 31, mistakenly attributed to Sargent), are two Bordighera works in plain batten frames that appear to be about three inches wide. Given Monet's business relationship with Theo van Gogh, it is worth noting a general similarity between this plain frame choice and rare surviving frames used by Vincent van Gogh. For more information, see Cahn.

16. One was in a white frame, a second in an oak frame, and a third in a frame made of wood from four (presumably poplar) trees. This last frame was probably for the unique *Poplars* composition featuring four trunks [W 1309] now at The Metropolitan Museum Art, New York. Again, given the Monet–van Gogh relationship, it is worth mentioning Vincent's decision in 1888 to frame three related garden paintings in frames made from walnut, chestnut, and pine woods (Gogh, 69).

17. W, III, letter 1301.

18. Contemporary photographs of three of the four tondo-format *Water Lilies* paintings included in the exhibition [W 1701, W 1724, W 1729] record the basic frame type quite clearly: two of the three have identical frames; the third has a frame similar in format but with a slightly different molding pattern.

Plates

Caricature of Léon Machon, **probably 1858 (cat. no. 1a.)**
Charcoal, with stumping, heightened with white chalk, on blue laid paper (discolored to gray)
61.2 × 45.2 cm; 24⅛ × 17¾ in.
The Art Institute of Chicago, Gift of Carter H. Harrison (1933.888) [WD 481]

This Le Havre lawyer, beginning in 1858, served as treasurer for the local art society.

Caricature of Henri Cassinelli: "Rufus Croutinelli," **probably 1858 (cat. no. 1b.)**
Graphite on tan wove paper, laid down on commercially prepared tan wove card
13.0 × 8.4 cm; 5⅛ × 3⁵⁄₁₆ in.
The Art Institute of Chicago, Gift of Carter H. Harrison (1933.893) [WD 495]

Like Monet, Cassinelli was an applicant for a Le Havre art scholarship in 1859. The derogatory inscription plays on the French word "croûte," which signified "bad painting."

Caricature of Jules Didier, **probably 1860 (cat. no. 1c.)**
Charcoal, heightened with white chalk, on blue laid paper (discolored to gray)
61.6 × 43.6 cm; 24¼ × 17¼ in.
The Art Institute of Chicago, Gift of Carter H. Harrison (1933.889) [WD 515]

Didier, an historical landscape painter in Paris, won a national scholarship to study in Rome beginning in 1857.

Haystacks at Chailly at Sunrise, 1865 (cat. no. 2)
30 × 60 cm; 11⅞ × 23¾ in.
San Diego Museum of Art, Museum Purchase (1982:020) [W 1989-55 bis]

The Bodmer Oak, Fontainebleau Forest, 1865 (cat. no. 3)
96.2 × 129.2 cm; 37⅞ × 50⅞ in.
The Metropolitan Museum of Art, New York, Gift of Sam Salz and Bequest of
Julia W. Emmons, by exchange, 1964 (64.210) [W 60]

This particular tree was nicknamed after the Swiss landscape painter Karl
Bodmer, who frequently painted it.

Headland of the Hève River at Low Tide, 1865 (cat. no. 4)
90.2 × 150.5 cm; 35½ × 59¼ in.
Kimbell Art Museum, Fort Worth, Texas (AP 1968.07) [W 52]

Luncheon on the Grass (central panel), 1865–66 (cat. no. 5)
248 × 217 cm; 97⅜ × 85½ in.
Musée d'Orsay, Paris (RF 1987-12) [W 63 (b)]

This is the larger of two fragments that Monet salvaged from a monumental
(4 × 6 m; 13 × 20 ft.) painting that had suffered serious damage from improper
storage.

***Cliffs and Sea, Sainte-Adresse,* c. 1865 (cat. no. 6)**
Black chalk on off-white laid paper
20.5 × 31.4 cm; 8⅛ × 12¼ in.
The Art Institute of Chicago, Clarence Buckingham Collection (1987.56)
[WD 421]

This drawing is one of five showing in sequence a sailboat running aground
and capsizing. The series is Monet's earliest specific attempt to make time his
principal subject.

Port of Honfleur at Night, 1866 (cat. no. 7)
    59.5 × 72.5 cm; 23½ × 28⅝ in.
    National Galleries of Scotland, Edinburgh (NG.2399) [W 71]

Fishing Boats off the Normandy Coast, c. 1866 (cat. no. 8)
 Pastel on brown paper
 21 × 42 cm; 8¼ × 16⅝ in.
 Parrish Art Museum, Southhampton, New York, Gift of Mrs. Lawrence B.
 Dunham in memory of Lillian Haines Chittenden (1978.2) [WP 29]

Sea Study, 1866 (cat. no. 9)
    42 × 59.5 cm; 16⅝ × 23½ in.
      Ordrupgaardsamlingen, Copenhagen [W 72]

Garden of the Princess, Louvre, 1867 (cat. no. 10)
91.8 × 61.9 cm; 36 ⅛ × 24 ⅜ in.
Allen Memorial Art Museum, Oberlin College, Ohio; R. T. Miller, Jr. Fund,
1948 (48.296) [W 85]

Garden at Sainte-Adresse, 1867 (cat. no. 11)
98.1 × 129.9 cm; 38⅝ × 51⅛ in.
The Metropolitan Museum of Art, New York, Purchase, special contributions
and funds given or bequeathed by friends of the Museum, 1967 (67.241)
[W 95]

Gathered informally on the terrace of his aunt Marie-Jeanne Lecadre's
summer house are members of Monet's family, including his father (seated).

The Beach at Sainte-Adresse, 1867 (cat. no. 12)
75.8 × 102.5 cm; 29¹³⁄₁₆ × 40⅜ in.
The Art Institute of Chicago, Mr. and Mrs. Lewis Larned Coburn Memorial
Collection (1933.439) [W 92]

Regatta at Sainte-Adresse, 1867 (cat. no. 13)
    75.2 × 101.6 cm; 29⅝ × 40 in.
    The Metropolitan Museum of Art, New York, Bequest of William Church
    Osborn, 1951 (51.30.4) [W 91]

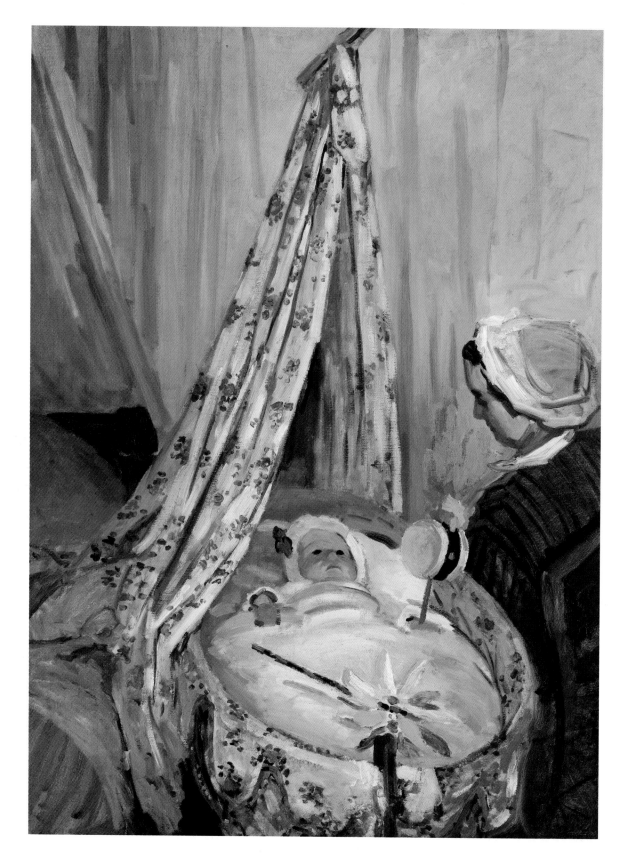

Jean Monet in His Cradle, 1867 (cat. no. 14)
116.2 × 88.8 cm; 45¾ × 35 in.
National Gallery of Art, Washington, D.C., Collection of
Mr. and Mrs. Paul Mellon (1983.1.25) [W 101]

The woman long thought to be Monet's wife Camille Doncieux may, in fact,
represent Camille Pissarro's companion Julie Vellay.

On the Bank of the Seine, Bennecourt, 1868 (cat. no. 15)
    81.5 × 100.7 cm; 32¹⁄₁₆ × 39⅝ in.
    The Art Institute of Chicago, Potter Palmer Collection (1922.427)[W110]

Rock Arch at Etretat (La Porte d'Amont), probably 1868–69
(cat. no. 16)
    81.3 × 100.3 cm; 32 × 39½ in.
    Fogg Art Museum, The Harvard University Art Museums, Gift of
    Mr. and Mrs. Joseph Pulitzer, Jr. (1957.163) [W 258]

The Magpie, 1869 (cat. no. 17)
    89 × 130 cm; 35 × 51³⁄₁₆ in.
    Musée d'Orsay, Paris (RF 1984-164) [W 133]

***La Grenouillère*, 1869 (cat. no. 18)**
74.6 × 99.7 cm; 29⅜ × 39¼ in.
The Metropolitan Museum of Art, New York, The H. O. Havemeyer
Collection, Bequest of Mrs. H. O. Havemeyer, 1929 (29.100.112) [W 134]

The Seine at Bougival, 1869 or 1870 (cat. no. 19)
   65.4 × 97.5 cm; 25¾ × 36⅜ in.
   The Currier Gallery of Art, Manchester, New Hampshire; Currier Funds, 1949
   (1949.1) [W 152]

Hôtel des Roches Noires, Trouville, 1870 (cat. no. 20)
80 × 55 cm; 31½ × 21⅝ in.
Musée d'Orsay, Paris, Gift of Jacques Laroche (RF 1947-30) [W 155]

The Beach at Trouville, 1870 (cat. no. 21)

    38 × 46 cm; 15 × 18⅛ in.

    The Trustees of the National Gallery, London (3951) [W 158]

At left is Camille Monet and at right, possibly, Madame Eugène Boudin.

Breakwater at Trouville, Low Tide, 1870 (cat. no. 22)
54 × 66 cm; 21¼ × 26 in.
Szépmüvészeti Múzeum, Budapest (367.B) [W 154]

Boats on the Thames, London, 1871 (cat. no. 23)
    47 × 72 cm; 18½ × 28⅜ in.
    Private Collection, Monte Carlo [W 167]

The Zaan River at Zaandam, 1871 (cat. no. 24)
   42 × 73 cm; 16½ × 28¾ in.
   Lent Anonymously [W 172]

The Red Kerchief: Portrait of Camille Monet, probably late
1860s–early 1870s (cat. no. 25)
99 × 79.3 cm; 39 × 31¼ in.
The Cleveland Museum of Art, Bequest of Leonard C. Hanna, Jr. (58.39)
[W 257]

The Reader (Springtime), 1872 (cat. no. 26)
   50 × 65 cm; 19¾ × 25⅝ in.
   The Walters Art Gallery, Baltimore (37.11) [W 205]

   The sitter has traditionally been identified as Camille Monet.

Jean Monet on His Horse-Tricycle, 1872 (cat. no. 27)
59.5 × 73.5 cm; 23½ × 29 in.
Sara Lee Corporation [W 238]

The Artist's House at Argenteuil, 1873 (cat. no. 28)
    60.2 × 73.3 cm; 23¹¹⁄₁₆ × 28⅞ in.
    The Art Institute of Chicago, Mr. and Mrs. Martin A. Ryerson Collection
    (1933.1153) [W 284]

The Highway Bridge under Repair, Argenteuil, 1872 (cat. no. 29)
54 × 73 cm; 21¼ × 28¾ in.
Fondation Rau pour le Tiers-Monde, Zurich (GR 1.805) [W 195]

The bridge had been destroyed in the recent Franco-Prussian war.

Harbor at Le Havre at Night, probably 1872 (cat. no. 30)
    60 × 81 cm; 23⅝ × 31⅞ in.
    Private Collection [W 264]

Spring (Fruit Trees in Bloom), 1873 (cat. no. 31)
62.2 × 100.6 cm; 24½ × 39⅝ in.
The Metropolitan Museum of Art, New York, Bequest of
Mary Livingston Willard, 1926 (26.186.1) [W 271]

Monet's Garden at Argenteuil (The Dahlias), 1873 (cat. no. 32)
   61 × 82.5 cm; 24 × 32½ in.
   Janice H. Levin [W 286]

Autumn on the Seine, Argenteuil, 1873 (cat. no. 33)
54 × 73 cm; 21¼ × 28¾ in.
Mrs. John Hay Whitney [W 291]

Sailboat at Le Petit Gennevilliers, 1874 (cat. no. 34)
    56 × 74 cm; 22 × 29⅛ in.
    Lucille Ellis Simon [W 336]

Fishing Boats Leaving the Harbor, Le Havre, 1874 (cat. no. 35)
60 × 101 cm; 23⅝ × 39¾ in.
Private Collection [W 296]

The Old Port of Le Havre, 1874 (cat. no. 36)
   60.3 × 101.9 cm; 23¾ × 40⅛ in.
   Philadelphia Museum of Art, Bequest of Mrs. Frank Graham Thomson
   (1961-48-3) [W 297]

The Highway Bridge at Argenteuil, 1874 (cat. no. 37)
60 × 79.7 cm; 23⅝ × 31⅜ in.
National Gallery of Art, Washington, D.C., Collection of
Mr. and Mrs. Paul Mellon (1983.1.24) [W 312]

The Railroad Bridge at Argenteuil, 1874 (cat. no. 38)
54 × 71.4 cm; 21¼ × 28⅛ in.
The John G. Johnson Collection at the Philadelphia Museum of Art
(J1050) [W 318]

Boulevard des Capucines, 1873–74 (cat. no. 39)
80.4 × 60.3 cm; 31⅝ × 23¾ in.
The Nelson-Atkins Museum of Art, Kansas City, Missouri (Purchase:
The Kenneth A. and Helen F. Spencer Foundation Acquisition Fund)
(F72-35) [W 293]

The Coal Workers, 1875 (cat. no. 40)
    55 × 66 cm; 21⅜ × 26 in.
    Musée d'Orsay, Paris (RF 1993.21) [W 364]

Meadow at Bezons, 1874 (cat. no. 41)
57 × 80 cm; 22½ × 31½ in.
Staatliche Museen zu Berlin-Preußischer Kulturbesitz, Nationalgalerie
(AI1013) [W 341]

The figures represent Camille and Jean Monet.

The Stroll, Camille Monet and Her Son Jean (Woman with a Parasol),
1875 (cat. no. 42)
100 × 81 cm; 39⅜ × 31⅞ in.
National Gallery of Art, Washington, D.C., Collection of
Mr. and Mrs. Paul Mellon (1983.1.29) [W 381]

Snow at Argenteuil, c. 1874 (cat. no. 43)
54.6 × 73.8 cm; 21½ × 29 in.
Museum of Fine Arts, Boston, Bequest of Anna Perkins Rogers
(21.1329) [W 348]

Train in the Snow at Argenteuil, 1875 (cat. no. 44)
    58.5 × 80 cm; 23 × 31½ in.
    Mr. and Mrs. Herbert Klapper [W 360]

Camille Monet in Japanese Costume, 1876 (cat. no. 45)
231.6 × 142.3 cm; 91¼ × 56 in.
Museum of Fine Arts, Boston, 1951 Purchase Fund (56.147) [W 387]

The Turkeys (Decorative Panel), 1876–77 (cat. no. 46)
172 × 175 cm; 67¾ × 68⅞ in.
Musée d'Orsay, Paris, Bequest of Princess Edmond de Polignac,
née Winnaretta Singer, 1944 (RF 1944-18) [W 416]

The Studio Boat, around 1873–76 (cat. no. 47)
54 × 65 cm; 21¼ × 25⅝ in.
Musée d'art et d'histoire, Neuchâtel, Switzerland [W 393]

Camille Monet in the Garden at Argenteuil, probably 1877 (cat. no. 48)
   71.8 × 53.3 cm; 28¼ × 21 in.
   San Francisco Museum of Modern Art, Bequest of Elise S. Haas (91.167)
   [W 415]

***Saint-Lazare Station,* 1877 (cat. no. 49)**
54.3 × 73.6 cm; 21⅜ × 29 in.
The Trustees of the National Gallery, London (6479) [W 441]

Arrival of the Normandy Train, Saint-Lazare Station, 1877
   (cat. no. 50)
      59.6 × 80.2 cm; 23½ × 31½ in.
      The Art Institute of Chicago, Mr. and Mrs. Martin A. Ryerson Collection
      (1933.1158) [W 440]

Saint-Lazare Station (sketch), c. 1874–77 (cat. no. 51)
      Graphite on paper
      24 × 31 cm; 9⁷⁄₁₆ × 12³⁄₁₆ in.
      Musée Marmottan, Paris (carnet II, folio 14 recto)
      (5130) [WD 153]

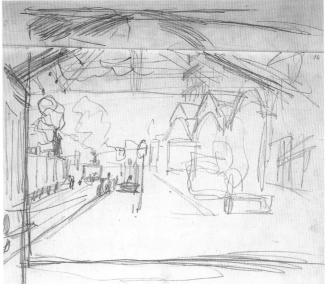

Tracks outside Saint-Lazare Station, 1877 (cat. no. 52)
60 × 80 cm; 23⅝ × 31½ in.
Private Collection, Japan [W 445]

Track Signals outside Saint-Lazare Station, 1877 (cat. no. 53)
65.5 × 81.5 cm; 25¾ × 32⅛ in.
Niedersächsisches Landesmuseum, Hannover (PNM 941) [W 448]

The Meadow, 1879 (cat. no. 54)
81.3 × 100.3 cm; 32 × 39½ in.
Joslyn Art Museum, Omaha, Nebraska, Gift of Mr. William Averell Harriman
(1944.79) [W 535]

Still Life with Apples and Grapes, 1880 (cat. no. 55)
  66.2 × 82.3 cm; 26⅟₁₆ × 32⅜ in.
  The Art Institute of Chicago, Mr. and Mrs. Martin A. Ryerson Collection
  (1933.1152) [W 546]

Floating Ice, 1880 (cat. no. 56)
97 × 150.5 cm; 38¼ × 59¼ in.
Shelburne Museum, Shelburne, Vermont (27.1.2-108) [W 568]

Sunset on the Seine in Winter, 1880 (cat. no. 57)
    60 × 80 cm; 23⅝ × 31½ in.
    Private Collection, Japan [W 574]

The Road to Vétheuil, 1880 (cat. no. 58)
68 × 90 cm; 26¾ × 35½ in.
Sallyan Windt [W 584]

The Wheatfield, 1881 (cat. no. 59)
　　65.4 × 81.3 cm; 25¾ × 32 in.
　　The Cleveland Museum of Art, Gift of Mrs. Henry White Cannon (47.197)
　　[W 676]

Vétheuil in Summer, 1880 (cat. no. 60)
60 × 99.7 cm; 23⅝ × 39¼ in.
The Metropolitan Museum of Art, New York, Bequest of
William Church Osborn, 1951 (51.30.3) [W 605]

Apple Trees in Bloom, 1880 (cat. no. 61)
   73 × 60 cm; 28¾ × 23⅜ in.
   Private Collection, Paris [W 585]

The Coast, Looking East from Fécamp, 1881 (cat. no. 62)
61 × 79 cm; 24 × 31⅛ in.
Private Collection, Canada [W 2004–656 bis]

The Sea at Fécamp, 1881 (cat. no. 63)
  65.5 × 82 cm; 25¾ × 32¼ in.
  Staatsgalerie Stuttgart (2410) [W 660]

The Artist's Garden at Vétheuil, 1881 (cat. no. 64)
80 × 65 cm; 31½ × 25⅜ in.
Mr. and Mrs. Herbert Klapper [W 682]

The Artist's Garden at Vétheuil, 1881 (cat. no. 65)
    100 × 80 cm; 39⅜ × 31½ in.
    Private Collection [W 684]

The children represent Jean-Pierre Hoschedé and Michel Monet.

Rough Sea, Normandy, 1881 (cat. no. 66)
60 × 73.7 cm; 23⅜ × 29 in.
National Gallery of Canada, Ottawa (4636) [W 663]

Abandoned Coast Guard's Post, East of Varengeville, 1882 (cat. no. 67)
   65.9 × 81.3 cm; 26 × 32 in.
   The Brooklyn Museum, Gift of Mrs. Horace Havemeyer (41.1260) [W 740]

Fishing Nets at Pourville, 1882 (cat. no. 68)
60 × 81 cm; 23⅝ × 31½ in.
Collection Haags Gemeentemuseum, The Hague (15-1932) [W 768]

Church at Varengeville, Morning Effect, 1882 (cat. no. 69)
  60.2 × 73.5 cm; 23¹¹⁄₁₆ × 28¹⁵⁄₁₆ in.
  Private Collection, Courtesy Richard L. Feigen and Company [W 795]

Etretat, Sunset, 1883 (cat. no. 70)
60.5 × 81.8 cm; 23¹³⁄₁₆ × 32³⁄₁₆ in.
North Carolina Museum of Art, Raleigh, Purchased with funds from the State
of North Carolina (67.24.1) [W 817]

Rock Arch West of Etretat (The Manneporte), 1883 (cat. no. 71)
    65.4 × 81.3 cm; 25¾ × 32 in.
    The Metropolitan Museum of Art, New York, Bequest of
    William Church Osborn, 1951 (51.30.5) [W 832]

Vase of Dahlias, 1883 (cat. no. 72)
    Oil on panel
    128.3 × 37.1 cm; 50½ × 14⅝ in.
    Private Collection [W 931]

Dahlias, 1883 (cat. no. 73)
    Oil on panel
    119 × 36.5 cm; 46¾ × 14¼ in.
    Private Collection [W 932]

Peaches, 1883 (cat. no. 74)
    50.5 × 37 cm; 19⅞ × 14⅝ in.
    Private Collection, Europe [W 935]

Gardener's House at Bordighera, 1884 (cat. no. 75)
73 × 92 cm; 28¾ × 36¼ in.
Joslyn Art Museum, Omaha, Nebraska (1943.39) [W 874]

Moreno Garden at Bordighera, 1884 (cat. no. 76)
   73 × 92 cm; 28¾ × 36¼ in.
   Norton Gallery of Art, West Palm Beach, Florida (53.134) [W865]

Bordighera, 1884 (cat. no. 77)
64.8 × 81.3 cm; 25½ × 32 in.
The Art Institute of Chicago, Potter Palmer Collection (1922.426) [W 854]

Coastal Road at Cap Martin, near Menton, 1884 (cat. no. 78)
    139 × 180 cm; 54¾ × 70⅞ in.
    Private Collection [W 891]

The Needle, Etretat, 1885 (cat. no. 79)
64.9 × 81.1 cm; 25⁹⁄₁₆ × 31¹⁵⁄₁₆ in.
Sterling and Francine Clark Art Institute, Williamstown, Massachussetts (528)
[W 1034]

Rain at Etretat, 1886 (cat. no. 80)
  60.5 × 73.5 cm; 23⅞ × 29 in.
  Nasjonalgalleriet, Oslo (M.368) [W 1044]

Etretat: The Beach and the Eastern Rock Arch, 1885 (cat. no. 81)
69.3 × 66.1 cm; 27¼ × 26 in.
The Art Institute of Chicago, Gift of Mrs. John H. (Anne R.) Winterbotham
in memory of John H. Winterbotham; Joseph Winterbotham Collection
(1964.204) [W 1012]

Storm at Belle-Ile, 1886 (cat. no. 82)
   60 × 73 cm; 23⅝ × 28¾ in.
   Private Collection, Chattanooga, Tennessee [W 1117]

Pyramids of Port-Coton, Belle-Ile, 1886 (cat. no. 83)
60 × 73 cm; 23⅝ × 28¾ in.
Ny Carlsberg Glyptotek, Copenhagen (I.N. 2820) [W 1086]

Pyramids of Port-Coton, Belle-Ile, 1886 (cat. no. 84)
　　65.5 × 65.5 cm; 25⅞ × 25⅞ in.
　　Fondation Rau pour le Tiers-Monde, Zurich (GR 1.564) [W 1087]

Snow at Giverny, **1886** (cat. no. 85)
66 × 81 cm; 26 × 31⅞ in.
Private Collection [W 1054]

View of Bennecourt, 1887 (cat. no. 86)
    81.6 × 81.6 cm; 32⅛ × 32⅛ in.
    Columbus Museum of Art, Columbus, Ohio, Gift of Howard D. and
    Babette L. Sirak, the Donors to the Campaign for Enduring Excellence, and
    the Derby Fund (91.1.42) [W 1125]

Antibes Seen from La Salis, 1888 (cat. no. 87)
73.3 × 92 cm; 28⅞ × 36¼ in.
The Toledo Museum of Art, Toledo, Ohio; Purchased with funds from the
Libbey Endowment, Gift of Edward Drummond Libbey (1929.51) [W 1168]

Antibes, 1888 (cat. no. 88)
    65.5 × 92.4 cm; 25¾ × 36⅜ in.
    Courtauld Institute Galleries, London (Samuel Courtauld Bequest 1948)
    [W 1192]

The Stroll at Giverny, 1888 (cat. no. 89)
80 × 80 cm; 31½ × 31½ in.
Private Collection [W 1204]

The figures in the foreground are (left to right) Michel Monet, Germaine
Hoschedé, and Jean-Pierre Hoschedé; in the background are Jean Monet and
Suzanne Hoschedé.

Bend in the River Epte, 1888 (cat. no. 90)
    74 × 92.7 cm; 29⅛ × 36½ in.
    Philadelphia Museum of Art, The William L. Elkins Collection (E24-3-16)
    [W 1209]

Study of Rocks, The Creuse (Le Bloc), 1889 (cat. no. 91)
73 × 92 cm; 28¾ × 36¼ in.
Her Majesty Queen Elizabeth The Queen Mother (469261) [W 1228]

Le Bloc was a catchword for the French Revolution coined by the politician
Georges Clemenceau, Monet's close friend and the picture's first owner.

The Petite Creuse River, 1889 (cat. no. 92)
65.9 × 93.1 cm; 25¹⁵/₁₆ × 36⅜ in.
The Art Institute of Chicago, Potter Palmer Collection (1922.432) [W 1231]

Young Women in a Boat, probably 1889–90 (cat. no. 93)
145.5 × 133.5 cm; 57¼ × 52⁹⁄₁₆ in.
The National Museum of Western Art, Tokyo, Matsukata Collection
(P.1959-148) [W 1152]

The figures represent Suzanne and Blanche Hoschedé.

Boating on the River Epte, 1890 (cat. no. 94)
133 × 145 cm; 52⅜ × 57¹⁄₁₆ in.
Museu de Arte de São Paulo Assis Chateaubriand [W 1250]

The figures represent Suzanne and Blanche Hoschedé.

***Poppy Field (Giverny)*, 1890–91 (cat. no. 95)**
61.2 × 93.1 cm; 24 1/16 × 36 3/8 in.
The Art Institute of Chicago, Mr. and Mrs. W. W. Kimball Collection
(1922.4465) [W 1253]

Wheatstacks (Sunset, Snow Effect), 1890–91 (cat. no. 96)
    65.3 × 100.4 cm; 25¹¹⁄₁₆ × 39½ in.
    The Art Institute of Chicago, Potter Palmer Collection (1922.431) [W 1278]

    Popularly known as *Haystacks,* Monet's famous series of paintings of 1890–91
    actually depict the storage of wheat (see Herbert 1979 and W, III, 13, in Works
    Cited). The recognition of this fact has initiated an ongoing sequence of title
    changes for these pictures.

Wheatstacks (End of Summer), 1890–91 (cat. no. 97)
60 × 100 cm; 23⅝ × 39⅜ in.
The Art Institute of Chicago, Arthur M. Wood in memory of
Pauline Palmer Wood (1985.1103) [W 1269]

Wheatstacks, 1890–91 (cat. no. 98)
65.8 × 101 cm; 25⅞ × 39¾ in.
The Art Institute of Chicago, Mr. and Mrs. Lewis Larned Coburn Memorial
Collection (1933.444) [W 1270]

Wheatstack (Snow Effect, Overcast Day), 1890–91 (cat. no. 99)
66 × 93 cm; 26 × 36⅝ in.
The Art Institute of Chicago, Mr. and Mrs. Martin A. Ryerson Collection
(1933.1155) [W 1281]

Wheatstack (Thaw, Sunset), 1890–91 (cat. no. 100)
64.9 × 92.3 cm; 25⁹⁄₁₆ × 36⅜ in.
The Art Institute of Chicago, Gift of Mr. and Mrs. Daniel C. Searle (1983.166)
[W 1284]

Wheatstack, 1890–91 (cat. no. 101)
65.6 × 92 cm; 25¹³⁄₁₆ × 36¼ in.
The Art Institute of Chicago, Restricted gift of the Searle Family Trust;
Major Acquisitions Centennial Endowment; through prior acquisitions of
the Mr. and Mrs. Martin A. Ryerson and Potter Palmer Collections; through
prior bequest of Jerome Friedman (1983.29) [W 1283]

Wheatstack (Sun in the Mist), 1891 (cat. no. 102)
    65 × 100 cm; 25⅝ × 39⅜ in.
    The Minneapolis Institute of Arts, Gift of Ruth and Bruce Dayton, The
    Putnam Dana McMillan Fund, The John R. Van Derlip Fund, The William
    Hood Dunwoody Fund, The Ethel Morrison Van Derlip Fund, Alfred and
    Ingrid Lenz Harrison, and Mary Joann and James R. Jundt (93.20) [W 1286]

Poplars along the River Epte, Autumn, 1891 (cat. no. 103)
100 × 65 cm; 39⅜ × 25⅝ in.
Private Collection [W 1297]

Spring Meadow, Giverny, 1894 (cat. no. 104)
    92 × 65 cm; 36¼ × 25⅝ in.
    New England Collector [W 1367]

Rouen Cathedral, Façade, 1894 (cat. no. 105)
100.5 × 66.2 cm; 39⅝ × 26 in.
Museum of Fine Arts, Boston, Juliana Cheney Edwards Collection (39.671)
[W 1356]

Church at Vernon, Fog, 1894 (cat. no. 106)
    65 × 92 cm; 25⅝ × 36¼ in.
    Shelburne Museum, Shelburne, Vermont (27.1.2-107) [W 1390]

Sandvika, Norway, 1895 (cat. no. 107)
73.4 × 92.5 cm; 28⅞ × 36⅜ in.
The Art Institute of Chicago, Gift of Bruce Borland (1961.790) [W 1397]

Branch of the Seine near Giverny (Mist), from the *Mornings on the*
   Seine Series, 1897 (cat. no. 108)
89.9 × 92.7 cm; 35⅜ × 36½ in.
The Art Institute of Chicago, Mr. and Mrs. Martin A. Ryerson Collection
(1933.1156) [W 1475]

Headland of the Petit Ailly River, 1897 (cat. no. 109)
73 × 92 cm; 28¾ × 36¼ in.
The Rothschild Art Foundation [W 1445]

Val-Saint-Nicholas, near Dieppe, Morning, 1896–97 (cat. no. 110)
    65.1 × 100 cm; 25⅝ × 39⅜ in.
    The Phillips Collection, Washington, D. C. (1377) [W 1466]

Pink Water Lilies, 1897–99 (cat. no. 111)
81 × 100 cm; 31⅞ × 39⅜ in.
Galleria Nazionale d'Arte Moderna e Contemporanea, Rome (5163) [W 1507]

The Garden (Irises), 1900 (cat. no. 112)
　　81 × 92 cm; 31⅞ × 36¼ in.
　　Ralph T. Coe [W 1625]

The Water Lily Garden, 1899 (cat. no. 113)
90.5 × 89.7 cm; 35⅝ × 35⁵⁄₁₆ in.
The Art Museum, Princeton University, from the Collection of William
Church Osborn, Class of 1883, Trustee of Princeton University (1914–1951),
President of The Metropolitan Museum of Art (1941–1947); gift of his family
(Y1972-15) [W 1509]

Water Lily Garden, 1900 (cat. no. 114)
89.9 × 100.1 cm; 35⅜ × 39⅜ in.
The Art Institute of Chicago, Mr. and Mrs. Lewis Larned Coburn Memorial
Collection (1933.441) [W 1628]

Vétheuil, 1901 (cat. no. 115)
90 × 93 cm; 35⅞₁₆ × 36⅝ in.
The Art Institute of Chicago, Mr. and Mrs. Lewis Larned Coburn Memorial
Collection (1933.447) [W 1643]

Vétheuil, 1901 (cat. no. 116)
    88.3 × 91.5 cm; 34¾ × 36 in.
    The Art Institute of Chicago, Mr. and Mrs. Martin A. Ryerson Collection
    (1933.1161) [W 1645]
    Withdrawn from the exhibition

Houses of Parliament, London, 1900–01 (cat. no. 117)
81 × 92 cm; 31⅞ × 36¼ in.
The Art Institute of Chicago, Mr. and Mrs. Martin A. Ryerson Collection
(1933.1164) [W 1600]

Houses of Parliament, London, Effect of Sunlight, 1903 (cat. no. 118)
    81.3 × 92 cm; 32 × 36¼ in.
    The Brooklyn Museum, Bequest of Grace Underwood Barton (68.48.1)
    [W 1597]

Houses of Parliament, London, Fog Effect, 1904 (cat. no. 119)
81 × 92 cm; 31⅞ × 36¼ in.
Museum of Fine Arts, St. Petersburg, Florida, Gift of Charles and Margaret
Stevenson Henderson and Friends of Art (1979.5) [W 1611]

Houses of Parliament, London, Symphony in Rose, possibly 1903
   (cat. no. 120)
   81 × 92 cm; 31⅞ × 36¼ in.
   Private Collection, Japan [W 1599]
   Withdrawn from the exhibition

Houses of Parliament, London, Sunset, 1904 (cat. no. 121)
80 × 91 cm; 31½ × 35⅞ in.
Kaiser Wilhelm Museum, Krefeld (87/1907) [W 1602]

Houses of Parliament, London, Sunset, 1904 (cat. no. 122)
  81 × 92 cm; 31⅞ × 36¼ in.
  Kunsthaus Zürich, Gift of Walter Haefner [W 1607]

Houses of Parliament, London, Sun Breaking through the Fog, 1904
(cat. no. 123)
81 × 92 cm; 31⅞ × 36¼ in.
Musée d'Orsay, Paris, Bequest of Comte Isaac de Camondo, 1911 (RF 2007)
[W 1610]

Houses of Parliament, London, 1905 (cat. no. 124)
    81 × 92 cm; 31⅞ in. × 36¼ in.
    Musée Marmottan, Paris (5007) [W 1606]

Water Lilies (The Clouds), 1903 (cat. no. 125)
74.6 × 105.3 cm; 29⅜ × 41⅞₆ in.
Private Collection [W 1656]

Water Lilies, 1903 (cat. no. 126)
   81.3 × 101.6 cm; 32 × 40 in.
   The Dayton Art Institute, Dayton, Ohio, Gift of Mr. Joseph Rubin (53.11)
   [W 1657]

Water Lilies, 1904 (cat. no. 127)
90 × 93 cm; 35⁷⁄₁₆ × 36⅝ in.
Musée des Beaux-Arts André Malraux, Le Havre (A 486) [W 1664]

Water Lilies, 1904 (cat. no. 128)
89 × 92 cm; 35⅛ × 36¼ in.
Denver Art Museum, The Helen Dill Collection (1935.14) [W 1666]

Water Lilies, 1904 (cat. no. 129)
    90 × 92 cm; 35⁷⁄₁₆ × 36¼ in.
    Musée des Beaux-Arts, Caen (75-1-23) [W 1667]

Water Lilies, 1906 (cat. no. 130)
87.6 × 92.7 cm; 34½ × 36½ in.
The Art Institute of Chicago, Mr. and Mrs. Martin A. Ryerson Collection
(1933.1157) [W 1683]

Water Landscape, 1907 (cat. no. 131)
　　81 × 92 cm; 31⅞ × 36¼ in.
　　Wadsworth Atheneum, Hartford, Connecticut, Bequest of
　　Anne Parrish Titzell (1957.622) [W 1696]

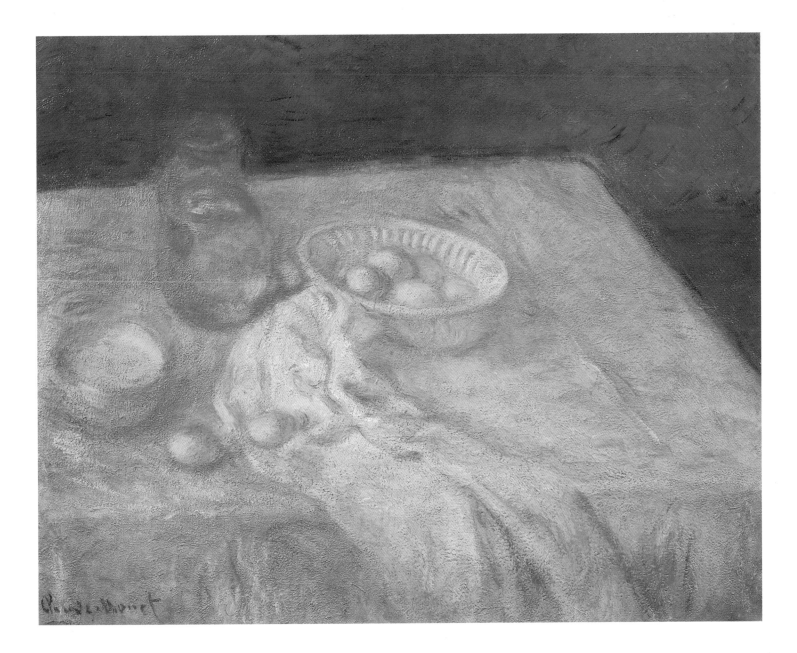

Still Life with Eggs, 1907 (cat. no. 132)
73 × 92 cm; 28¾ × 36¼ in.
Private Collection [W 1692]

Water Lilies, 1907 (cat. no. 133)
92.1 × 81.2 cm; 36¼ × 31¹⁵⁄₁₆ in.
The Museum of Fine Arts, Houston, Gift of Mrs. Harry C. Hanszen (68.31)
[W 1703]

Pond with Water Lilies, **1907 (cat. no. 134)**
107 × 73 cm; 42⅛ × 28¾ in.
The Israel Museum, Jerusalem, The Sam Spiegel Collection (L-B90.20)
[W 1710]

Water Lilies, 1907 (cat. no. 135)
100 × 81 cm; 39⅜ × 31⅞ in.
Kuboso Memorial Museum of Art, Osaka [W 1713]

Water Lilies, 1907 (cat. no. 136)
100.5 × 73.4 cm; 39⅝ × 28⅞ in.
Bridgestone Museum of Art, Ishibashi Foundation, Tokyo (F.P. 23) [W 1715]

Water Lilies, 1908 (cat. no. 137)
90 × 94 cm; 35⁷⁄₁₆ × 37 in.
Private Collection, Japan [W 1721]

Water Lilies, 1908 (cat. no. 138)
92 × 81 cm; 36¼ × 31⅞ in.
Gregory Callimanopulos, New York [W 1725]

Water Lilies, 1908 (cat. no. 139)
100 × 100 cm; 39⅜ × 39⅜ in.
Private Collection, Courtesy Sotheby's London [W 1730]

Water Lilies, 1908 (cat. no. 140)
  94.7 × 89.9 cm; 37¼ × 35⅜ in.
  Worcester Art Museum, Worcester, Massachusetts (1910.26) [W 1733]

Water Lilies, 1908 (cat. no. 141)
diameter 81 cm; 31⅞ in.
Dallas Museum of Art, Gift of the Meadows Foundation Incorporated
(1981.128) [W 1729]

Water Lilies, 1908 (cat. no. 142)
    100 × 90 cm; 39⅜ × 35½ in.
    Tokyo Fuji Art Museum [W 1731]

San Giorgio Maggiore by Twilight, 1908 (cat. no. 143)
63.5 × 88.9 cm; 25 × 35 in.
The National Museum of Wales, Cardiff (NMW A 2485 [793]) [W 1768]

Self-Portrait, around 1915–17 (cat. no. 144)
    70 × 55 cm; 27⁹⁄₁₆ × 21⅜ in.
    Musée d'Orsay, Paris, Gift of Georges Clemenceau, 1927 (RF 2623) [W 1843]

Water Lilies, 1914–17 (cat. no. 145)
200 × 200 cm; 78¾ × 78¾ in.
Musée Marmottan, Paris (5115) [W 1811]

Water Lilies, probably 1914–17 (cat. no. 146)
    130 × 150 cm; 51¼ × 59¹⁄₁₆ in.
    Musée Marmottan, Paris (5085) [W 1783]

Water Lilies, probably 1915 (cat. no. 147)
160.5 × 180.5 cm; 63¼ × 71⅛ in.
Portland Art Museum, Portland, Oregon, Helen Thurston Ayer Fund (59.16)
[W 1795]

Water Lily Pond, probably 1918 (cat. no. 148)
   130.2 × 201.9 cm; 51¼ × 79½ in.
   Mrs. Harvey Kaplan [W 1889]

Water Lily Garden with Weeping Willow, 1916–19 (cat. no. 149)
200 × 180 cm; 78¾ × 70⅞ in.
Musée Marmottan, Paris (5125) [W 1848]

Water Lilies: Reflection of a Weeping Willow, 1916–19 (cat. no. 150)
200 × 200 cm; 78¾ × 78¾ in.
Musée Marmottan, Paris (5122) [W 1862]

Water Lily Garden, 1918 (cat. no. 151)
117 × 83 cm; 46⅛ × 32¹¹⁄₁₆ in.
Musée de Grenoble (MG 2168) [W 1878]

Weeping Willow, 1918 (cat. no. 152)
131.2 × 110.3 cm; 51⅝ × 43⁷⁄₁₆ in.
Columbus Museum of Art, Columbus, Ohio, Gift of Howard D. and
Babette L. Sirak, the Donors to the Campaign for Enduring Excellence, and
the Derby Fund (91.001.041) [W 1869]

Water Lily Pond, 1918 (cat. no. 153)
    100 × 200 cm; 39⅜ × 78¾ in.
    Musée des Beaux-Arts de Nantes (938-6-1-P) [W 1886]

The Japanese Bridge, 1919 (cat. no. 154)
66 × 107.5 cm; 26 × 42⅜ in.
Kunstmuseum, Oeffentliche Kunstsammlung Basel (G1986.15) [W 1916]

The Japanese Bridge, probably 1918–24 (cat. no. 155)
   89 × 116 cm; 35 × 45¾ in.
   The Minneapolis Institute of Arts, Bequest of Putnam Dana McMillan
   (61.36.15) [W 1931]

Wisteria, 1919–20 (cat. no. 156)
diptych: each canvas, 149.9 × 200.6 cm; 59 × 79 in.
Private Collection [W 1906-7]

181

Water Lilies (Clouds), c. 1920 (cat. no. 157)
triptych: each canvas, 200 × 425 cm; 78¾ × 167⁵⁄₁₆ in.
The Museum of Modern Art, New York, Mrs. Simon Guggenheim Fund
(666.59.1-3) [W 1972–74]

Water Lily Garden, probably 1922 (cat. no. 158)
198 × 596.6 cm; 77¹⁵⁄₁₆ × 234⅞ in.
The Carnegie Museum of Art, Pittsburgh, Acquired through the generosity of
Mrs. Alan M. Scaife, 1962 (62.19.1) [W 1983]

Water Lilies (Evening), c. 1920 (cat. no. 159)
diptych: each canvas, 200 × 300 cm; 78¾ × 118⅛ in.
Kunsthaus Zürich (1952/64) [W 1964–65]

Chronology

1. Gustave Le Gray, *An Effect of the Sun, Normandy*, 1856/59. Albumen print from wet collodion on glass negative; 32.5 × 41.5 cm, 12¹³⁄₁₆ × 16⅜ in. Board of Trustees of the Victoria and Albert Museum, London, Townsend Collection (67.998). Le Gray's seascape photographs from the late 1850s appear to be precedents for Monet's compositions of the early 1860s.

2. Eugène Boudin, *Cloud Study, Sunset*, probably 1859. Pastel on beige paper; 21.5 × 29.1 cm, 8½ × 11⁷⁄₁₆ in. Musée du Louvre, Paris (RF 4029).

1840–57

November 14, 1840 Birth of Oscar-Claude Monet at 45, rue Lafitte, Paris. Monet will later point out that this street was "the street of picture dealers." He is the second child of Claude Adolphe Monet and Louise Justine Aubrée. Monet's older brother, Léon, was born in 1836.[1]

March 1841 John G. Rand, an American portrait painter living in London, patents the collapsible paint tube, revolutionizing the history of landscape painting by enabling painters to work away from their studios.

May 20, 1841 Monet's baptism at Notre-Dame-de-Lorette, Paris.[2]

c. 1845 The Monet family moves to 30, rue d'Eprémenil, Ingouville, outside of Le Havre, so that Monet's father can take a job with his half-sister's husband, Jacques Lecadre, a wholesale grocer and ship supplier. The Lecadres also have a summer house at the neighboring resort town of Sainte-Adresse.[3]

1851 Monet enrolls at Le Havre primary school. His drawing teacher is Jacques-François Ochard, a friend of Eugène Boudin. From 1844 to 1846 Boudin, who will exert a profound influence on Monet's career, had been a partner in a Le Havre paper goods shop that did picture framing and exhibited in its shop windows works by artists working in and around the city, including Thomas Couture, Eugène Isabey, Jean-François Millet, and Constant Troyon. After 1846 Boudin devoted himself full-time to an art career, and in late 1850–early 1851, he successfully applies for a three-year municipal art stipend with recommendations from Couture and Troyon.[4]

August and October 1855 Publication in *Magasin pittoresque* of translated excerpts from C. R. Leslie's *Memoirs of the Life of John Constable, Esq., R.A.,* including a synopsis of Constable's pioneering lectures on the history of landscape painting (which stress the preeminence of Claude Lorrain) and an account of his early 1820s experiments with studies of clouds and skies. The article describes around fifty of Constable's paintings as oil studies of clouds on heavy paper, each inscribed on the reverse with the date, time of day, and weather conditions, and quotes from the artist's letters in which he emphasizes the importance of painting skies: "That landscape painter who does not make his skies a very material part of his composition, neglects to avail himself of one of his greatest aids. . . . It will be difficult to name a class of landscape in which the sky is not the key note, the standard of scale, and the chief organ of sentiment."[5]

December 3, 1856 Describing the attempt to render ephemeral natural effects—which will become a central tenet of Impressionism—Boudin writes in his diary: "To swim in the open air. To attain the tenderness of the cloud. To suspend these masses in the background, very far off in the gray haze, to make the azure shine out. I sense all that coming, dawning in my designs. What a joy and what a torment!— if the background were motionless, perhaps I would never arrive at these depths. Has anyone ever done better? Did the [seventeenth-century] Dutch [landscape] masters attain this cloud poetry that I am seeking? These tendernesses of the sky that go as far as praise, as far as adoration: that is not an exaggeration."[6]

1856–57 Monet's earliest surviving sketchbooks, including several sheets dated 1856, include quick drawings of landscape subjects and boats, the first indication of his interest in seascape painting. During this period, Monet exhibits some of his caricatures in an art supply store in Le Havre. There he meets Boudin, who invites a skeptical Monet to join him painting out-of-doors. Later Monet will recall: "It was as if a veil suddenly lifted from my eyes and I knew that I could be a painter." As an aspiring caricaturist, Monet admires Etienne Carjat, Paul Hadol, and one of the era's outstanding humorists and photographers, Nadar, some of whose works (published in *Le Gaulois* and *Journal amusant* in 1856) Monet copies, as he will five individual figures in the *Panthéon Nadar*, a lithograph with caricatures of 249 notable contemporary figures published in March 1854 (Monet will probably refer to the December 1858 printing of the lithograph, with 270 figures).[7]

January 28, 1857 Death of Monet's mother. Monet, his father, and brother move to 13, rue Fontenelle (the Lecadre house), in Le Havre, where his aunt Marie-Jeanne Lecadre, an amateur artist, has her own studio. She knows painter Amand Gautier, a close friend of controversial Realist painter Gustave Courbet.[8]

Autumn 1857 Charles-François Daubigny, one of the Barbizon artists who pioneered out-of-doors landscape painting, builds a studio boat. He depicts his life as an itinerant painter of riverscapes in a portfolio of etchings published in 1862 as *Le Voyage en bateau*. Monet will build his own floating studio in 1872.[9]

1858

August–September Monet shows a landscape painting of Rouelles, where Boudin had taken him, at a Le Havre contemporary art exhibition organized by the Société des amis des arts, of whose treasurer Monet draws a caricature (cat. no. 1a).[10]

August 6 Monet submits an unsuccessful application for a Le Havre scholarship to study art in Paris. He draws a caricature of a rival applicant (cat. no. 1b).[11]

September 30 Death of Jacques Lecadre. Monet's father takes over Lecadre's business until he retires around 1860.[12]

October 9 France establishes official relations with Japan. Late in life Monet will recall that he bought his first Japanese print in Le Havre when he was a teenager.[13]

1859

At some point during this year, Monet exhibits caricatures of actors and musicians (now lost) in the window of an art and photography shop in Le Havre.[14]

January–February Courbet purchases adjoining plots of land in his hometown, Ornans; his never-realized plan is to construct a studio and to plant varieties of trees nearby so that he can paint landscapes with ideal convenience.[15]

March 21 Monet submits a still life as part of his second unsuccessful application for a city art scholarship.[16]

Around April 24–May Visiting his mother's seaside house in Honfleur, the poet Charles Baudelaire informs Nadar that he would like to review the Salon of 1859 without ever seeing it. In fact, Baudelaire had already visited the prestigious and popular national contemporary art exhibition, if only to look for novelties, of which he found few. In his review, Baudelaire takes note of a "super-naturalist" painting by Octave Penguilly l'Haridon of gulls on the coast of Belle-Ile (where Monet will paint in 1886).[17]

Mid-May Monet goes to Paris to see the Salon, open since April 15. This year Boudin participates for the first time, exhibiting a painting based on his 1857 and 1858 sojourns in Brittany. Also for the first time, a section of photographs is incorporated at the Salon, including landscape and seascape photographs by Gustave Le Gray (see fig. no. 1). (Le Gray in 1859 has his business at 35, boulevard des Capucines, Paris; Nadar rents and expands the studio beginning in 1860, and in 1874 it will be the site of the first Impressionist exhibition.)

With introductions from Boudin, Monet seeks art advice from Gautier and shows his

3. Claude Monet, *In the Studio*, 1861. Oil on canvas; 182 × 127 cm, 71⅝ × 50 in. Musée d'Orsay, Paris (MNR 136) [W 6].

works to Troyon, the acclaimed self-taught Barbizon landscape painter. Monet stays in Paris (35, rue Rodier), summering in Le Havre, but he is unable or unwilling to follow Troyon's advice that he enroll as a student under figure painter Couture, with whom Edouard Manet had studied from 1850 to 1856. While in Paris, Monet uses the studio of Boudin's friend Charles Monginot. Writing to Boudin about the Salon, Monet praises the skies in large paintings by Troyon; the landscapes by Théodore Rousseau, Daubigny, and Camille Corot; and the warm light in the Oriental views by Théodore Frère. Monet finds the works by Eugène Delacroix too unfinished. He concludes the letter to Boudin: "There are no seascape painters at all, and it is the road that will take you far."[18]

June Boudin meets Courbet in Le Havre and then takes him to his studio in Honfleur. Lodging at the Ferme Saint-Siméon, an inn popular with artists, Courbet makes his first Normandy coastscapes. In Honfleur they meet Baudelaire, a close associate of Courbet from the late 1840s. During a visit to Boudin's studio, Baudelaire is deeply impressed by his pastel studies of skies (see fig. no. 2), and he celebrates these unexhibited works in a July installment of his review of the Salon of 1859 in the *Revue française*: "Boudin, who could gorge himself with devotion to his art, shows his curious collection quite modestly. He knows well that each must become a picture by the means of the poetic impression recalled at will; and he has no pretension of considering these notes as pictures.

4. Charles Lhuillier, *The Soldier (Portrait of Monet)*, 1862. Oil on canvas; 37 × 24 cm, 14⁹/₁₆ × 9⁷/₁₆ in. Musée Marmottan, Paris (5041).

Later, certainly, he will astound us with realized paintings of the prodigious magic of air and water. The studies so quickly and faithfully sketched after what is most transient, what is impossible to grasp in form or color, after waves and clouds, are always inscribed marginally with the date, the hour, and the wind condition, thusly, for example: October 8, noon, northwest wind. . . . In the end all these clouds with fantastic and luminous forms, these yawning furnaces, these firmaments of black or violet satin . . . mount to the brain like a heady drink or the eloquence of opium. Curiously enough, it never once occurred to me in front of one of these liquid, aerial forms of magic to complain about the absence of man."[19]

1860

January 3 Armande-Célestine Vatine, the companion of Monet's sixty-year-old widowed father, gives birth in Le Havre to a daughter, Marie, who now competes with Monet for disposable family resources.[1]

Early 1860 Monet enrolls at the Académie Suisse, located at 4, quai des Orfèvres, Paris, to improve his ability to render the figure. This inexpensive "art school" provides models but no instruction. Possibly he meets Camille Pissarro here.

5. Eugène Delacroix, *Cliffs at Etretat*, date unknown. Watercolor; 17.4 × 22.9 cm, 6⅞ × 9 in. Musée du Louvre, Paris (RF 35828).

6. Johan Barthold Jongkind, *Sainte-Adresse*, 1862. Oil on canvas; 27 × 41 cm, 10¹¹⁄₁₆ × 16³⁄₁₆ in. Phoenix Art Museum, Mrs. Oliver B. James Bequest (70.37).

Monet's aunt Lecadre gives him a small painting by Daubigny, *Harvest with Crescent Moon*. Gautier made an engraving after it, but no example is known. The now-lost Daubigny painting may be the canvas Monet depicts on the wall in an 1861 work, *In the Studio* (fig. no. 3). Within a few years, the impoverished Monet will sell the Daubigny to a dealer.[2]

February Monet moves to 18, rue Pigalle, Paris. He frequents the Brasserie des Martyrs, where modern-minded writers and artists mingle and debate. Monet will later recall that he wasted a great deal of time there.[3]

February 20 Having visited the so-called Salon Intime of Romantic and Barbizon art, including works by Corot, Courbet, Delacroix, Millet, Rousseau, and Troyon, at a commercial gallery at 26, boulevard des Italiens, Monet again writes encouragingly to Boudin: "Our only good seascape painter, Jongkind, is dead as an artist; he is completely mad. . . . [In seascape painting] you have a fine place to take." Dutch landscapist Johan Barthold Jongkind had received considerable official recognition in the 1850s; Monet would soon paint subjects similar to Jongkind's.[4]

March 24 Monet's caricature of an actor appears in *Diogène*. Commissions in August of other caricatures (never realized) suggest that he intends to use his skill to help support himself.[5]

Spring Monet plans (but perhaps never takes) a trip to paint river landscapes around Champigny with two friends.[6]

June Daubigny purchases land in Auvers and builds a house, studio, and garden.[7]

1861

Around February Boudin comes to Paris, staying at 66, rue Pigalle, up the street from Monet. In April Troyon hires Boudin to help him paint the skies for his pictures.[8]

March 2 Monet receives a low number in the lottery for the military draft and faces seven years of duty. His family is unwilling to pay the required 2,500 francs for a replacement unless he gives up painting. On April 29 Monet enlists in the elite first regiment of the African Cavalry. According to army records, he is 1.65 meters (5 ft. 5 in.) tall and has brown eyes. Monet arrives at barracks in Mustapha, Algeria, on June 10. He later recalls the experience with enthusiasm, telling one journalist in 1889 that the landscape there prepared him to become an Impressionist painter.[9]

December The postscript of a letter (now unlocated) from Baudelaire to the writer Arsène Houssaye indicates that earlier the poet had come into possession of "japonneries" and distributed them to friends. This year, for the first time, stores specializing in Japanese art and curios are listed in the Didot-Bottin annual directory of Paris businesses.[10]

1862

Summer Having fallen ill, Monet returns to Le Havre on convalescent leave (see fig. no. 4).[11]

Autumn While working on the coast, Monet meets Jongkind, who provides insights into out-of-doors painting. Monet will later recall that Jongkind worked out-of-doors on watercolors, often making fifteen or twenty a day and using the most promising of these as studies for a

group of oil paintings, which Monet finds relatively unsuccessful. By mid-September Monet introduces Jongkind to Boudin. Jongkind's pictures from this time (see fig. no. 6) will serve as the basis for compositions developed by Monet in the summer and autumn of 1864 (see cat. no. 4). Although no paintings by Monet survive from 1862, a number of pastels evidently date from around the time of this encounter (see fig. no. 7).[12]

November 21 Monet receives an honorable discharge from the military five and a half years early. His aunt Lecadre has decided to pay the replacement fee in order to help him proceed with his art career.[13]

Late 1862 Monet returns to Paris, where his career is guided by Auguste Toulmouche, a successful young genre painter who had recently married a cousin of Monet's aunt Lecadre. Monet shows Toulmouche a still life, *The Cutlet* (private collection), in order to demonstrate his painting skill, and, with Toulmouche's help, Monet begins to study under Charles Gleyre, a Swiss history painter who had stopped exhibiting at Salons after 1849. Gleyre's studio is in the same building where Toulmouche lives, 70 bis, rue Notre-Dame-des-Champs. James McNeill Whistler had studied under Gleyre since 1856.

Since late 1861, Pierre-Auguste Renoir had been a student there. Simultaneously enrolled at medical school, Frédéric Bazille enrolls with Gleyre in November 1862 and shortly afterwards brings his friend Alfred Sisley there as well. Ludovic-Napoléon Lepic, who will later participate in the first two Impressionist exhibitions, enters Gleyre's studio in early 1863. Gleyre's studio thus provides the first opportunity for the future Impressionists to come

7. Claude Monet, *View of the Sea at Sunset*, c. 1862. Pastel on paper; 15.3 × 40 cm, 6 × 15¾ in. Museum of Fine Arts, Boston, Bequest of William P. Blake in memory of his sister, Anne Dehon Blake (22.604) [WP 34].

8. Portrait photograph of Monet, taken by Etienne Carjat in Paris around 1864.

together as a group. Renoir will later recall: "Back then Monet amazed everyone, not only with his virtuosity, but also with his ways. Jealous of his superb appearance when he arrived in the studio, the students nicknamed him the 'dandy.' He didn't have a cent and wore shirts with ruffled cuffs."[14]

1863

March 1 Group exhibition of modern paintings opens at the Martinet Gallery, boulevard des Italiens, with fourteen Manets, including *Music in the Tuileries Gardens* (National Gallery, London), among his most influential proto-Impressionist works.

Early April For the Easter holidays, Monet and Bazille go to Chailly, south of Paris, just outside of Barbizon. They stay at the Cheval-Blanc Inn. Obsessed with landscape painting, Monet stays on in Chailly through May, initiating a lifelong pattern of extending work campaigns beyond his original plans. It seems that only one of the works he made during this time (a farmyard scene) survives.[15]

May 15 Opening of the Salon. This year the admissions jury excludes so many submitted works that the emperor, in response to complaints, authorizes an annex salon to exhibit the works not accepted. This controversial Salon des Refusés includes paintings by Paul Cézanne, Henri Fantin-Latour, Jongkind, Manet, Pissarro, and Whistler.

Summer When Gleyre temporarily closes his studio, Monet visits his family in Le Havre and Sainte-Adresse. Monet resumes his studies with Gleyre in the fall, probably continuing to attend until 1864, when the "school" closes for good.[16]

November 26–December 3 Publication in *Le Figaro* of Baudelaire's highly influential three-installment essay entitled "The Painter of Modern Life," which is devoted to the newspaper illustrator Constantin Guys and encourages painters to follow Guys in portraying contemporary urban subjects. At some unknown date, Monet will acquire an ink wash drawing by Guys, *Woman in Black with White Gloves* (Musée Marmottan, Paris).

1864

February 16–29 At the posthumous auction of works by Delacroix at the Hôtel Drouot, Paris, Georges de Bellio and Victor Chocquet, two collectors who will later become important in Monet's career, purchase works. Among the items auctioned are previously unknown cloud and sky studies on paper (see fig. no. 5).

March Monet resides in a fourth-floor apartment at 20, rue Mazarine, Paris. A photograph of the young artist by Carjat (fig. no. 8) seems to date from around this time. Possibly around now, Monet meets medical student Georges Clemenceau in the Latin Quarter through mutual friends.[17]

April Monet returns to Chailly.[18]

May 1 Opening of the Salon. Boudin for the first time exhibits one of his beach scenes peopled with vacationing Parisians. Future Impressionists Berthe Morisot, Pissarro, and Renoir exhibit for the first time at this Salon.

In terms of Monet's immediate development, the most notable Salon paintings are views of the beach of Villerville (just west of the village of Honfleur) by Daubigny and his son Karl. The paintings by the Daubignys are comparable in appearance to those that Monet will exhibit in the Salon of 1865. According to his biographer Frédéric Henriet, Charles Daubigny painted his work entirely out-of-doors: "The *Villerville-sur-mer* of the 1864 Salon was . . . completely executed on the spot. Daubigny attached his canvas to stakes solidly planted in the ground; and there it stayed, exposed to the attacks of goats and bulls and to the pranks of naughty children, until it was perfectly finished. The painter had chosen a gray sky filled with fat clouds chased by the angry wind. He was constantly on the alert for the right moment and ran to take up his work the moment the weather corresponded to that of his painting."[19]

Late May–Early June Bazille and Monet go by boat down the Seine to Honfleur for two weeks and work around the Ferme Saint-Siméon from 5 A.M. until 8 P.M.[20]

May–November Monet remains in Normandy, running up a considerable bill at the Ferme Saint-Siméon. He reports his excitement to Bazille: "Every day I discover still more beautiful things. It's enough to drive one mad, I've got such a desire to do everything, my head explodes. . . . I want to struggle, scrape off, begin again. . . . It seems to me, when I see nature, that I will do it all, write it all down."

In July Monet meets Boudin and Jongkind at Honfleur, and in September he works there with Jongkind. Together they paint some of the same motifs. Arguments with his family during visits to Sainte-Adresse in August and October result in the suspension of their financial support. Monet asks Bazille to lend him money and arranges for him to take three paintings in October to show to the important Montpellier collector Alfred Bruyas, a major supporter of Courbet. Monet intends to send finished versions of landscapes painted out-of-doors, but he eventually decides that the studies are superior and sends them instead.[21]

June–July On his annual summer vacation to Boulogne, Manet undertakes a group of starkly modern marine paintings, including two depicting the iron-clad Union battleship that had defeated a wooden Confederate warship in the French harbor on June 19. One or more of these paintings is probably included in a group exhibition at the Martinet Gallery in February 1865. Whistler and Monet take immediate inspiration from these Manet seascapes.

October 16 Monet goes to Rouen to see the Twentieth Annual Municipal Fine Arts Exhibition, where his still life of flowers is poorly displayed and not listed in the catalogue. Monet admires still lifes by Boudin's friend Théodule Ribot.[22]

Late October–Early November Monet is commissioned to paint two works for the Le Havre collector Louis-Joachim Gaudibert, who has also commissioned four or five paintings from Gautier.[23]

Early November Bazille works every day on "life-size studies" at Monet's studio. A collector (possibly Gaudibert) has just commissioned three paintings from Monet at 400 francs apiece. Bazille asks family friend and collector Commandant Hippolyte Lejosne to help sell works by Monet.[24]

Around December 15 Monet's father visits Paris and gives Monet 250 francs with which to rent a studio with Bazille.[25]

1865

January Bazille and Monet rent a living/work space at 6, rue de Furstenberg, Paris. Bazille paints a view of the studio (Musée Fabre, Montpellier), and Monet awakens Bazille early every morning so that the two can paint from models together. Monet paints large versions (see cat. no. 4) of marine studies made on the Normandy coast in 1864 to submit in March to the selection jury for the Salon of 1865.[1]

April Monet returns to Chailly to paint.[2]

May 1 Opening of the Salon. Monet's two large marine paintings, including *Headland of the Hève River at Low Tide* (cat. no. 4), are well received by the press. Monet has photographs of these made by a commercial photographer named Jacob; in December 1920 Monet will send these photographs to a biographer, commenting that they represent the first works he ever sold: to the print publisher and art dealer Alfred Cadart, for 300 francs each. Around this time, Cadart exhibits several works by Manet (whose *Olympia* [fig. no. 9] creates a scandal at this Salon). Mistakenly complimented for Monet's Salon paintings, signed with a name much like his own, Manet takes notice of Monet.

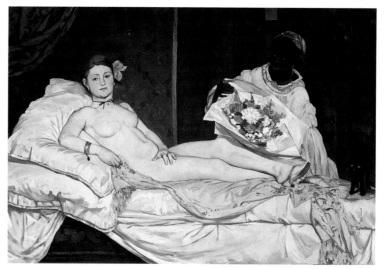

9. Edouard Manet, *Olympia*, 1863. Oil on canvas; 130.5 × 190 cm, 51⅜ × 74¾ in. Musée d'Orsay, Paris (RF 644). In 1889 Monet conducted a fundraising campaign to purchase Manet's masterpiece for the French National Museums.

10. Claude Monet, preliminary portable version of *Luncheon on the Grass*, 1865–66. Oil on canvas; 130 × 181 cm, 51³⁄₁₆ × 71¼ in. Pushkin State Museum of Fine Arts, Moscow [W 62].

Immediately after the opening, Monet returns to Chailly and the Cheval-Blanc Inn to begin drawings and oil studies (see fig. no. 10) for his monumental *Luncheon on the Grass* (cat. no. 5), a painting that will include a dozen life-size figures assembled for a picnic in the forest of Fontainebleau. Monet undertakes such an ambitious figure painting, despite the promise of his Normandy seascapes, perhaps to prove to his still-skeptical family that he is capable of succeeding as a Salon painter.[3]

May Bazille comes with art supplies to Chailly to pose for Monet but instead finds the artist temporarily bedridden with a leg injury. Monet ends up posing for an informal portrait by Bazille (Musée d'Orsay, Paris). Around this same time, Renoir is working nearby in Marlotte; by August, Sisley joins him. In response

to Monet's urgent requests, Bazille returns to Chailly on August 26 in his model's role, although rainy weather slows progress. Both artists stay at the Hôtel du Lion d'Or.[4]

September–Mid-November Courbet paints in Trouville. About his three-month stay, he writes to Bruyas: "I took eighty sea baths. . . . I did thirty-eight paintings in that place, including twenty-five seascapes [see fig. no. 11] similar to yours and to those I did in Sables d'Olonne; and twenty-five autumn skies, one more extraordinary and free than the next." By mid-October Whistler has joined Courbet, and he paints some half-dozen starkly modern seascapes of his own. These important paintings mark the entry of two of the era's foremost avant-garde figure and landscape painters into the genre of marine painting, which

11. Gustave Courbet, *Seascape*, 1865. Oil on canvas; 54 × 64 cm, 21¼ × 25¼ in. Wallraf-Richartz-Museum, Cologne (WRM 2905).

12. Claude Monet, *The Road to Chailly*, 1864. Oil on canvas; 98 × 130 cm, 38⁹⁄₁₆ × 51¹³⁄₁₆ in. Private Collection [W 19].

Boudin and Monet had been exploring in an aesthetically innovative manner since the 1850s.

At this same time, the Goncourt brothers, Edmond and Jules, are also staying in Trouville, finishing their novel about modern painters, *Manette Salomon*.[5]

October Monet, back in Paris, undertakes a large version of *Luncheon on the Grass* in his rue de Furstenberg studio in anticipation of exhibiting the work at the Salon of 1866. He sells 1,000 francs' worth of paintings.[6]

December Courbet and many other painters come to admire Monet's work in progress. But Bazille's decision to move out of their shared studio forces Monet to suspend work in early January 1866.[7]

1866

January Monet rents a small fourth-floor studio at 1, place Pigalle, for 800 francs a year. Unable to finish his oversized *Luncheon on the Grass* (cat. no. 5) in time for the March 20 Salon entry deadline, Monet decides to submit a large landscape, *The Road to Chailly* (fig. no. 12), painted at the same site in 1864 and showing carters transporting felled trees out of the forest. He also quickly begins a life-size painting of a young woman modeling a satin dress and jacket indoors, *Camille in a Green Dress* (fig. no. 13). The model for this work is Camille Doncieux, whose family lives in Monet's new neighborhood. She becomes Monet's companion, and they will marry in 1870. In June Bazille will prepare a very large genre painting (never realized), which would have included a woman wearing a rented green satin dress.[8]

March Courbet exhibits twenty-five works, among them his 1865 Trouville seascapes, at Cadart's gallery and writes that "those seascapes done in two hours sold for twelve to fifteen hundred francs apiece."[9]

Mid-April An exhibition in New York and Boston of the French Etching Club, arranged by Cadart, includes some paintings by Boudin, Corot, Courbet, and Jongkind, and one by Monet, entitled *Sea Shore*.[11]

Mid-April–Summer Monet rents a little house in suburban Sèvres, near Ville d'Avray. Doncieux poses for at least three of the four stylishly dressed women represented in *Women in the Garden* (fig. no. 14). At more than eight feet high, the painting is a monumental version of the sort of illustration used in fashion magazines. Determined to paint this work out-of-doors as a record of strictly firsthand observations, Monet digs a trench into which the canvas can be lowered on pulleys, easing access to its upper portion. Courbet may have visited him in the beginning of July. Impatient creditors in Paris contact his father for payment and threaten to seize Monet's belongings. As late as 1878, Monet is still repaying a January 16, 1867, lawsuit for debts incurred this summer. Monet may have destroyed some two hundred works to prevent their seizure; still others may have been seized and sold.[11]

May 1 Opening of the Salon, with both works submitted by Monet accepted. *Camille in a Green Dress* (listed in the Salon catalogue as *Woman in a Green Dress*) is very well received by newspaper critics. Walter Bürger claims that Monet executed it in only four days. Emile Zola, referring to the work familiarly as *Camille*—

his favorite in the entire exhibition—claims that he does not know the artist, although the two will soon become close friends.

Monet is again compared with Manet, this time by the caricaturist-critic André Gill, and the two artists now meet. Monet's aunt Lecadre, who had been threatening to cut off her support, is convinced by his Salon success to sustain it. Cadart, now back from America and planning a second exhibition there to open December 8, 1866, commissions a reduced-scale replica of the painting *Camille in a Green Dress* (Muzeal de Arte al Republicii Populaire Romaniei, Bucharest), advancing Monet 800 francs.[12]

Late Summer Monet and Doncieux travel to Normandy, bringing *Women in the Garden* along to complete in a studio maintained at the Ferme Saint-Siméon.[13]

Around September Courbet invites Monet and Doncieux, as well as Boudin and his wife, Marie-Anne Guédès, to dinner at the opulent summer home in Deauville of the Count de Choiseul, where Courbet is a guest. Courbet apparently paints his first Etretat coastscapes on this visit to Normandy.

Anticipating Monet's famous subjects of the 1870s, Boudin had painted sailboats at Argenteuil this summer, possibly in the company of Jongkind, and is now working on Jongkind-like harbor scenes at Le Havre, in addition to his signature genre pictures of vacationers on the beach at Trouville.[14]

December Monet asks Bazille to send from Paris *Camille in a Green Dress* and the reduced-scale replica that he had begun for Cadart, but these paintings are still in Paris on December 22, when Cadart demands delivery of the replica

13. Claude Monet, *Camille in a Green Dress*, 1866. Oil on canvas; 228 × 148.9 cm, 89¾ × 58⅝ in. Kunsthalle, Bremen [W 65].

14. Claude Monet, *Women in the Garden*, 1866. Oil on canvas; 256 × 208 cm, 104⅜ × 81⅞ in. Musée d'Orsay, Paris (RF 2773) [W 67]. In 1920 Monet arranged for this important early work to be purchased by the Louvre.

within four days (so that it can be shipped to America), threatening to cancel the sale. However, the painting never goes to America but remains the property of Cadart and is sold at auction in Paris in 1876.[15]

1867

January 18–July 10 In installments, *Le Temps* publishes Edmond and Jules Goncourt's *Manette Salomon*, a Realist novel set in the art world of the 1850s. With its enthusiastic descriptions of photography and Japanese prints, as well as its episodes set in the forest of Fontainebleau and on the beach at Trouville, the novel actually provides a vivid description of Monet's early career. One character, a landscape painter named Crescent, "gave the feeling, almost the emotion, of summer, autumn, morning, afternoon, evening, in admirable paintings of sensations. What he sought and rendered above all was the vivid, profound impression of the place, of the moment, of the season, of the hour . . . —the atmosphere. . . . The penetration of things by the sky was the major study of his eyes and of his spirit, which were always absorbed in the contemplating and coming to know the fairytale effects of sunshine, rain, fog, and haze; the metamorphoses and the infinite variety of celestial tonalities, changing vaporizations, floating rays of light, the decomposition of clouds, the wonderful richness and divine caprice of our

northern skies. Also, for him the sky was never an *isolated fact*, the top and back of a painting; rather, it enveloped the landscape, giving the whole and the details all the relationships of tone . . . from which arose all of nature's mirages and all of the transfigurations of the earth." The novel is published in book form in October.[16]

February Still at Honfleur, Monet works on paintings for the Salon. He also paints a group of related snowscapes. A recollection of Monet at work out-of-doors will be included in a review of the Le Havre International Maritime Exhibition (October 9, 1868): "It was during winter, after several snowy days, when communications had almost been interrupted. The desire to see the countryside beneath its white shroud had led us across the fields. It was cold enough to split rocks. We glimpsed a little heater, then an easel, then a gentleman swathed in three overcoats, with gloved hands, his face half-frozen. It was M. Monet studying an aspect of the snow." This month Courbet, at home in Ornans, also undertakes "a series of snow landscapes that will be similar to the seascapes."[17]

February–March Monet returns to Paris, staying at Bazille's studio at 20, rue Visconti, where Renoir is also a temporary resident.[18]

April 1 Opening of the Universal Exposition, which includes an international art exhibition and sections on Japanese art and manufactures. Opting not to show his luxury textile items

with other specialists within the Exposition galleries, Ernest Hoschedé (whose father died this year, leaving him 200,000 francs), has a special pavilion constructed in the Renaissance style for his company.[19]

April 8 Informed of Doncieux's pregnancy, Monet's father advises his son to abandon her.[20]

May 1 Opening of the Salon. Both of the works submitted by Monet, including *Women in the Garden* (fig. no. 14), are refused by the jury, as are those submitted by Bazille, Pissarro, Renoir, and Sisley. With the support of more established artists Corot, Courbet, Daubigny, and Narcisse Virgile Diaz de la Peña, they try unsuccessfully to pool funds for an independent exhibition, to capitalize on the large crowds in Paris for the Universal Exposition.

Instead, two Paris dealers, Cadart and Louis Latouche, exhibit Monet's intended Salon paintings in the windows of their shops. The former buys a small seascape and the latter a cityscape from a group of such subjects painted in the spring by Monet and Renoir. As a subtle gesture of protest, Monet paints one of his views of Paris, *Garden of the Princess, Louvre* (cat. no. 10), from a balcony of the Louvre, his back turned on the collected art paradigms within. Bazille agrees to buy *Women in the Garden* for 2,500 francs, to be paid in small monthly installments.[21]

May 22 or 24 Opening of a retrospective of fifty paintings by Manet in a self-financed gallery building at the intersection of avenue de l'Alma and avenue Montaigne.[22]

May 30 Opening of a retrospective exhibition of more than 130 paintings by Courbet in a self-financed gallery and studio building constructed on Place de l'Alma. In the catalogue, he categorizes his 1865 Trouville seascapes (see fig. no. 11) as "Paysages de mer," his neologism perhaps guiding Monet to categorize his water lily paintings as "Paysages d'eau" in 1909.[23]

Summer Having arranged for a doctor friend to look after Doncieux, Monet moves in with his family in Sainte-Adresse. He begins a work for the 1868 Salon and by the end of the month has twenty paintings well under way, including seascapes, figures, gardens, and genre paintings of the Le Havre regattas. Doncieux remains in Paris at their rented apartment (8, de l'impasse Saint-Louis). At this time, Sisley is staying in Honfleur, west along the coast from Sainte-Adresse.[24]

Early July Troubled by his eyes, Monet receives medical advice to give up painting out-of-doors.[25]

August 8 Birth of Jean-Armand-Claude Monet, registered three days later as Monet's son and witnessed by Zacharie Astruc and Alfred Hatté. Monet is in Paris briefly for the birth. He makes other short visits from Sainte-Adresse throughout the summer and fall.[26]

Late 1867 Monet, in Paris for the holidays, faces extreme financial pressures. Bazille arranges the sale of a Monet still life to Lejosne.[27]

1868

January–March Monet works in Le Havre on the shipping and pier scenes he will submit to the Salon, and he returns to Paris shortly after March 1 to finish them in their frames before the March 20 entry deadline. Bazille allows Monet to use his new studio at 9, rue de la Paix (today rue de la Condamine).[28]

March 21–? Monet exhibits three works at the annual exhibition of the Société des Beaux-Arts of Bordeaux.[29]

March 26 Monet attends a Hôtel Drouot, Paris, auction of paintings, watercolors, pastels, and drawings by Boudin.[30]

April 2 Baptism of Jean Monet at Sainte-Marie des Batignolles, Paris, with Julie Vellay, Pissarro's companion since 1860, named godmother and Bazille named godfather. Although there is no record that Pissarro is Monet's neighbor at this time, Vellay gives her address as the same building where Monet and Doncieux are living, suggesting that Vellay could be the nursemaid portrayed by Monet in his first painting of Jean (cat. no. 14).[31]

Spring Monet, Doncieux, and son Jean leave Paris to stay at the Gloton Inn in the village of Bonnières-sur-Seine, where Zola and Cézanne had stayed in 1866. Presumably, *On the Bank of the Seine, Bennecourt* (cat. no. 15) is begun at this time. Unable to pay, they must leave the inn at the end of June. His family lodged elsewhere in the vicinity, Monet returns to Le Havre, via Paris, desperately trying to raise money. He suggests to Bazille that he had attempted to drown himself, claiming that his father and aunt will do nothing more to help him.[32]

May 1 Opening of the Salon. Thanks to Daubigny's advocacy, the Salon jury accepts one of Monet's two entries, a Le Havre shipping scene (seized by creditors after the Salon's closing). In his review of the Salon, Zola, very familiar with Monet by now, praises his works at length, including those refused by the jury this year and the year before. Zola mentions racetrack subjects (although no such works are otherwise documented), and he concludes that Monet is a leading painter of contemporary life *(actualiste)*. Zola's reference to a subject more typical of Edgar Degas and Manet than Monet raises the possibility of an early dialogue among them.[33]

May 26 Monet is listed, along with Manet and Fantin-Latour, as "a faithful emulator of Hokusai," among the eighteen leading French enthusiasts of Japanese art by Astruc in his article "Le Japon chez nous," published in *L'Etendard*.[34]

Mid-July–October/November Five works by Monet are included in the art section of the Le Havre International Maritime Exhibition, along with paintings by Courbet, Daubigny, Manet, and Pissarro.[35]

August 1 Monet, Doncieux, and Jean take a hotel room at Fécamp on the Normandy coast; by September they are renting a small furnished house on the rue de Coudriers.[36]

September 7 Monet returns to Le Havre to paint commissioned portraits of the Gaudibert family, working there and at their country home in Montivilliers through October. Courbet, in Le Havre to see the International Maritime Exhibition, introduces Monet to the playwright Alexandre Dumas.[37]

October 6 Houssaye, director of the prestigious periodical *L'Artiste*, buys *Camille in a Green Dress* (fig. no. 13) from the Le Havre exhibition for 800 francs, vowing to donate it one day to the French contemporary art museum at the Luxembourg Palace.[38]

October 25 The jury for the Le Havre exhibition awards Monet one of the four supplementary silver medals added to the forty they distribute to outstanding participating artists.[39]

15. Claude Monet, *The Lunch*, 1868. Oil on canvas; 230 × 150 cm, 90⅝ × 59⅛ in. Städtische Galerie at the Städelisches Kunstinstitut, Frankfurt (S.G. 170) [W 132].

Late October Monet and his family move to route du Havre, Etretat. Although there are several signed and dated pastels from around this time, it is a difficult period for him. He writes to Bazille, "Nothing manages to rekindle my old ardor. Painting is not going well, and decidedly I no longer count on glory. . . . I have become lazy; everything bores me as soon as I want to work; I see everything in black."[40]

Late 1868–Early 1869 Monet's four unsold works are seized and auctioned by creditors at the closing of the Le Havre exhibition. Gaudibert buys them back for the artist. Regaining his high spirits, Monet writes to Bazille that he wants to paint two figure paintings for the upcoming Paris Salon, an interior with his family (*The Lunch*, fig. no. 15) and sailors out-of-doors. He remarks: "I assure you that I don't envy your being in Paris, and I hardly miss the get-togethers [at the Café Guerbois]. . . . One gets too preoccupied with what one sees and hears in Paris . . . and what I will do here will at least have the merit of resembling no one else's work. . . . I honestly believe that I will not return to Paris for a long time now, at most a month each year." Monet asks Bazille to send all of his paintings to his aunt's address in Le Havre so that he may sell some and settle permanently in Normandy. Monet also asks Bazille to send paints, including lots of white, black, and cobalt blue.[41]

16. Pierre-Auguste Renoir, *La Grenouillère*, 1869. Oil on canvas; 66 × 86 cm, 26 × 33⅞ in. Nationalmuseum, Stockholm (NM 2524).

1869

January Paris art supply dealer Latouche exhibits one of Monet's views of Paris in his gallery window.[42]

March Monet returns to Paris, where Bazille gives him access to his rue de la Paix studio so that he can finish the works to be submitted to the Salon jury, *Fishing Boats in the Sea* (Hill-Stead Museum, Farmington, Connecticut) and *The Magpie* (cat. no. 17).[43]

Spring With help from Gaudibert, Monet rents a small house in the village of Saint-Michel, situated in the hills above the Seine resort of Bougival, where Pissarro had spent the summer of 1868. Courbet may visit Monet at this time. By May, Pissarro and his family settle in neighboring Louveciennes.[44]

May 1 Opening of the Salon. Monet learns that his request for an extension has been denied and his Salon submissions are refused. Instead, Latouche shows one of Monet's views of Sainte-Adresse, and it draws fanatical crowds.[45]

Late Summer The penniless Monet gets food from Renoir, who is staying with his parents at nearby Voisins. After selling a still life, Monet buys badly needed art supplies and works in tandem with Renoir at the nearby boating and bathing resort of La Grenouillère (see cat. no. 18 and fig. no. 16). Both hope to develop these works into entries for the Salon of 1870. Their invention of a stenographic style of brushwork to render the choppy, sun-dappled river initiates the pictorial language of classic Impressionism.[46]

Late July–Early August Degas, now a close associate of the Morisot family, vacations around Houlgate on the Normandy coast west of Le Havre, where he makes a series of more than forty remarkably modern pastels on paper with coastal motifs and sky effects (see fig. no. 17). He signs and dates eight of these, which suggests that he had the opportunity to exhibit them.

The striking similarities between Degas's pastels and a group that Monet had done the year before suggest a dialogue between these artists. Regardless of whether they actually met, the similarities indicate that both artists were responding to the sudden interest in pastels that followed the dispersal of Delacroix's works on paper in 1864 and Millet's output of pastels commissioned beginning around 1865.[47]

August–September Staying in a little house on the beach at Etretat, Courbet paints around thirty variations on the single pictorial motif of a crashing wave, again vividly demonstrating a serial approach to landscape and the ultimate challenge of instantaneity. He also paints more views of the picturesque western cliff with its pierced rock (see fig. no. 18), a motif favored by Monet around this same time (see cat. no. 16 and fig. no. 19) and again in the early 1880s (see cat. no. 70). Courbet will exhibit one large version of each motif at the Salon of 1870.[48]

Winter 1869–70 Monet paints snowscapes and several views of the Versailles road at Louveciennes. Pissarro lives on this road, and his paintings of the same subject suggest a close dialogue between the two painters. Probably around this time, Monet paints the frozen river Seine, a subject that he will treat frequently in ensuing severe winters.

Monet poses for two group portraits of artists assembled in a studio, one by Bazille, *Rue de la Condamine Studio*, the other by Fantin-Latour, *A Studio in the Batignolles Quarter* (both Musée d'Orsay, Paris), the latter an homage to Manet that is exhibited at the Salon of 1870.[49]

1870

Early January Monet returns to the forest of Fontainebleau.[1]

May 1 Opening of the Salon. One of Boudin's works is lent by Ernest Hoschedé. Monet's two paintings, *The Lunch* (fig. no. 15) and a lost version of *La Grenouillère*, are refused; Daubigny and then Corot resign from the jury in protest. Of Monet's colleagues, only Cézanne is similarly excluded.

Around this time, Monet sells two paintings, *The Seine at Bougival* (cat. no. 19) and *Camille on the Beach at Trouville* (Mrs. John Hay Whitney Collection), to art dealer Pierre Ferdinand Martin, with whom Jongkind, Boudin, and Pissarro are already doing business. As partial payment for the first of these works, Monet receives a small painting by Cézanne, *Picnic by a River* (Yale University Art Gallery, New Haven, Connecticut), apparently the beginning of what will become Monet's remarkable collection of works by Cézanne.[2]

June 28 Marriage in Paris of Camille Doncieux and Monet, who is still living in Saint-Michel. Courbet, who has just refused the Legion of Honor, is a witness. The marriage documents indicate review by authorities of Monet's military service status. War with Prussia is becoming increasingly likely.[3]

Summer Leaving a number of canvases in safekeeping with Pissarro in Louveciennes, the Monets leave Saint-Michel for the Channel resort of Trouville, registering at the Hôtel Tivoli. Of the 1,500 works by Pissarro stored in Louveciennes, only forty will survive the ensuing Franco-Prussian War.[4]

July 7 Death of Monet's aunt Lecadre at Sainte-Adresse.[5]

July 19 Official declaration of the Franco-Prussian War. Bazille had enlisted for military service on July 10; Renoir will be drafted into the Tenth Cavalry Regiment on August 26.[6]

August 12 The Boudins arrive in Trouville, where Monet is painting Boudinesque subjects of vacationers relaxing along hotel beachfronts and several astonishing genre-portraits of Camille seated on the beach with a sunshade (see cat. no. 21).[7]

17. Edgar Degas, *Houses beside the Sea*, probably 1869. Pastel on paper; 81.3 × 116.8 cm, 32 × 46 in. Musée d'Orsay, Paris (RF 31199).

18. Gustave Courbet, *Rock Arch at Etretat*, 1869. Oil on canvas; 76.2 × 123.1 cm, 30 × 48½ in. The Barber Institute of Fine Arts, The University of Birmingham, Great Britain.

19. Claude Monet, *Rough Sea at Etretat*, 1868–69. Oil on canvas; 66 × 131 cm, 26 × 51⅝ in. Musée d'Orsay, Paris (RF 1678) [W 127].

August 31 Surrounded and trapped by Prussian forces at Sedan, the main French army, led by Marshal MacMahon, surrenders on September 2.

September 4 Anticipating a Prussian advance on Paris, a provisional government of national defense led by Léon Gambetta declares itself as the Third Republic. The Prussians begin to besiege the city on September 19, and Gambetta escapes from the capital in a balloon and tries to organize the French armies in the countryside. Sometime in September, Degas and Manet, who had remained in Paris, as had Morisot, volunteer for the artillery of the National Guard.[8]

September 5 Monet gets a passport. Four days later, visiting his sick father in Le Havre, Monet observes boats departing full of passengers seeking refuge in neutral London from war in France.[9]

September 28 Bazille dies in combat.

Before October 6 The Monets flee to London, temporarily settling at 11 Arundel Street, Piccadilly Circus (today Coventry Street, W1).[10]

October 31 Monet's father marries Armande-Célestine Vatine and acknowledges his paternity of their daughter, Monet's half-sister.[11]

December Monet paints the Thames Embankment and the Houses of Parliament for the first time. One of Monet's recent Trouville paintings, *Breakwater at Trouville, Low Tide* (cat. no. 22), is included in Paul Durand-Ruel's First Exhibition of the Society of French Artists at his German Gallery, 168 New Bond Street, London. Daubigny, also in London, had introduced Monet to the similarly exiled dealer. Another Monet Trouville painting is included in the Exhibition for the Benefit of the Distressed Peasantry of France, held at the Gallery of the Society of British Artists, London. Daubigny serves on the organizing committee for this exhibition.[12]

1871

January 1 The Monets move to 1 Bath Place (today Kensington High Street) in the West End, London.[13]

January 17 Monet's father dies in Sainte-Adresse. There is no record of any inheritance received by Monet.[14]

January 21 Durand-Ruel puts Pissarro, who settled in the London suburbs the previous month, in touch with Monet. Together the friends visit museums and galleries, taking particular inspiration from Constable and Turner, according to Pissarro's later recollections. They also dine together at the home of Whistler's friend Alphonse Legros, the French Realist artist who had settled in London in 1863.[15]

20. Portrait photograph of Monet, taken by A. Greiner in Amsterdam, 1871.

21. Claude Monet, *Sailboats at Argenteuil*, 1872. Oil on canvas; 48 × 75 cm, 17¾ × 29½ in. Musée d'Orsay, Paris, Caillebotte Bequest (RF 2778) [W 233].

January 28 With the surrender of Paris, an armistice provides for a new French National Assembly to negotiate peace with Prussia.

March 18–May 28 Fearful that the conservative National Assembly meeting in Versailles might restore the monarchy, an insurrection in Paris results in the formation of a Republican municipal government, the Commune, on March 26. Troops of the Versailles government attack Paris on May 21, initiating a "Bloody Week" of civil war that results in 20,000 fatalities and the fall of the Commune.

May 1 Opening of the International Exhibition at the South Kensington Museum, London (today the Victoria and Albert Museum), including works by Pissarro and Monet, the latter contributing two figure paintings (*Meditation, Camille Monet on the Couch* [Musée d'Orsay, Paris] and *Camille* [the reduced-scale version of *Camille in a Green Dress*]) and perhaps a seascape. Works submitted by both artists to the Royal Academy exhibition are not accepted.[16]

May Durand-Ruel makes his first recorded purchase of Monet paintings.

The Monets leave London for Holland. Although evidently unfamiliar with the Hague School of out-of-doors coastal landscape painting under way by 1871, Monet would have been made aware of rich subjects in Holland by Daubigny, Jongkind, and others. During his stay in Holland, Monet perhaps acquires some Japa-

nese prints and some flower pots with blue oriental-style designs. Amsterdam photographer A. Greiner takes portraits of the Monets (see fig. no. 20).[17]

June 2 The Monets arrive in remote Zaandam, a picturesque town of 12,000 citizens surrounded by canals and dotted with windmills. Staying at the Beurs Hotel, Monet paints twenty-four works, some related to pencil notebook sketches, while Camille gives French lessons.[18]

June Monet meets the French painter Henri Michel-Lévy, probably in Amsterdam. Along with influential decorative arts historian Henry Havard, who had been active in the Commune, Monet and Michel-Lévy visit the Rijksmuseum on June 22. Later that same day, Michel-Lévy and Havard join the Monets at the Beurs Hotel, staying until late July.[19]

October 8 The Monets leave Zaandam for Amsterdam. A few days later, Monet visits the Frans Hals Museum in Haarlem.[20]

Before Mid-November The Monets return to Paris and register at the Hôtel de Londres et de New York (near the Saint-Lazare train station). Monet rents a nearby studio, formerly occupied by Gautier, on the fifth floor of 8, rue de l'Isly, for 450 francs a year. Since Monet does not paint any Paris scenes during the next few years, this evidently serves more as a business office and storage facility. Boudin lives nearby. Monet soon sells at least one Holland painting to Latouche.[21]

December 21 Monet rents a house (for 1,000 francs yearly) in Argenteuil with a river view and a garden at 2, rue Pierre Guienne, owned by the widow of one of Manet's friends. With 8,000

inhabitants, this town on the Seine is linked to the Saint-Lazare train station by an hourly service. Asking Pissarro to send the remaining paintings stored in Louveciennes when the Monets went to Trouville the previous year, Monet writes of his intention to commute to Paris daily to work in his studio there from 10 A.M. to 4 P.M.[22]

1872

At intervals throughout 1872, Durand-Ruel buys twenty-nine paintings from Monet for a total of 9,800 francs, and Manet buys *The Highway Bridge under Repair, Argenteuil* (cat. no. 29). The dealer also begins to buy works from Degas, Manet, Pissarro, Renoir, and Sisley, his support effectively shaping the group of artists soon to be publicized as Impressionists.

Monet's total sales this year, including sales to other dealers, will amount to 12,100 francs. Monet's personal account ledger for the period when he is living in Argenteuil indicates expenditures for two domestic servants and a gardener and purchases of considerable amounts of wine. Although his income is comparable to that of a doctor in Paris or roughly six times greater than that of an Argenteuil workman, such comparisons are misleading unless overhead expenses like art supplies are taken into account.

With this increased income, Monet buys a boat and fits it with a cabin to serve as a floating studio, following the precedent set by Daubigny, who is still using his own studio boat in Auvers in the early 1870s.[23]

January Courbet asks Boudin to bring Monet and Gautier to visit him at a clinic in Neuilly, where he is being treated for hemorrhoids after

22. Claude Monet, *Impression, Sunrise*, 1872. Oil on canvas; 48 × 63 cm, 17¾ × 21¾ in. Musée Marmottan, Paris, Donop de Monchy Bequest, 1957 (4017) [W 263].

four months in prison for political crimes during the Commune.[24]

Winter Monet and Sisley paint together in Argenteuil.[25]

March Encouraged by his brother Léon, who lives outside of Rouen, Monet shows two paintings at the Twenty-third Municipal Fine Arts Exhibition there. While in Rouen for this exhibition, Monet paints around a dozen paintings, several incorporating the gothic towers of Rouen Cathedral in the background and several apparently painted from a boat.[26]

Spring Posing his wife and guests in his own garden, Monet establishes a lifelong tendency to integrate his roles as family member and painter (see cat. no. 27). Several very similar works by his guest Sisley indicate that the two artists are working in tandem.

The similarity between woodblock prints by Hiroshige and 1872 paintings by Monet of sailboats at Argenteuil (see fig. no. 21) suggests that he is adding to his collection of Japanese art around this time.[27]

Summer Durand-Ruel's Fourth Exhibition of the Society of French Artists at his German Gallery, London, includes two paintings by Monet, as well as works by Degas, Manet, Pissarro, and Sisley, prefiguring the group that will soon exhibit together in Paris. The Monet painting listed in the catalogue as *Havre* was either a large 1860s Salon painting or the painting, dated 1872, now known as *Impression, Sunrise* (fig. no. 22), which will become notorious at the April 1874 Impressionist exhibition in Paris. Living in London, Whistler paints

harbor scenes similar to Monet's *Impression, Sunrise*.

November 2 Durand-Ruel includes two paintings by Monet in the Fifth Exhibition of the Society of French Artists at his German Gallery, London, along with works by Degas, Pissarro, Renoir, Sisley, and Whistler.

December Sisley paints his first set of "flood" paintings at Port-Marly. Monet, too, will often paint floods of the Seine.

1873

January Durand-Ruel sells one of Monet's Holland paintings to Daubigny (cat. no. 24). Starting now, recent works by Monet are sold occasionally in Paris auctions.[28]

January 18 Whistler shows a group of his works (which remain unidentified) at Durand-Ruel's Paris gallery that are, in his own words, "intended to indicate . . . my theory in Art— The *Science* of color and *'picture* pattern' as I have worked it out for myself during these years. . . . My frames I have designed as carefully as my pictures . . . [and] they form as important a part as any of the rest of the work— carrying on the particular harmony throughout. . . . By the names of the pictures also I point out something of what I mean in my theory of painting." Whether or not Monet and Whistler influence each other is unknown.[29]

February 28 Durand-Ruel buys twenty-five paintings from Monet for 12,100 francs. Four works by Monet are illustrated in the four-volume *Recueil d'estampes* (1873), a sampling

of works by artists represented by Durand-Ruel's gallery. In the preface (previously published in installments from August 17 to September 28, 1872, in *La Renaissance litteraire et artistique*), the influential critic Armand Silvestre characterizes Monet as the most daring painter of his generation and compares his mode of rendering objects in discontinuous brushstrokes to children's puzzles and Japanese prints.[30]

April 22 Monet writes to Pissarro expressing the hope that he can come to Argenteuil to have lunch with Sisley. In what seems to be the earliest reference to the plan to organize an independent artists' exhibition society, which will make its debut in April 1874, Monet explains that the idea is favored by everyone except Manet.[31]

April 25–May 7 Durand-Ruel's Sixth Exhibition of the Society of French Artists at the German Gallery, London, includes two paintings by Monet, as well as works by Degas, Manet, Pissarro, Sisley, and Whistler.

May 5 Paul Alexis, a close friend of Cézanne and Zola, publishes an article in *L'Avenir national*, encouraging the formation of an "artistic corporation" to give artists exhibition opportunities outside of the Salon. On May 7, assuming a leader's role in the nascent independents group, Monet writes to Alexis that "a group of painters assembled in my home has read with pleasure [your] article . . . and we hope [that your newspaper will help] when the society which we are about to form is completely constituted." Alexis publishes Monet's letter in the May 12 issue of *L'Avenir national* and names Jongkind, Pissarro, and Sisley—but not Boudin, Cézanne, Degas, Morisot, and Renoir—among those who had already joined.[32]

May 5–8 Sale, in Paris, of John Constable's *Weymouth Bay* (fig. no. 24) to John W. Wilson, who presents the painting to the Louvre later in the year.

May 24 Back from a trip to Japan, Théodore Duret, art critic and friend of Manet, buys a little 1867 Monet painting for 1,200 francs, to be paid in installments. When Duret disregards his payment schedule, Monet threatens to take the work back.[33]

September 12 Monet invites Pissarro to Argenteuil to discuss improvements to the bylaws under consideration for the independent artists' exhibition society. Explaining that Renoir is away, Monet invites Pissarro to spend the night. This suggests that Renoir is often at Argenteuil around this time, sometimes working in tandem with Monet, as they had on occasion during the 1860s. Renoir paints at least four portraits of Camille Monet in Argenteuil. Renoir's portraits of Monet dressed in black (see frontispiece and fig. no. 25) amount to a

23. Claude Monet, *The Drawbridge, Amsterdam*, 1874. Oil on canvas; 53.5 × 63.5 cm, 21 1/16 × 25 in. Shelburne Museum, Shelburne, Vermont [W 306].

24. John Constable, *Weymouth Bay*, c. 1818–19. Oil on canvas; 88 × 112 cm, 34¾ × 44 in. Musée du Louvre, Paris (RF 39).

"series." It is unknown whether Renoir intends to be ironic by portraying Monet in a dark manner altogether at odds with his colorful style. Monet's paintings of his studio boat amount to a "series" of self-portraits, by proxy.[34]

September 22 Death of Camille Monet's father. The following month, she receives 4,000 francs as part of her inheritance.[35]

November 3 Durand-Ruel's Seventh Exhibition of the Society of French Artists at the German Gallery, London, includes two paintings by Monet and works by Degas, Manet, Pissarro, Sisley, and Whistler.

November–December In Paris Monet tries to convince more artists, including caricaturists Carjat and Gill, to take part in the forthcoming independents group exhibition. At this time there are fifteen members.[36]

December Durand-Ruel buys nine paintings from Monet for 7,000 francs. Altogether,

according to Monet's notebook ledger, he sells 24,800 francs' worth of paintings this year. Thanks to a severe economic recession, however, Durand-Ruel is unable to make more purchases from Monet or his colleagues until February 1881.[37]

December 27 Official incorporation of the "Société anonyme des artistes peintres, sculpteurs, graveurs, etc." Various drafts of the articles of incorporation explain that its goals are to stimulate sales with a jury-free and prize-free exhibition around the time of the official Salon, and it is hoped that the corporation can publish its own magazine.

Once arrangements are made to rent the former studio of the photographer Nadar at 35, boulevard des Capucines, Paris, as galleries for the first Impressionist group exhibition, to open the following April, Monet goes to Paris to paint two views of the busy street from the gallery window (Pushkin State Museum of Fine Arts, Moscow, and cat. no. 39). His intention is to allow exhibition visitors to make a direct comparison between the view of the street from the window and the view as represented in the paintings.[38]

December 1873–January 1874 Monet goes to Le Havre over the holidays, lodging at the Hôtel de l'Amirauté, and paints views of the port (see cat. nos. 35 and 36).[39]

1874

January 14 Auction at the Hôtel Drouot, Paris, of eighty-four works, mostly landscapes, from the collection of Ernest Hoschedé, whose straitened circumstances force him to sell part of his collection of contemporary art. Included are thirteen works by Impressionist artists Degas, Monet, Pissarro, and Sisley, all of which sell at good prices, raising hopes that the recent recession is coming to an end. The Rumanian-born homeopath Dr. Georges de Bellio buys the first of over thirty works by Monet that he will acquire by 1881. Ernest Chesnau writes the catalogue preface.[40]

February–March? Monet takes undocumented working trip(s) to Amsterdam, producing a dozen paintings, including two snowscapes. None is ever exhibited or listed in Monet's sales ledger; and indeed early 1873 needs to be considered as another possible time frame for this campaign. The uncharacteristic absence of documentation for these important paintings might indicate that Monet exhibited or sold them outside of Paris. New Yorker Louisine Elder—who will marry Horace Havemeyer in 1883—buys one of these paintings (fig. no. 23) around 1877 on the advice of Mary Cassatt, marking the first purchase of a Monet work by an American collector.[41]

25. Pierre-Auguste Renoir, *Claude Monet Reading*, probably 1873. Oil on canvas; 61 × 50 cm, 24 × 19⅝ in. Musée Marmottan, Paris (5013a).

26. Claude Monet, *Train in the Snow*, 1875. Oil on canvas; 59 × 78 cm, 23³⁄₁₆ × 30¹¹⁄₁₆ in. Musée Marmottan, Paris (4017) [W 356]. Monet painted this picture from the Argenteuil train station, which faced his house on boulevard Saint-Denis.

March 5 Early Cézanne supporter Dr. Paul Gachet urges Pissarro, his Auvers neighbor, to organize an auction of paintings by Cézanne, Degas, Manet, Monet, Sisley, and "everyone in the cooperative" in order to help Honoré Daumier, the great cartoonist and Realist artist, who had become virtually blind.[42]

April 15–May 15 Historic first exhibition of the Société anonyme at 35, boulevard des Capucines, Paris, including more than 165 works in various media by thirty artists. Of these, Cézanne, Degas, Morisot, Pissarro, Renoir, and Sisley will achieve legendary status, along with Monet, as the core Impressionists. Among the etchings exhibited by Félix Bracquemond is a reproduction of Turner's *Rain, Steam, and Speed* that prefigures Monet's 1877 paintings of the Saint-Lazare train station (see cat. nos. 49, 50, and 52). The walls of the gallery are brownish red, as is typical for commercial and municipal art installations at the time.

Monet shows five paintings, including *The Lunch* (fig. no. 15), which had been refused at the Salon of 1870; *Poppy Field at Argenteuil* (fig. no. 27); *Fishing Boats Leaving the Harbor, Le Havre* (cat. no. 35); and seven pastels, some perhaps done as early as 1862. One painting is listed under a title suggested by Renoir's brother: *Impression, Sunrise* (fig. no. 22). The term "Impressionist" is subsequently used to describe works by the entire group. According to Littré's 1866 dictionary, "impressions" are the sensory stimuli caused by objects preceding any mental categorization. The most serious argument in favor of the term appears in an April 29 review by Jules Castagnary, who had already used it to refer to Jongkind's paintings. The humorist Louis Leroy, skeptical of both Salon and independent artists, uses the word less seriously in his April 25 review, "Exposition des impressionnistes," published in the satirical journal *Le Charivari*.[43]

April Durand-Ruel's Eighth Exhibition of the Society of French Artists at the German Gallery, London, includes three paintings by Monet, as well as works by Manet, Pissarro, and Sisley.

Monet's idyllic garden world is threatened when Argenteuil municipal authorities approve the construction of a new ironworks.[44]

June With Manet's help, Monet sells three very large early works to Opéra baritone Jean-Baptiste Faure; this is the single most important purchase from Monet by any collector until now. Faure also acquires recent works from Monet during this year. In all, Monet's sales for 1874 will amount to around 10,500 francs, down roughly sixty percent from his 1873 art income.

Monet signs a lease for a new house, with occupancy on October 1, 1874. Monet's willingness to pay 1,400 francs yearly (up from 1,000) suggests that he needs more space. Before moving, Monet makes an ambitious painting, *The Lunch (Decorative Panel)* (fig. no. 28), of his family in their garden after breakfast, combining elements of still life, genre, and landscape. Not since his 1868 paintings intended for the Salon has he worked on such a large scale. When he finally exhibits this work in 1876, he lists it without a title in the catalogue as a "decorative panel," indicating an ambition to go beyond easel painting and to conceive works as modern domestic murals.[45]

Summer Durand-Ruel's Ninth Exhibition of the Society of French Artists at the German Gallery, London, includes two paintings by Monet, as well as works by Degas, Pissarro, Renoir, and Sisley. The financially troubled Durand-Ruel will close his London gallery the following year.

July–August Manet vacations in Gennevilliers, near Argenteuil, where he spends most of the month with Monet and Renoir, adopting their broad, controversial style in his own works. Renoir (National Gallery of Art, Washington, D.C.) and Manet (Metropolitan Museum of Art, New York) both paint the Monet family in their garden, and in turn Monet paints a portrait (now lost) of Manet at work there. Manet makes two large Impressionist "portraits" of Monet and his wife on his studio boat (Staatsgalerie Stuttgart, and fig. no. 29), perhaps intending to submit one to the Salon of 1875. Neither painting is fully realized, because Monet is unwilling to pose for long periods of time.[46]

October Monet moves to a recently constructed house—it is pink with green shutters—on boulevard Saint-Denis in Argenteuil, across from the train station.[47]

December 17 Renoir presides over a meeting to dissolve the indebted Société anonyme.[48]

27. Claude Monet, *Poppy Field at Argenteuil*, 1873. Oil on canvas; 50 × 65 cm, 19⅝ × 25⅝ in. Musée d'Orsay, Paris (RF 1676) [W 274].

28. Claude Monet, *The Lunch (Decorative Panel)*, 1873–76. Oil on canvas; 162 × 203 cm, 63 × 79 in. Musée d'Orsay, Paris (RF 2774) [W 285].

29. Edouard Manet, *Monet Painting in His Studio Boat*, 1874. Oil on canvas; 80 × 98 cm, 31½ × 38½ in. Bayerische Staatsgemäldesammlungen, Neue Pinakothek, Munich (8759).

1875

January 30 The National Assembly, although divided by significant demands for the restoration of the monarchy, declares that France will remain a republic.

March 23–24 Desperate to find buyers, Monet, Morisot, Renoir, and Sisley auction seventy-three of their works at the Hôtel Drouot, Paris (see cat. nos. 40 and possibly 41). Their unconventional paintings nearly cause a riot, obliging the auctioneer to call in the police. The catalogue preface is by critic and Japanese art enthusiast Philippe Burty. Only about half of Monet's twenty works find buyers, among them Degas's friend the painter Henri Rouart, who had exhibited at the April 1874 independents group exhibition, and Chesnau, another champion of Japanese art. Asked by Manet to publicize the event in the press, Albert Wolff gives the works a mixed review in *Le Figaro* (March 24), saying that the Impressionist paintings make him think of "a cat walking on a piano keyboard or a monkey who has got hold of a box of paints." Off to a bad start with this sale, Monet's 1875 art income will amount to only 9,765 francs.[1]

June Manet, to whom Monet turns in desperation for small loans throughout the year, buys five paintings from Monet for 440 francs. Monet's first major figure painting since the Franco-Prussian War, *The Stroll, Camille Monet and Her Son Jean (Woman with a Parasol)* (cat. no. 42), is a testament to his ongoing dialogue with Manet, Renoir, and now Morisot, all of whom are seeking to adapt the brushwork of classic Impressionist landscape to figure painting.[2]

October 2 Camille Monet transfers the rights to a 2,000-franc inheritance that she is due to receive on January 1, 1877, to the art supply dealer Carpentier in order to settle Monet's bill.[3]

October 10 Writing to Burty, Monet expresses excitement about a work in progress: *Camille Monet in Japanese Costume* (cat. no. 45), a Salon-scale painting of Camille in a blonde wig, wearing a red Japanese actor's robe, posed in a setting decorated with fifteen Japanese-style fans. Monet is probably directly inspired by Manet's never-exhibited portrait of art-world hostess Nina de Callias (Musée d'Orsay, Paris), which includes a similar background of Japanese fans.[4]

1876

February 5 Brought to Argenteuil by Cézanne, collector Victor Chocquet buys a painting, *Autumn on the Seine, Argenteuil* (cat. no. 33), and a pastel, *Fishing Boats off the Normandy Coast* (cat. no. 8), for 120 francs, the first of around a dozen Monet works he will assemble. Cézanne had met Chocquet through Renoir, who had

30. Claude Monet, *Domestic Interior*, 1875. Oil on canvas; 80 × 60 cm, 31¼ × 23½ in. Musée d'Orsay, Paris (RF 2776) [W 365]. Camille and Jean Monet are shown in the second Argenteuil house.

31. Claude Monet, *Gladioli*, probably 1876. Oil on canvas; 60 × 81.5 cm, 56 × 83 in. The Detroit Institute of Arts, City of Detroit Purchase (21.71) [W 414]. Monet made several paintings of Camille in the garden of the second Argenteuil house during the summer of 1876 (see also cat. no. 48).

painted portraits of the collector (Collection of Oskar Reinhart, Winterthur, Switzerland) and his wife (Staatsgalerie Stuttgart) in 1876.

Prompted by Degas, Renoir and Rouart write to painter Gustave Caillebotte, explaining that the independents group has decided to resume its exhibitions with a month-long show to open in March. Inviting him to join the group, they explain that each participant will be limited to five works.[5]

March 30–End of April Second exhibition of the independents group opens at the Durand-Ruel Gallery at 11, rue Le Peletier, with 252 works by nineteen artists. Of the eighteen works exhibited by Monet, nine are borrowed from Faure and one from Chocquet, leaving only eight for sale. These eight include Monet's two major 1875 "portraits" of Camille Monet, *The Stroll, Camille Monet and Her Son Jean (Woman with a Parasol)* (cat. no. 42) and *Camille Monet in Japanese Costume* (cat. no. 45), as well as *The Beach at Sainte-Adresse* (cat. no. 12), *The Reader (Springtime)* (cat. no. 26), and *Meadow at Bezons* (cat. no. 41). Installed next to Monet's group, Morisot's presentation includes five extremely sketchy 1875 views of one harbor locale on the Isle of Wight. Her works amount to the first exhibited "series"

of related Impressionist landscapes. The exhibition attracts extensive but mixed press coverage.

Bazille's family, learning that Manet has lent Renoir's 1867 *Portrait of Bazille* (Musée d'Orsay, Paris) to this exhibition, arranges to acquire it. In exchange, Manet receives Monet's large *Women in the Garden* (fig. no. 14).

Edmond Duranty's *The New Painting*, a thirty-eight-page pamphlet published in response to the exhibition, is the first attempt to trace the roots of Impressionism back to Boudin, Constable, Corot, Courbet, Jongkind, and other older painters.[6]

April 14 Sale at the Hôtel Drouot, Paris, apparently organized by Hoschedé, includes eleven paintings that he did not sell at his own 1875 sale, and at least three works by Monet, among them the controversial *Camille Monet in Japanese Costume*, which the artist removes from the group exhibition and offers for sale. Although *Camille Monet in Japanese Costume* supposedly sells for 2,020 francs, the "buyer" could have been Monet. The 12,300 francs of art income recorded in Monet's account book for this year includes this questionable sale, as well as some advances on paintings not yet realized. The total might therefore be exaggerated by as much as twenty percent.[7]

April 22 Monet formalizes arrangements to borrow 1,500 francs from Morisot and Eugène Manet, her husband, with fifteen paintings as collateral. Throughout this year, Monet is desperate to raise money.[8]

Late April Initiating an extraordinary support for Monet, Caillebotte buys several Monet works. Beginning this year, the independently wealthy Caillebotte frequently advances sums to Monet against future purchases.[9]

May From Chocquet's fourth-floor apartment at 198, rue de Rivoli, Paris, Monet initiates his series procedure by painting four views of the Tuileries Gardens, a motif also painted by Renoir. Around this time, Monet also makes three paintings of the Parc Monceau in Paris, a subject painted by Caillebotte.[10]

July Manet spends two weeks at Rottenbourg, the Hoschedés' country home in Montgeron inherited by Alice Hoschedé, née Raingo, in 1870.[11]

August Camille Monet poses for a group of garden paintings that combine elements of landscape, genre, and still-life painting (see cat. no. 48 and fig. no. 31).

September Monet is invited to Rottenbourg to paint four large decorative works, one of which is *The Turkeys (Decorative Panel)* (cat. no. 46). The artist remains, probably returning periodically to Argenteuil and Paris, through December. It seems likely that Alice Hoschedé and Monet fall in love during Ernest Hoschedé's absences on business in Paris and that Monet is the father of Alice's youngest son, Jean-Pierre, born in August 1877.

Given the proximity of the Hoschedé properties to Yerres, where Caillebotte works during the summers until 1879, Monet has the opportunity to strengthen this friendship.[12]

November 3 Caillebotte writes his will, naming Renoir as executor. He guarantees funds for an Impressionist group exhibition in 1878 and states that his art collection is to be donated to France—on condition that the works be exhibited at the contemporary art museum in the Luxembourg Palace in Paris, and later in the Louvre.[13]

1877

January Monet moves to a ground-floor studio at 17, rue Moncey, near the Saint-Lazare train station. Caillebotte pays the 700 francs yearly rent for this studio through 1878, advancing Monet further sums of nearly 1,000 francs during this year.

Monet obtains permission to paint at Saint-Lazare, the terminus for trains to most of his destinations, including Argenteuil and Normandy. According to Renoir, this subject gives Monet the opportunity to respond to critics who had lampooned the hazy effects of some of the works in the 1874 independents group exhibition. Monet allegedly claims, "At departure times, the locomotives' smoke is so thick there that almost nothing is clearly visible. It is an enchantment, a true *féerie*. . . . They will need to delay the Rouen train. The light is better a half-hour after its departure time." Renoir recalled that Monet put on his best suit, fluffed his ruffled cuffs, and while playing nonchalantly with a gold-tipped cane, had his card presented to the station's manager: "I have decided to paint your station. For a long time I have hesitated between North station and yours, but in the end I think yours has more character."

As a result, Monet has the full cooperation of the station personnel: they stop trains, empty platforms, and load engines with coal to make them generate the smoke that suits his pictorial needs. Monet plans the compositions of some of the twelve paintings he makes there in pencil notebook sketches (see cat. no. 51). Monet's in-depth treatment of a single locale marks an important stage in the evolution of his working methods, henceforth often designed around serial variations on a group of subjects adjacent to one another.

Ernest Hoschedé obtains twenty-seven paintings from Durand-Ruel without paying for them, including works by Manet, Monet, Morisot, Pissarro, and Sisley. Durand-Ruel gives a painting by Monet and one by Pissarro to Chesnau as a fee for this sale. Still faced with financial problems, Durand-Ruel has arranged to rent all his gallery premises for a year.[14]

32. Gustave Caillebotte, *The Pont de l'Europe*, 1876. Oil on canvas; 124.7 × 180.6 cm, 49⅛ × 71⅛ in. Musée du Petit Palais, Geneva. The tracks leading to Saint-Lazare train station are visible through the bridge's girders.

March Ernest Hoschedé buys six works directly from Monet including three Saint-Lazare paintings, among them *Arrival of the Normandy Train, Saint-Lazare Station* (cat. no. 50), thus initiating a new kind of collecting in series. But within a year, Hoschedé will sell all three, perhaps not ever having taken possession of them. Chesnau and de Bellio also buy works from this new series.[15]

April 4 Opening of the third exhibition, on the second floor of a building at 6, rue Le Peletier, near the Durand-Ruel Gallery, of independent artists who now refer to themselves as "Impressionists." Eighteen artists present 241 works. A special periodical, *L'Impressionniste*, is published in conjunction with the exhibition. Seven of the thirty works exhibited by Monet depict the Saint-Lazare station (see cat. nos. 50 and possibly 53). Eleven Monet paintings are lent by Hoschedé, including the large (and unfinished) *Turkeys* (cat. no. 46) from the decorative scheme conceived for Rottenbourg possibly in competition with Whistler, who had undertaken his famous Peacock Room decorations in London in 1876. Caillebotte (see fig. no. 32) and Renoir also show relatively large-scale works. Pissarro presents his entries in white frames. Extensive press coverage ranges from hostile to enthusiastic.[16]

May 28 Auction at the Hôtel Drouot, Paris, of works by Caillebotte, Pissarro, Renoir, and Sisley with poor results. Monet, despite his pressing need to raise money, does not take part.[17]

June–July De Bellio buys ten Monet paintings for 1,000 francs (in the course of the year, he buys sixteen works, often advancing small sums to the artist between acquisitions). Although

Monet's personal account book records an income of 15,197.50 francs this year, his real art sales amount to only around 9,000 francs, not counting some 2,000 francs' worth of advances. When possible, he barters art to settle debts, for example trading sixteen works to his art supplier Voisinot.[18]

July Monet's ledger indicates that he sold two frames, two Japanese robes, and three plates for 200 francs.[19]

Summer–Winter Camille Monet, who became pregnant in June, is gravely ill from an ulcerating uterus, and the bulk of Monet's time is spent caring for her and their son.[20]

August 20 Alice Hoschedé, who may have been leaving Paris to avoid the embarrassment of her husband's forthcoming bankruptcy declaration, gives birth to Jean-Pierre Hoschedé on a train to Biarritz.[21]

October 6 Premiere of *La Cigale*, a short play spoofing Impressionist landscape painters, written by Degas's friends Ludovic Halévy and Henri Meilhac. Monet and Renoir may have helped to paint the sets. This autumn Monet spends afternoons in his Paris studio, presumably in an effort to produce and sell enough paintings to settle debts so that his family can leave Argenteuil without creditors seizing furnishings or paintings.[22]

December Monet sells five oil sketches to pastry chef/restaurateur Eugène Murer, who hosts Wednesday dinners for Impressionist artists and their critic friends in the back room of his 95, boulevard Voltaire, establishment, decorated by Pissarro and Renoir. As a rule, Murer buys small, inexpensive works for his collection, on this occasion paying only 125 francs to Monet for all five works.[23]

1878

January 5 Manet lends 1,200 francs to Monet. Unclear entries in both artists' account books suggest that the loan will be renegotiated in March and may remain unpaid for more than a year. An undated letter from Manet to Duret, perhaps written around this time, proposes that, acting anonymously, they jointly buy 1,000 francs' worth of paintings from Monet. Sometime later this year, Manet makes a most generous trade with Monet: Monet returns a little 1874 Argenteuil painting by Manet in exchange for his own 1866 *Women in the Garden* (fig. no. 14), which Manet had acquired in a trade with the Bazille family in 1876. Monet will never exhibit this important painting but will sell it in 1921 to the Louvre.[24]

Late January The Monets move back to Paris, taking a large apartment on the second floor of 26, rue d'Edimbourg, for an annual rent of 1,360 francs.[25]

March Caillebotte chooses *The Lunch (Decorative Panel)* (fig. no. 28) as well as three Saint-Lazare paintings in return for funds advanced to Monet the previous year.[26]

March 17 Birth of Michel Monet. Manet and his close friend the composer Emmanuel Chabrier are witnesses for the birth certificate.[27]

March 25 Meeting held at the gallery of Alphonse Legrand at 22a, rue Lafitte, near the Durand-Ruel Gallery, to discuss plans for a never-realized June 1878 independents group exhibition. Degas advocates a new guideline, barring artists who send works to the Salon from participating in these independent group shows.

Also in 1878 Legrand seems to have been organizing an exhibition of Impressionist paintings in America, apparently unsuccessfully, since Legrand later notifies Pissarro that his paintings are being returned.[28]

April Chabrier buys three paintings from Monet for 300 francs, including one recent work from a group painted on the island of Grande Jatte, just outside Paris.[29]

May 1–November 15 Universal Exposition, incorporating the 1878 Salon, in which Renoir participates for the first time in the hope of increasing his marketability. The fair also contains an international art exhibition and an extensive exhibition of Japanese art at the Trocadero Palace.[30]

May Publication of Duret's pamphlet *Les Peintres impressionnistes*, with brief biographies and commentaries on the work of Monet, Morisot, Pissarro, Renoir, and Sisley; Monet is singled out as "the Impressionist par excellence." Duret relates their unconventional

33. Claude Monet, *The Rue Montorgueil, Celebration of June 30, 1878*, 1878. Oil on canvas; 80 × 48.5 cm, 31½ × 19⅛ in. Musée d'Orsay, Paris (RF 1982.71) [W 469].

34. Claude Monet, *The Rue Saint-Denis, Celebration of June 30, 1878*, 1878. Oil on canvas; 76 × 52 cm, 29¹⁵⁄₁₆ × 20⁷⁄₁₆ in. Musée des Beaux-Arts, Rouen (09.1.34) [W 470].

brushwork to the tradition initiated by Corot, Courbet, and Manet, and argues that their bold use of color is indebted to the example of recently imported Japanese prints. He adds that the Impressionists already have the support of distinguished collectors and critics.[31]

June 5–6 Bankruptcy forces Ernest Hoschedé to sell, at the Hôtel Drouot, Paris, his art collection, which includes sixteen works by Monet (see cat. no. 26). Low bids indicate that the market for Monet's art remains depressed. This sale initiates a relationship between Monet and Georges Petit, who has been in charge of his family's art gallery since the death of his father the previous year. Petit buys three paintings at this sale, at least one on behalf of Monet; Petit will soon become Durand-Ruel's chief rival in the Impressionist market.[32]

June 30 National Sunday holiday to celebrate the recovery of France after the Franco-Prussian War. Monet obtains permission to make two paintings of the festivities from balconies overlooking the flag-bedecked rue Montorgueil and rue Saint-Denis in central Paris: *The Rue Montorgueil, Celebration of June 30, 1878* (fig. no. 33) and *The Rue Saint-Denis, Celebration of June 30, 1878* (fig. no. 34), both of which he sells within a matter of days (one to the recently bankrupted Hoschedé). Manet also makes two paintings of flags decorating rue Mosnier, Paris

(Bührle Collection, Zurich, and the Mr. and Mrs. Paul Mellon Collection).[33]

August–September Monet leaves his Paris apartment for Vétheuil, a small Seine-side village with 600 inhabitants. Access to Paris involves a carriage service from Vétheuil to the train station at Mantes. Monet and his family move into a small house on the road to Mantes, sharing the premises with the Hoschedé family, Alice and Ernest Hoschedé and their six children: Marthe, Blanche, Suzanne, Jacques, Germaine, and Jean-Pierre (see fig. nos. 47 and 48). Ernest Hoschedé receives 500 francs per month from his mother, who also rents an apartment for him in Paris. Camille Monet's health is rapidly deteriorating.

Monet often paints at the village of Lavacourt, across the Seine, and works from his studio boat. Anticipating his 1892–93 *Rouen Cathedral* paintings, his earliest views of the church at Vétheuil initiate an obsession with this single motif that will last more than two decades.[34]

October The Monets and Hoschedés rent a house on the Chantemesle–La Roche-Guyon road (which becomes a favorite painting subject; see cat. no. 58) in Vétheuil for 600 francs a year. The rented property includes an orchard leading down to the bank of the Seine, where Monet can dock his studio boat. Although

35. Claude Monet, *Vétheuil in Fog*, 1879. Oil on canvas; 60 × 71 cm, 23¼ × 27¾ in. Musée Marmottan, Paris (5024) [W 518].

36. Pierre-Auguste Renoir, *The Wave*, 1879. Oil on canvas; 64.8 × 99.2 cm, 35½ × 39 in. The Art Institute of Chicago, Potter Palmer Collection (1922.438).

Monet sells Vétheuil landscapes to the dealer Jules Luquet and to de Bellio during October, this year his art sales will amount to only around 4,000 francs. Meanwhile Monet moves his Paris "studio" to a ground-floor apartment at 20, rue Vintimille, again rented for him by Caillebotte for 700 francs a year. The "studio" serves as a convenient storage space, readily accessible to potential collectors, for Monet's works and for works by his colleagues such as Pissarro.

Thanks to Manet, Ernest Hoschedé is employed by the Paris newspaper *Le Voltaire*, but as the financial situation of the two families worsens, the children's nanny and tutor both quit over unpaid wages.[35]

Around December 10 Monet goes to Paris for two weeks, trying without much success to raise sufficient funds to care for his wife, who desperately needs medical attention, and to pay his household staff.[36]

December 30 Monet inscribes a small portrait of Jean-Pierre Hoschedé (private collection) as a gift to the boy's mother, Alice.[37]

1879

January 27 This especially harsh winter provides Monet with snowscape motifs, four of which he sells in Paris for his only significant income aside from loans until October. Later in life Monet will recall the complete indifference of collectors to perhaps his most remarkably minimal Vétheuil winter scene (fig. no. 35), with its reflection of the town's church-dominated skyline in the rippling waters of the Seine. The same subject observed in sunlight, and appar-

ently painted from the studio boat, was a favorite of Monet's during this and the following summer (see cat. no. 60).[38]

March 10 Monet writes to de Bellio that he has lost hope, and learning of his friends' plans for a new independents group exhibition, he decides not to participate.[39]

Mid-March Monet receives an undated letter from Caillebotte, who tries to persuade him to participate in the independents group exhibition: "Since you are not working, come to Paris, you have time to collect all the possible pictures from lenders. I will take care of M. de Bellio. If there isn't a frame on the 'Flags' [fig. nos. 33 and 34], I will take care of it. I will see to everything."[40]

April 10–May 11 The fourth independents group exhibition in five specially decorated rooms (perhaps with electric lighting) on the first floor of a new building at 28, avenue de l'Opéra, includes around 250 works by sixteen artists. The hastily prepared catalogue gives an inaccurate account of what is actually on view; for example, Degas shows eight works at most, while the catalogue lists twenty-five. Missing from the original group of painters are Cézanne, Renoir, and Sisley (who submitted works to the Salon jury), and Morisot. Gauguin and Cassatt participate in an independents group exhibition for the first time, the latter presenting works in painted frames (vermilion and green).

Monet's works are hung with Pissarro's in the last room. Twenty-nine works by Monet (see cat. nos. 11, 22, and 40) are listed in the catalogue, some dating back to the 1860s, twenty-four borrowed from collectors; since no newspaper account refers to it, there is the

possibility that a major early work, *Garden at Sainte-Adresse* (cat. no. 11), may not have been sent in time from Montpellier. The works most acclaimed by reviewers are his two views of flag-bedecked streets painted the year before (fig. nos. 33 and 34). Monet does not go to Paris for this exhibition.[41]

May 1 Acknowledging the receipt of two (additional) works for the exhibition, Caillebotte assures Monet that he will quickly have the rips in them repaired and reports that Cassatt is ready to buy the larger one. Thanks to good attendance, each exhibitor receives 439 francs after the closing, at which time Caillebotte, who had sent Monet 2,900 francs on account in April, arranges to return Monet's paintings to their owners.[42]

May 14 Unable to pay for his family's share of expenses, Monet considers moving and asks Ernest Hoschedé to calculate what is owed. The same day he writes a deeply discouraged letter to Manet, explaining that he cannot repay any loans, since all his money goes to doctors and medicine for his suffering wife; moreover, the poor weather has prevented him from painting new works to sell.[43]

July Five canvases by Monet (see cat. no. 26), Pissarro, and Sisley are exhibited in the offices of the newspaper *L'Evénement*. Monet is in Paris in mid-July for a few days, trying in vain to sell paintings.[44]

Summer Renoir is on the Normandy coast at Wargemont and Dieppe working on a decorative ensemble for a client's summer house and painting coastscapes, including a crashing wave (fig. no. 36) of the sort Courbet had painted a decade before and that Monet will render in 1881 (see cat. no. 66). Renoir will return to the same area in the following summers.

August 17 Monet writes to de Bellio that Camille Monet can no longer get out of bed or hold down any food. Totally preoccupied with nursing her, the painter is out of art supplies and unable to purchase new ones.[45]

August 31 Thanks to Alice Hoschedé, a devout Catholic, Camille Monet receives the last rites and church sanction of her civil marriage to Monet.[46]

September 5 Camille Monet dies at the age of thirty-two. After her death, Monet paints a portrait, *Camille Monet on Her Deathbed* (fig. no. 37). The burial follows on September 7.[47]

September–October Behind two quarters on his rent, Monet continues to rely on Caillebotte for substantial advances. Urged by Caillebotte, Monet takes works to Paris, desperate to find buyers. Sales amount to about 1,000 francs.[48]

November Back in Vétheuil, where the temperature is low and there is considerable snowfall, Monet paints still lifes (see cat. no. 55).[49]

November 16 Monet writes to Ernest Hoschedé that he should return to Vétheuil, where his presence will help quiet rumors about the relationship between the painter and Alice Hoschedé. Ernest wants Alice to leave Vétheuil and settle the family in Paris.[50]

November 25 According to Pissarro, Impressionist works sent to America have been returned with "jeers." It is not known whether or not these works were actually exhibited and where, or whether any Monets were in this group.[51]

December The Seine freezes in record cold temperatures. Monet braves the sub-zero conditions to begin an extraordinary series of riverscapes documenting the freeze and subsequent thaw.[52]

December 25 Ernest Hoschedé, who is acting as Monet's sales agent in Paris, does not come to Vétheuil to spend Christmas with his family.[53]

December 29–30 Borrowing money for train fare, Monet takes several new still lifes and snow paintings to Paris and sells more than 1,000 francs' worth of them. The dealer Petit makes a down payment on a still life and promises to buy more, urging Monet—whose 1879 art income totals 12,285 francs—to stop selling cheaply. Meanwhile, rising temperatures and pouring rain cause flooding in Vétheuil.[54]

1880

January 5 As the Seine thaws, crashing blocks of ice wake the Monet and Hoschedé families. Monet makes roughly two dozen paintings of

37. Claude Monet, *Camille Monet on Her Deathbed*, 1879. Oil on canvas; 90 × 68 cm, 35 × 26½ in. Musée d'Orsay, Paris (RF 1963.3) [W 543].

the awesome spectacle (see cat. no. 56). Ironically, the compositions of these stark paintings of scattered blocks of ice directly anticipate the summertime *Water Lilies* paintings he begins two decades later. Monet also paints more salable still lifes.[1]

January 24 *Le Gaulois* predicts that in several days the independents will learn of the "death" of Monet, whose funeral will be celebrated on the date of the opening of the Salon. The malicious article says that Monet lives in Vétheuil in a white house with his "wife" (i.e., Alice Hoschedé) and supports his former patron Ernest Hoschedé, who is now ruined and living in the artist's studio. *L'Artiste* reprints the article in February. Letters to the editor of *Le Gaulois* from Monet and Ernest Hoschedé go unpublished.[2]

February 14 The Hoschedé–Monet household servants quit and file suit because of unpaid wages.[3]

March Monet decides to send works to the Salon again, hoping that success there will improve sales, especially with Petit. Five days after the deadline, Monet submits two paintings, *Lavacourt* (Dallas Museum of Art), based on studies made a year or two earlier, and *Floating Ice* (cat. no. 56), to the Salon jury.[4]

April 1–30 Fifth independents group exhibition, without the participation of Cézanne,

Monet, Morisot, Renoir, or Sisley. Pissarro presents his works on lilac walls with canary-yellow borders. After this month, Caillebotte apparently no longer pays rent for the rue Vintimille studio, although Monet uses it for another year.[5]

Mid-April Monet goes to Paris for a few days, possibly to discuss a one-artist exhibition at the gallery adjoining the offices of *La Vie moderne*, a weekly publication that had been launched in April 1879 by Georges Charpentier, publisher of Zola's novels and host since the mid-1870s of Parisian art-world soirées at his townhouse at 11, rue de Grenelle, for which Renoir had provided staircase decorations around 1876–77. Emile Taboureux travels to Vétheuil this month to interview Monet for an article intended to appear in *La Vie moderne* at the time of the show. Monet lends his book of press clippings to Taboureux to read as background.[6]

April 30 Opening of the Salon. Monet's one accepted painting, *Lavacourt*, is installed disadvantageously high on the uppermost row of paintings on crowded walls. In his review in *Le Voltaire*, Zola devotes considerable attention to the history of the major artists of the independents group in and out of the Salon; he concludes that Monet, the leading Impressionist, now paints too quickly because he needs sales, but that in ten years he will be universally acclaimed.[7]

May 25 Monet goes to Paris to help Duret prepare the catalogue and negotiate loans for the exhibition at *La Vie moderne*'s gallery, planning to return later to help with installation.[8]

June 6 Monet attends the private opening at the gallery of *La Vie moderne* at 7, boulevard des Italiens, of his first one-artist exhibition, which includes eighteen works (see cat. nos. 54, 56, 61, and possibly 55), many borrowed from collectors for the month-long show. The first painting listed in the catalogue is *Floating Ice* (cat. no. 56), recently refused by the Salon jury, which Mme Charpentier will buy as a present for her husband. According to a review in the June 19 issue of *La Vie moderne,* many works sell immediately. In his introduction to the little catalogue, Duret claims that Monet begins and finishes all his paintings directly from nature (rather than in a studio with the aid of preparatory studies), a method which frequently requires the artist to return to a given site several times before a painting can be completed. However, it is known that Monet already sometimes makes exceptions to this principle.[9]

June 12 Taboureux's interview with Monet in *La Vie moderne* describes Monet's makeshift "port" and his studio boat. Exaggerating, the artist tells Taboureux that he has never had a traditional studio. Alluding to his absence from this year's group show, Monet claims that he "is always and wants always to be an Impressionist." This spring and summer, Monet again paints riverscapes and views of Vétheuil from his studio boat (see cat. no. 60).[10]

July Despite art sales for this year that will total more than 12,000 francs, old creditors are still a problem.[11]

August 5–September 3 Three works by Monet, including the one exhibited at the Salon, are included in an exhibition of the Société des amis des arts in Le Havre.[12]

Around September 10 Monet spends a few days with his brother Léon in Rouen and accompanies him to his vacation home at Petites-Dalles on the Normandy coast. Several works painted there mark the beginning of Monet's six-year preoccupation with the churning surf and sublime cliffs along the Channel coast.[13]

October 3 Monet writes to Duret that he cannot leave Vétheuil just now without losing a whole "series of studies" (partially completed works needing more working sessions). He abandons two studies of apple trees because, when he goes to the site, the apples have been picked.[14]

December 9 Monet writes to Duret that he wishes he could spend a month in London to seek sales there and to paint several views of the Thames.[15]

38. Claude Monet, *Sunset on the Seine, Winter Effect,* 1880. Oil on canvas; 100 × 152 cm, 39 × 59¼ in. Musée du Petit Palais, Paris (439) [W 576].

December 10 Death of Ernest Hoschedé's mother. Monet attends the funeral in Paris on December 12.[16]

1881

January An injured finger prevents Monet from painting. He hopes to arrange for a Paris exhibition, either at *La Vie moderne* or at the gallery of another publication, *L'Art.*[17]

January 24 Writing to Pissarro, Caillebotte confides: "One could write a book with everything [Degas] has said against Manet, Monet, and you," adding that "he went so far as to tell me, referring to Renoir and Monet, 'You receive those people in your home?' "[18]

February 17 With the financial backing of Jules Féder, director of the Union Générale bank, Durand-Ruel reinitiates business with the Impressionists that had been suspended since 1873. He comes to Monet's rue Vintimille studio and buys fifteen recent paintings for 4,500 francs, including at least two coastscapes painted at Petites-Dalles. The purchase is not recorded in his gallery's records until April, suggesting that some of the paintings may have been incomplete when the purchase was decided.[19]

March 9–Around April 10 At the fishing port of Fécamp, Monet begins a group of coastscapes, realizing subjects that he had prospected during the winter of 1868–69. Assuming viewpoints on the coastal clifftops as well as on the beaches, Monet addresses vast barren spaces with activated stenographic brushwork suggesting the tossing sea (see cat. nos. 62, 63, and 66). The work produced during this campaign marks a dramatic departure from his generally idyllic 1870s suburban landscapes with figures. Monet plans to remain in Normandy for just three weeks, but he stays longer when Durand-Ruel advances money.

Renoir, who is also a beneficiary of Durand-Ruel's renewed patronage, travels to Algeria in March and April (see fig. no. 39). In 1900 one of Renoir's Algerian pictures will become a centerpiece in Monet's private collection, and in December 1883 Renoir will take Monet to the Mediterranean coast to stake out similar lush motifs.[20]

April 2–May 1 Sixth independents group exhibition is staged, without the participation of Caillebotte, Cézanne, Monet, Renoir, or Sisley.

April 29 Monet takes his brand-new coastal works to Paris. Durand-Ruel immediately buys four, and then buys eighteen more a few days later, for 300 francs each.[21]

May 7 Caillebotte and his brother Martial buy property at Petit Gennevilliers (across the Seine from Argenteuil) and begin to plan construction of buildings and a garden.[22]

May 24 With his lease due to expire in October and realizing that Vétheuil provides no suitable school for his son Jean, Monet writes to Zola for information about the town of Poissy.[23]

June Durand-Ruel buys another 3,000 francs' worth of paintings, reestablishing a more or less regularly executed exclusive option on Monet's output. Thanks to this renewed business rela-

39. Pierre-Auguste Renoir, *Banana Plantation*, 1881. Oil on canvas; 51 × 63 cm, 19⅝ × 27⅞ in. Musée d'Orsay, Paris (RF 1959.1).

40. Claude Monet, *Road at La Cavée, Pourville*, 1882. Oil on canvas; 60.4 × 81.5 cm, 23¾ × 32⅛ in. Museum of Fine Arts, Boston, Bequest of Mrs. Susan Mason Loring (24.1755) [W 762]. In 1882 Monet undertook a small "series" of three paintings of the road that descends from the cliffs of Varengeville, near Pourville.

tionship, Monet's total art sales for 1881 will total 20,400 francs, making it his best year since 1873. Alice Hoschedé writes to her husband that she plans to return to Paris with the children in October and that he should find an appropriate home for them.[24]

October 1 Monet writes to Durand-Ruel that he has begun a large work, presumably *The Artist's Garden at Vétheuil* (National Gallery of Art, Washington, D.C.), the last of a series of four paintings of the stairs in the garden leading up to the Vétheuil house, from which he is about to move (see cat. nos. 64 and 65).[25]

October 31 Monet delivers eleven paintings to Durand-Ruel in Paris. This month the dealer buys two still lifes of gladioli in an elongated vertical Japoniste format. In the next year, Durand-Ruel will commission similar still lifes from Monet for the doors of his sitting room (see fig. no. 42).[26]

Late October–November After his annual summer stay on the Normandy coast, Renoir leaves for Italy. The daringly stenographic views of Venice painted on this trip are the closest counterparts by any artist to Monet's landscapes of the late 1870s and early 1880s (see fig. no. 38), widely criticized for being painted too quickly and without sufficient detail.[27]

November 18 Baptism in Vétheuil of Michel Monet at the request of Alice Hoschedé.[28]

Mid-December The Monets, along with Alice Hoschedé and her children, rent the Villa Saint-Louis, a large house with a view of the river at 10, cours de 14-Juillet, in the northern sector of Poissy, a town with a population of 5,600 on the left bank of the Seine, twenty kilometers west of Paris. Alice Hoschedé's decision to move to Poissy with Monet amounts to open acknowledgment of their spousal relationship.[29]

1882

February 1–2 Bankruptcy is filed by the Union Générale bank. The bank's director, Jules Féder, had advanced funds to Durand-Ruel and now asks for reimbursement.[30]

February 4 Not at all inspired to paint Poissy subjects, Monet goes to the town of Dieppe on the Normandy coast and stays at the Grand Hôtel du Nord et Victoria. On this and subsequent trips, Monet corresponds almost daily with Alice Hoschedé.[31]

February 9–10 Monet writes to Pissarro and Durand-Ruel that he has no interest in participating in another independents group exhibition. He cannot imagine returning from the coast so quickly and would wish to choose and install his works personally.[32]

February 15 Uninspired by the motifs around Dieppe, which he finds too urban, Monet moves on to Pourville, a fishing village five kilometers to the west, where he stays at a modest beachside hotel-restaurant. Pencil sketches in one of his notebooks indicate how Monet would scout an area at the beginning of any campaign. In mid-winter he finds the resort beaches to be empty and sublime, with the year's highest tides, but the cold makes work out-of-doors very difficult. Monet's only complaint is that the Pourville cliffs have no caves similar to those around Dieppe, where he was able to shelter during bad weather.[33]

February 23–24 Monet writes to Durand-Ruel that he has changed his mind and now agrees to participate in the independents group exhibition, on condition that Renoir also participate and that Monet's train fare to Paris be paid. However, Monet remains on the coast until the end of the month, while the exhibition is organized and installed by Pissarro and Caillebotte. Renoir agrees to let Durand-Ruel oversee his participation in the exhibition because he has contracted

41. Marcellin Desboutin, *Paul Durand-Ruel,* 1882. Drypoint; 19.5 × 15 cm, 7¹¹⁄₁₆ × 5¹⁵⁄₁₆ in. Document Archives Durand-Ruel, Paris.

42. In addition to Monet's decorative still lifes, two large paintings by Renoir are visible in this photograph of the sitting room of Paul Durand-Ruel's home at 35, rue de Rome, Paris.

pneumonia while visiting Cézanne in L'Estaque. Cézanne, despite Pissarro's efforts, does not take part.[34]

March 1–April 2 Seventh group exhibition of independent artists at 251, rue Saint-Honoré, in the Salle Valentino (near the Place Vendôme), on the floor above a panorama depicting the August 6, 1870, defeat of France at Reichshoffen. There are approximately 210 new works shown by nine artists, including thirty-five by Monet (see cat. nos. 56 and possibly 65), almost all of them from Durand-Ruel's stock. The dealer now prices Monet's works at 2,000 to 2,500 francs each. As at earlier exhibitions, several artists use white frames, and Pissarro's paintings are glazed. Electric lighting allows the exhibition to remain open until 11 P.M.

Many critics this year suggest that the pervasive blue-violet tonality of Impressionist paintings is indicative of abnormal vision. In the artists' defense, Chesneau argues in *Paris-Journal* that Impressionism is first an exploration of retinal sensation and only secondarily a description of reality.[35]

March 5 Monet is back at Pourville, intending to return home to Poissy for Easter on April 9. Once again, however, he underestimates how much time he will need to paint there, and bad weather impedes his progress.[36]

March 25 Monet explains to Durand-Ruel that he cannot send new paintings from Pourville until he can see the "series" all together. During this period, most of Monet's "series" consist of two to four treatments of the same motif. However, by the end of the year, he makes fourteen

different paintings of the abandoned Napoleonic coast guard's post, now used by fishermen, that overlooks the English Channel at Petit Ailly (see cat. no. 67). Most of his "studies," he tells Alice Hoschedé in April, have required at least ten working sessions, some as many as twenty. On any given workday, he might work on eight different canvases at disparate sites. This method requires him to hire someone to carry all these wet canvases and his other art supplies from site to site.[37]

Mid-April Monet returns home to Poissy with about three dozen new works in a special case, the dimensions of which will oblige him on this and subsequent campaigns away from home to make works on a few standard-sized canvas formats that can be shipped this way. By April 15 Monet transfers his belongings at the rue de Vintimille, Paris, studio to another studio in the same building.[38]

April 22 Monet brings sixteen paintings to Durand-Ruel, who pays 6,000 francs for them. Three days later, the dealer pays 400 francs each for another seven works.[39]

May Courbet retrospective at the Ecole des Beaux-Arts, Paris. Among the 135 works are many paintings of the Normandy coast from the 1860s, which provide a clear historical perspective for Monet's newest efforts at related sites. Moreover, the fact that variations by Courbet of a single composition are installed in tandem at this exhibition provides an important precedent for Monet's ongoing effort to exhibit similar works together in groups or series.

May 26 Durand-Ruel mentions that he has commissioned Monet to make a suite of still-life paintings for the panels of the doors in the sitting room of his home at 35, rue de Rome, Paris (see fig. no. 42).[40]

June 17 With advances from Durand-Ruel, Monet and his extended family rent a summer house, the Villa Juliette, in Pourville. Alice Hoschedé's daughter Blanche joins Monet in painting out-of-doors. Durand-Ruel and Renoir visit Monet in July, and Renoir evidently stays on through August. Monet also sees Chocquet frequently.[41]

Mid-July Four works by Monet are included in an Impressionist exhibition organized by Durand-Ruel in London at 13 King Street, St. James's.[42]

September 16 Monet asks Pissarro for information about schools for the children in Pontoise, evidently hoping to move from Poissy.[43]

Autumn Three works by Monet are included in a group exhibition at the Gurlitt Gallery in Berlin, where his works will be exhibited the following year as well.[44]

October 5 Monet returns to Poissy after the summer in Pourville with about sixty new paintings (see cat. nos. 67 and 68), some not finished to his satisfaction. Eleven days later, he delivers thirteen paintings to Durand-Ruel for 5,200 francs, followed shortly thereafter by thirteen more for 5,900 francs. This year's art income will amount to 24,700 francs, not including additional advances from his dealer.[45]

November 4 Monet goes to Paris to see Sisley and Durand-Ruel and to discuss future Impressionist exhibitions. Unenthusiastic about more group shows, Monet recommends to Durand-Ruel that one-artist exhibitions, alternating between landscape and figure painters, would be more appropriate to the dealer's intimate gallery spaces.[46]

December 22 Monet and Pissarro visit an "International" group exhibition staged by Durand-Ruel's rival Georges Petit. Although they are disinterested in the works on view, they realize that Petit's deluxe gallery space (with several exhibition rooms, one 2,700 square feet, with electric lighting) at 8, rue de Sèze, would provide an ideal setting for an Impressionist group show. Therefore, they urge Durand-Ruel to consider a business relationship with Petit. Durand-Ruel explores this possibility in June–July 1883.[47]

1883

January 31 After stopping in Le Havre on January 25, Monet checks in at the beachside Hôtel Blanquet ("Where artists get together," according to its signboard) in familiar Etretat, where he will stay for nearly a month. "My motifs are right outside the door, and my window even looks out on one," Monet writes home enthusiastically.[48]

February 2 For his rapidly approaching one-artist exhibition at Durand-Ruel's newly rented Paris gallery at 9, boulevard de la Madeleine, Monet makes studies for two large works, one of the famous western cliff with its flying-buttress-like rock formation that Courbet had painted in 1869 and one of fishing boats. Monet never realizes the latter idea and, ultimately, withholds all his new Etretat pictures from his upcoming show.[49]

February 3 Disregarding the easily accessible motifs that excited him when he arrived in Etretat, Monet decides to paint at the isolated beach just west of town, inaccessible except by scaling the steep vertical cliff at low tide. At this time, Monet devotes only three canvases to the cliffs and beaches, although in 1885 he will return and realize a more extensive group of works here. Monet's innovative method of bringing many canvases to remote sites, so that he can put one down and start another as light conditions change, is imperfect for coastscapes, since not only the light but the height of the tide has to be similar from one day to the next in order for him to progress with any single canvas based on particular conditions. For these coastscapes, Monet must synchronize his work sessions with both solar and tidal clocks.[50]

February 10 In order to work productively despite heavy rain, Monet turns a room with a

43. James McNeill Whistler, *Design for a Parasol for Lady Archibald Campbell*, 1881–82. Pencil and watercolor on off-white wove paper; 29.3 × 23.2 cm, 11⁹⁄₁₆ × 9⅛ in. Hunterian Art Gallery, University of Glasgow, Birnie Philip Bequest. Whistler's use of the water lily motif exemplifies its widespread popularity decades before it became Monet's principal subject.

view in the hotel's annex into a studio. He cannot sleep with worry about the forthcoming exhibition.[51]

Mid-February Whistler exhibits a suite of Venice etchings in an elaborate installation in London, which in some ways prefigures the yellow décor that Monet will provide for his Giverny dining room in the early 1890s: "[Whistler] decorated the gallery in a scheme of white and yellow. The wall was white with yellow hangings, the floor was covered with pale yellow matting, and the couches were pale yellow serge. The few light cane-colored chairs were painted yellow. There were yellow flowers in the pots, a white and yellow livery for the door attendant."[52]

February 18 Ernest Hoschedé visits Poissy to discuss his family's future, causing Monet to worry that Alice Hoschedé might be persuaded to return to her marriage. Monet himself returns to Poissy three days later with about two dozen paintings (see cat. nos. 70 and 71), most, if not all, finished later.[53]

February 28–March 27 Monet's second one-artist exhibition at the Durand-Ruel Gallery. Around sixty works, many lent by collectors, are included; fifty-six are listed in the catalogue (see cat. no. 24). Monet complains that his dealer has not enlisted sufficient press coverage and that the back room needs shades to control overly strong light. Evidently Durand-Ruel complies, for one press account reports that the room is too dark.

Taking the exhibition's press coverage into his own hands, Monet sends a small painting to Burty and provides him with first-hand information about his career in order to encourage him to review the show. Burty writes the best of all the generally positive reviews and one of the most important early accounts of Monet's life and work; it appears in *La République française* on March 27. Gustave Geffroy writes about the artist for the first time in Clemenceau's *La Justice* on March 15. Acclaiming the poetic nature of Monet's new images and his innovative brushwork, Alfred de Lostalot's review in the *Gazette des Beaux-Arts*, which generally limits its coverage to acknowledged old and modern masters, is particularly noteworthy. Lostalot goes to great lengths to explain the paintings' controversial violet tonalities with reference to recent scientific discoveries about exceptional individuals sensitive to the ultraviolet end of the spectrum. Monet provides two drawings to illustrate the article, and gives one to the magazine's director, Louis Gonse.[54]

March 9 From Vernon, where he is house-hunting (his Poissy lease expires on April 15), Monet goes to Paris to see an exhibition of Japanese art (it is unknown which exhibition he sees).[55]

April 20–July 7 Paintings by Monet are included in the Société des impressionnistes exhibition organized by Durand-Ruel at the Dowdeswell & Dowdeswell Gallery, 133 New Bond Street, London.[56]

April 29 With considerable financial support from Durand-Ruel, Monet moves to what will be his final home, in Giverny, a village of 279 inhabitants eighty kilometers northwest of Paris and across the Seine from the town of Vernon, where the older children will go to school. The rental consists of a large house along with a smaller one on ninety-six acres. The property extends from the village's major east–west road on the north to the Gisors–Vernon road and railroad on the south, both of these following the river Ru, which empties into the Seine.[57]

April 30 Death of Manet in Paris. With Burty, Duret, Fantin-Latour, and Zola, among others, Monet serves as pallbearer at the funeral in Paris on May 3.[58]

Early June Monet builds a boathouse on a small, nettle-covered island in the Seine a kilometer away from his house. This first summer in Giverny, he explores the surrounding area by boat, encountering a repertoire of motifs that will be hallmarks of his career. He also starts to plant his garden, explaining to Durand-Ruel that he wants "to have flowers to pick for rainy days" so as not to lose a single working moment.[59]

44. Paul Cézanne, *The Sea at L'Estaque*, 1882–85. Oil on canvas; 73 × 92 cm, 28¾ × 36¼ in. Musée Picasso, Paris (RF 1973.59).

45. Claude Monet, *Villas at Bordighera*, 1884. Oil on canvas; 115 × 130 cm, 45¼ × 51³⁄₁₆ in. Musée d'Orsay, Paris [W 857].

September–December Durand-Ruel takes three works (see cat. no. 28) by Monet to Boston for the "American Exhibition of Foreign Products, Arts and Manufactures," which runs from September 1 until December 1. Franco-American relations had recently been celebrated by the French gift of Frédéric Bartholdi's *Statue of Liberty* to the United States.

On November 9 Monet sends Durand-Ruel his first paintings of motifs around Giverny. When the weather is rainy, Monet arranges flowers in large vases sent by Durand-Ruel and works on still-life panels for the dealer's sitting-room doors. Monet apparently delivers an installment of decorative still-life panels, including *Vase of Dahlias, Dahlias,* and *Peaches* (cat. nos. 72, 73, and 74), to Durand-Ruel in mid-December and decides which six should go together on each door (fig. no. 42). His art income for 1883 amounts to over 29,000 francs.[60]

Last Half of December Monet accompanies Renoir on a quick trip to the Mediterranean coast, from Marseilles to Genoa, perhaps to allow Ernest Hoschedé an opportunity to see his children over Christmas. They visit Cézanne at L'Estaque. Considering the many compositional similarities between the mid-1880s landscapes by Cézanne (see fig. no. 44) and Monet, this brief meeting may have marked a turning point for either or both artists.[61]

1884

January 6–28 Memorial retrospective of Manet's works at the Ecole des Beaux-Arts, Paris. At the opening, Monet promises Morisot that he will make a decorative painting of a Mediterranean subject for the drawing room in her newly finished home on the rue Villejust, Paris (fig. no. 45).[62]

January 17 Having explained to Durand-Ruel his need for solitude while working, Monet instructs the dealer not to tell anyone, not even his best friend Renoir, that he is returning to the picturesque Italian seaside resort town of Bordighera for what he plans as a three- to four-week-long campaign, but which lasts for three months. He stays at the Pension Anglaise.[63]

January 23 Monet asks Durand-Ruel to buy him a work by Manet from the artist's estate sale to be held February 4–5. The pastel purchased for Monet for 250 francs disappoints him, but he nevertheless keeps it.

Determined to make paintings at the lavish guidebook-acclaimed palm garden of Francesco Moreno in Bordighera, Monet asks his dealer, among others, to provide a letter of introduction. Monet also refers in his letter to a never-realized *La Vie moderne* monograph which is to include photographs of the artist and his works; the whereabouts of any photographs remain unknown.[64]

January 25 Monet's Argenteuil landlord writes to claim payment of a six-year-old debt, initiating negotiations that will lead to the return of Monet's most ambitious 1860s painting, *Luncheon on the Grass* (cat. no. 5), left with this man as collateral in 1878.[65]

January 27 Monet makes pencil sketches in his notebooks on trips with two English painters to the mountain villages of Borghetto, Sasso, and Valbona. Monet returns to these villages later during his stay to make six paintings.[66]

January 28–29 Excited by the prospect of a new "series," Monet makes arrangements to order gilded frames to be ready for his return. Bordighera works in these frames are recorded the following February in an unfinished sketch of Monet seated in his studio painted by Swiss artist Charles Giron (private collection). Working in Bordighera on six canvases at one time, Monet devotes as many as six sessions to refining each. By March 27 he has reworked some of the canvases as many as fifteen times.[67]

February 2 Writing to Duret that "one needs a palette of diamonds and jewels here because of the blues and pinks," Monet uses the term *féerique* (fairytale-like) to describe the landscape. The mood defined by this term becomes central to an increasing number of Monet's important works.[68]

February 5 Moreno receives Monet in the "pure fairyland" garden, surely an inspiration for the lavish Giverny garden that Monet will fashion in coming years. Two days later, Monet begins to work there (see cat. nos. 75, 76, and 77). While he is painting Renoiresque palm tree subjects, he receives a letter from Renoir in which he describes himself as a figure painter and wishes Monet well on his landscapes. Renoir reports that Chocquet bought Manet's 1874 portrait of Monet in his studio boat (fig. no. 29) for around 1,500 francs at Manet's estate sale and that Durand-Ruel has given up the new gallery space that he had rented in 1883.[69]

February 6 Monet takes a day trip to Menton, just across the border in France, choosing two sea motifs that he will come back to paint on his return trip home in April. Other day trips to Menton follow.[70]

February 10 Although Alice Hoschedé has just written that she is considering separating from the constantly absent painter, Monet takes a day trip to gamble in Monte Carlo.[71]

February 17 Wishing to avoid the Bordighera winds that have blown over his umbrella and broken his easel, Monet and some English painters staying at his hotel make a day excursion to the picturesque mountain village of Dolceacqua in the Nervia valley. Monet returns alone two days later to paint.[72]

March 6 With about thirty paintings under way, Monet takes a larger room where he can better see his works in progress. His supplies from France exhausted, Monet has arranged for more oils to be sent from Turin, Italy. On rainy days, he works on more still-life panels for Durand-Ruel's sitting-room doors (see fig. no. 42).[73]

March 10 Monet writes, "Now I grasp this fairytale-like country and it is precisely this marvelous side that I so want to render. People will surely scream that it is madly unrealistic, but too bad, they say that anyway when I paint our climate. . . . Everything I do is flaming punch or pigeon's throat."[74]

Late March–Early April Finally ready to return home to Giverny, Monet crates more than three dozen paintings and overcomes aggravating Italian art export regulations. Monet stops at Menton on April 6, checking into the Pavillon du Prince de Galles, which is located near motifs he had scouted out in February 1884. Nine days later, he continues by train to Giverny.[75]

April 27 Monet informs Durand-Ruel that he will bring a few new paintings to Paris on condition that he may take them back to Giverny for reworking. Durand-Ruel, who is short on capital, is arranging to sell some of the new paintings to Petit.[76]

May When Monet is in Paris from May 4 to May 7, he learns from Renoir and others about the slump in the art market. Monet is anxious that he will be forced to rely on selling works directly to collectors without the assistance of a dealer, as he had to do in the late 1870s.

Renoir hopes to organize a society of *irregularistes* to present exhibitions bringing together all sorts of artists (painters, decorators, architects, metalworkers, embroiderers, etc.) whose works are founded on the infinite variety of natural forms.[77]

May 15 Opening of the first exhibition of the Society of Independent Artists, committed to showing works outside the Salon. Contributions by Odilon Redon, Georges Seurat, and Paul Signac mark a new "Post-Impressionist" phase in French painting.

Early July Visiting his brother in Rouen, Monet accompanies Caillebotte on his prize-

46. John Singer Sargent, *Claude Monet Painting at the Edge of a Wood*, 1885. Oil on canvas; 54 × 64.8 cm, 21 × 25¼ in. Tate Gallery, London.

winning yacht, *Cul-blanc*. Monet invites Caillebotte to come see his Giverny home, hinting that he could transport by boat the large painting now stored in Argenteuil (*Luncheon on the Grass*, cat. no. 5).[78]

Late August Monet paints half a dozen works during a brief visit to the Normandy coast with his family.[79]

September–November Monet works on Giverny subjects, including a group of paintings of haystacks in a field bordered by poplars.[80]

October A picture framer named Nivard, to whom Monet has owed 1,550 francs since 1875, threatens litigation. Monet will settle, with considerable accumulated interest, the following February.[81]

November Monet proposes to Renoir and Pissarro that the three longtime colleagues have monthly dinners in Paris with their Impressionist associates at the Café Riche. Monet attends these dinners, held on the first Thursday of every month, irregularly for years to come.[82]

November 17 Monet, whose art income for 1884 will amount to around 45,000 francs, goes to Paris to deliver twelve works for 6,600 francs to Durand-Ruel, who is preparing to reoccupy his rue Lafitte premises after a lapse of seven and a half years. The dealer has arranged for Monet to meet Octave Mirbeau, an influential conservative journalist who has begun to publish a series of articles based on interviews with artists represented by Durand-Ruel.

Monet also delivers to Morisot the promised, large, still-unframed decorative panel (fig. no. 45) based on his Bordighera paintings.[83]

November 21 Mirbeau's enthusiastic article on Monet is published in *La France*. Mirbeau stresses Monet's ability to capture nature's most transient moods and reveries. Monet sends Mirbeau a painting in appreciation.[84]

1885

January 5 Monet attends a dinner in Paris organized in memory of Manet.[1]

Late January Monet begins a group of snowscapes that he later refers to as his "Giverny roads."[2]

March Monet works on more decorative still-life panels for Durand-Ruel's sitting-room doors, delivering them on April 2.[3]

May 15 Opening of the Fourth International Exhibition at Petit's gallery at 8, rue de Sèze, Paris, with works by nineteen invited painters. Monet's ten exhibited works (see cat. no. 71) strike some reviewers as fantasies comparable to the *One Thousand and One Nights*. Today, some scholars charge Monet with abandoning his colleagues to dedicate himself to the art market, but in fact he will make considerable efforts to arrange for the other Impressionists to show together at Petit's gallery during the next few financially difficult years.[4]

May 27 Monet writes to Durand-Ruel that he has taken on the role of gardener.[5]

July 13–19 Cézanne and his family, who had been visiting the Renoirs (brand-new parents) at La Roche-Guyon, stay at the Hôtel de Paris, Vernon, while awaiting the opportunity to visit Zola at Medan. It seems likely that Cézanne would have seen Monet at Giverny.[6]

47. The Monet and Hoschedé families at Giverny, mid-1880s (clockwise from lower left): Michel Monet (seated on the ground), Alice Hoschedé, Claude Monet (standing), Jean-Pierre Hoschedé, Blanche Hoschedé, Jean Monet, Jacques Hoschedé (standing), Marthe Hoschedé, Germaine Hoschedé, and Suzanne Hoschedé.

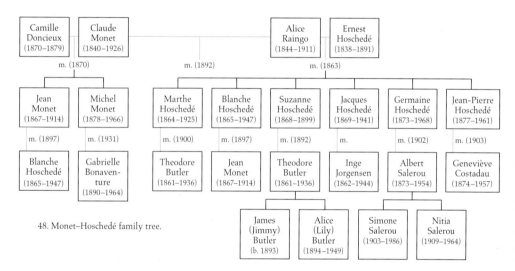

48. Monet–Hoschedé family tree.

July 28 Monet confides to Durand-Ruel, who has begun arrangements for a large group exhibition to take place in New York in April 1886, that he is upset by the prospect of his works leaving for the "land of the Yankees" and hopes that some can be kept in Paris, which is, he believes, the only place where there is still a little taste.[7]

Late Summer American artist John Singer Sargent visits Giverny and paints Monet at work out-of-doors on a painting of haystacks in a poplar-bordered field (fig. no. 46).[8]

September–October Monet and his extended family leave on September 17 for Rouen (where Jean Monet takes a school examination) and continue on to Etretat, where Faure has put a house at their disposal. Three pastel versions of Etretat motifs may have entered Faure's collection around this time as a token of gratitude.

Monet sees Guy de Maupassant frequently during this period, and the writer draws upon these meetings for an eloquent account of Monet's working methods published the following September in *Gil Blas*. Describing Monet at work this fall, Maupassant recalls that the children accompany the artist, carrying five or six canvases to a given site so that he can change from one work in progress to another when the light changes.

Alice Hoschedé and the children return to Giverny on October 10, but Monet remains in Etretat at the Hôtel Blanquet. Because of cold, rainy weather, Monet at first paints in a hotel staircase with windows overlooking the sea.[9]

Late October–November Monet paints the herring-boat fleet assembled on the beach; he also returns to the almost inaccessible beach just west of Etretat where he had begun a few paintings in February 1883. On November 27, hav-

ing incorrectly calculated the time of the incoming tide, Monet is thrown against the cliff by a large wave and loses his easel, brushes, and paints to the sea.

Monet makes arrangements to exhibit again with Petit, although Durand-Ruel hopes to organize an eighth Impressionist group exhibition for 1886.[10]

Late November–Early December Monet goes to Paris, where Petit invites him to participate in his 1886 International Exhibition on condition that he not exhibit elsewhere with his friends.[11]

December 6–13 Back in Etretat, Monet crates more than fifty unfinished paintings for his return to Giverny. He intends to take up the Etretat campaign again the following March. By mid-January 1886 Monet will enlarge a room on the west end of his house specifically as a work space, referred to as his "first studio."[12]

December 17 Monet explains to Durand-Ruel that his decision to exhibit with Petit is in everyone's interest, since recognition by another dealer will bolster interest in Durand-Ruel's stock and future enterprises. Monet also promises Durand-Ruel that he will soon produce some large works. He sells eleven paintings to the dealer for 10,400 francs, bringing his art income for 1885 to 25,400 francs.[13]

1886

January 22–24 "Do you really need so many paintings for America?" Monet asks Durand-Ruel, who will send nearly fifty of Monet's paintings to New York for a spring exhibition. "People are forgetting about us here because as soon as you have a new painting you make it disappear. My paintings from Italy, for example; they are unique among what I am doing otherwise, and no one has seen them here."[14]

February 6 Opening of the third annual Les XX exhibition in Brussels at the Palais des Beaux-Arts. There are ten works by Monet (see cat. nos. 75 and possibly 71) in this invitational exhibition of modern art, which also includes works by Redon and Renoir. Monet wants to send his paintings of train stations to this exhibition but cannot convince their owners to lend.[15]

February 19 Leaving Alice Hoschedé to celebrate her birthday with her husband, Monet arrives in Etretat, too distraught about his domestic situation to concentrate on painting. On February 26 Monet learns that she has decided to remain with him; he returns home a few days later.[16]

March 13 Durand-Ruel and his son Charles leave for New York with about three hundred Impressionist paintings (valued at $81,799 for customs) to exhibit there.[17]

49. Claude Monet, *Study of a Figure Out-of-Doors (Facing Left)*, 1886. Oil on canvas; 131 × 88 cm, 51 × 34¼ in. Musée d'Orsay, Paris (RF 2621) [W 1077].

50. Claude Monet, *Study of a Figure Out-of-Doors (Facing Right)*, 1886. Oil on canvas; 131 × 88 cm, 51 × 34¼ in. Musée d'Orsay, Paris (RF 2620) [W 1076].

April 2 Monet becomes a member of Mirbeau's Les Bons Cosaques, a literary group with monthly dinner meetings. Stéphane Mallarmé and Renoir are among the members.[18]

Spring Monet paints two relatively large figure paintings as decorative pendants (fig. nos. 49 and 50). The model, Suzanne Hoschedé, faces left in one and then right, in reprises of Monet's 1876 painting of Camille with a parasol (cat. no. 42). Monet later tells his American neighbor in Giverny, the painter Lilla Cabot Perry, that he kicked a hole in one of these canvases out of dissatisfaction.[19]

April 5 Monet writes to Zola, who has sent him a copy of his newly published novel, *L'Œuvre*. Its protagonist is a failed modern painter named Claude Lantier, whose story seems to include details from Monet's experiences. Monet points out that some readers might see parallels between Lantier and Manet or Cézanne. He complains to Zola that the novel, with its pessimistic conclusion, is potentially damaging to the cause of modern painting.[20]

April 10 Opening at the American Art Galleries, Madison Square, New York, of "Works in Oil and Pastel by the Impressionists of Paris." Some forty works (the most by any artist in the exhibition) by Monet (possibly cat. no. 24) span his career from 1864 to the present. The reception of Monet's art in the New York press is enthusiastic; a notable example is a twenty-page pamphlet, *Science and Philosophy in Art*, by

Celen Sabbrin (pseudonym of Helen De Silver Abbot), which includes an analysis of the underlying triangulated structures of Monet's works. This publication will be translated into French by Pissarro in July.[21]

April 27–May 6 Monet leaves from Paris for Holland at the invitation of Baron d'Estournelles de Constant, the diplomatic secretary to the French legation in The Hague. Monet paints five pictures in the picturesque tulip fields at Sassenheim and Rijnsburg, east of Leiden.[22]

May 25–June The successful American Art Association Impressionists exhibition, enlarged with twenty-one works (eight by Monet; see cat. no. 75) borrowed from American collectors such as Louisine Havemeyer and Alexander Cassatt (brother of the painter), is moved to the National Academy of Design, New York, and a new catalogue is printed. Durand-Ruel sells $18,000 worth of pictures as a direct result of this American venture, with works by Monet selling best. Among the important new collectors of his works are William Fuller, Alden Wyman Kingman, Catholina Lambert, and Albert Spencer.[23]

June 15 Opening of the Fifth International Exhibition at Petit's gallery, with twelve recent works by Monet (see cat. nos. 80 and 85) and five by Renoir. Many critics, both pro and con, feel that Monet's paintings are more fantastical than realistic. Joris-Karl Huysmans writes to Redon that he is astounded by Monet's tulip

paintings. Nine works by Monet sell, five to Faure. Monet's proceeds amount to 15,100 francs, which, added to 10,000 francs' worth of sales to Durand-Ruel this year, suggests that Monet's art income will total around 25,000 francs.[24]

June Morisot writes to her niece that Monet has "exhausted the subject of landscape, so to speak; no one has the courage to try that which he has already done perfectly."[25]

Summer Perhaps inspired by Renoir's enthusiasm for the landscape of Brittany, Monet confides to Morisot and Duret that he would like to go there. On August 11 he requests a 3,000-franc advance from Durand-Ruel to realize his travel plans.[26]

September 12 Leaving the French mainland, Monet crosses to the town of Le Palais on the island of Belle-Ile-en-Mer, staying at the Hôtel France. He plans a two-week campaign, to be concluded with a visit to Mirbeau at his country house at Noirmoutier, Brittany.[27]

September 15 Seeking an uninhabited locale, Monet reaches Kervilahouen, a village made up of about ten buildings, on the "savage" (Atlantic) coast of the island. He rents a peasant house, which he has all to himself (excepting the mice, rats, and pig), for four francs a day, including meals (mostly eggs and lobster).[28]

September 18 The Australian-born painter John Peter Russell, who has been staying at nearby Bangor for the last four months, visits Monet, who is at work on four paintings. Russell and his wife, Marianna, invite Monet to dinner on several occasions.[29]

Late September Monet hires a porter for his art supplies on September 22 and begins to paint a single motif on three or four different canvases. He expects to head home in ten days, but his porter quits two days later, by which time Monet has already started all the canvases that he brought with him. The weather, too, makes it difficult for him to carry on without assistance: he writes to Alice Hoschedé on September 27 that high winds make it necessary to lash down his painting parasol and his canvas. Moreover, the equinoctial tides delay the return of identical conditions needed for Monet to continue with works in progress. Having decided on September 28 to prolong his stay, Monet hires Hippolyte (known as Pauli or Poly) Guillaume, formerly a lobster fisherman, to porter his art supplies for two francs a day. Although rainy days slow the pace of his work, Monet finds the lugubrious rock motifs to be still richer under such gray light.[30]

October 2 At dinnertime Monet meets a newly arrived tourist, Gustave Geffroy, who since 1883 has written in support of the artist in *La Justice*. Geffroy departs on October 13, leaving *Anna Karenina* and an anthology of short stories by Tolstoy for Monet to read. The two men will remain friends until Geffroy's death forty years later, eight months before Monet's.[31]

October 8–15 Monet has ordered new canvases shipped to him, although after three weeks none of his paintings is finished. He regrets that he has no canvases on which to capture the more than week-long tempest that is under way. More canvases arrive by October 12, and Monet reports that he has acquired a waterproof outergarment (fashioned by his porter Guillaume). On October 15 he finds a sheltered spot in an isolated cove from which to render the spectacle of the waves crashing against the coast fifty meters above sea level (cat. no. 82).[32]

October 14 Durand-Ruel is enthusiastic for Monet to visit the United States, which he believes might offer better motifs than Belle-Ile. Monet has asked the dealer to get him a new watch, to replace the one now ruined.[33]

October 23 Asking Alice Hoschedé to send another empty case for transport, Monet reports that he has painted thirty-eight canvases, twenty-five of which seem promising, seven or eight merely rough sketches. "I must make great efforts to make them somber, to render this sinister, tragic aspect, me, more inclined to soft tender colors. . . . Today this sea with a leaden sky was so green that I was powerless to render the intensity." Monet eats porpoise for breakfast.[34]

October 29–30 Better weather permits Monet to work on a "series" of six variations, to begin to grasp and articulate what would several years later become the essence of his series concept: "I know very well that really to paint the sea, one must observe it every day, at every hour and from the same place."[35]

November 3–10 Tired of waiting for Monet to visit Noirmoutier as promised, Mirbeau and his friends instead go to Belle-Ile for a week. Mirbeau writes to the sculptor Auguste Rodin: "This will be a new aspect of his talent: a terrible and formidable Monet, unknown until now. But his works will please the common public less than ever. . . . [He] will bring home only three or four finished paintings and thirty more in which he has indicated his intentions." Monet realizes by now that he will need to finish his Belle-Ile paintings in the studio in Giverny, despite his efforts to progress as far as possible in front of the motifs themselves. To be ready for any and every last opportunity for first-hand study, he goes to work with a cart filled with numerous unfinished canvases.[36]

November 11 Monet paints through a hailstorm and, in the evening, goes eel fishing by moonlight.[37]

51. Auguste Rodin, *The Burghers of Calais*; from *L'Art français*, July 6, 1889. This photograph of Rodin's plaster cast of his famous sculptural group was taken at the Monet–Rodin exhibition held at the Georges Petit Gallery, Paris, in the summer of 1889.

November 14 Monet's forty-sixth birthday. Characteristically, he worries that his haste makes him ruin his works: "This morning I totally lost one canvas that satisfied me after at least twenty sessions: it was necessary to scrape it completely off; what a rage I was in!"[38]

November 16 Monet prepares to send the children some live seagulls with clipped wings to be released in the Giverny garden after they can acclimate in the pheasant pen.[39]

November 17 Staying indoors all day for only the second time, Monet fulfills a desire to make figure paintings of the townsfolk by painting a portrait of his porter Guillaume (Musée Marmottan, Paris).[40]

End of November In the evenings, Monet packs crates to send to Giverny, reminding his family not to open anything, since he is fanatical about doing that himself. He leaves for Mirbeau's country home in Noirmoutier on November 25 and arrives home in Giverny with around forty paintings four days later. Durand-Ruel comes to see the works two weeks later.[41]

December 1886–January 1887 Nine paintings by Monet are exhibited at the Modern Paintings exhibition at the American Art Galleries, New York.

1887

Early January Monet sells Durand-Ruel a group of five works, which include two Belle-Ile paintings, for 5,700 francs. Pissarro sees these works in the company of R. Austin Robertson,

an agent for the American Art Association (a partnership formed in 1883 by Robertson, James Fountain Sutton, and Thomas E. Kirby to promote American art and, eventually, to conduct estate auctions), and describes one of them, rendered in full sunlight, as "an incomprehensible fantasy" unlikely to appeal to the international art market.[42]

March 2 In Paris to attend a Bons Cosaques dinner, Monet meets with Durand-Ruel and then with Petit, at whose International Exhibition (slated for mid-May or mid-June) he intends to present the Belle-Ile works. Monet and Renoir apparently propose to Petit that Degas, Morisot, Pissarro, Rodin, Sargent, Sisley, and Whistler be invited to participate this year. Although Degas will not accept the invitation, otherwise the Impressionist group from the mid-1870s is mostly reconstituted, albeit in conjunction with other non-Impressionist artists associated with Petit.[43]

April 7–8 In Paris again making arrangements for Petit's International Exhibition, Monet makes his first sale to Goupil–Boussod et Valadon Successeurs (Boussod & Valadon), whose contemporary art transactions at their 19, boulevard Montmartre, branch are managed by Theo van Gogh. This sale involves two Belle-Ile paintings; as partial payment for one of them, Monet acquires a Degas pastel. Delivery of the pastel is delayed so that it can be framed to Degas's specifications, with a slate-gray satin border.[44]

April 22 At Monet's invitation, Theo van Gogh, who has already sold the two Belle-Ile paintings, comes to Giverny and buys four more, on

52. Monet at Giverny, photographed by the American painter Theodore Robinson, probably in 1887.

53. John Leslie Breck (seated on the ground), with (from left to right) Blanche Hoschedé, Alice Hoschedé, Germaine Hoschedé, Suzanne Hoschedé (seated in a chair), Claude Monet, Jean Monet, and Henry Fitch Taylor, probably around 1887.

the understanding that they will be included in the forthcoming Petit International Exhibition (see cat. no. 84). Monet now has three competing galleries interested in the same pictures, which assures his financial stability.[45]

May 8–June 8 Sixth Annual International Exhibition at the Georges Petit Gallery at 8, rue de Sèze, Paris, includes at least seventeen works by Monet (see cat. nos. 50 and 77), fifteen of them listed in the catalogue. Most notable are the daringly abbreviated *Vétheuil in Fog* (fig. no. 35), exhibited for the first time, and a group of ten Belle-Ile paintings (among them the *Portrait of Poly*); the paint is still wet on some of them. The press has never acclaimed Monet's art so enthusiastically, and particular praise comes from Geffroy, Huysmans, Lostalot, and Mirbeau. In a two-part article published on May 25 and June 2 in Clemenceau's *La Justice*, Geffroy acknowledges Monet as the first history painter of the raging ocean, comparing his views of the Belle-Ile rocks to cathedrals about to tumble into the deep. Saluting Monet as the greatest modern landscape painter, Huysmans writes in *La Revue indépendante* on June 1: "The savagery of this [mode of] painting seen by the eye of a cannibal is at first disconcerting, then, before the force which it emanates, before the faith which animates it, before the powerful inspiration of the man who brushes it, one submits to the grim charms of this unpolished art."

In this exhibition, Rodin includes his *Burghers of Calais* (fig. no. 51) and Renoir presents his *Bathers, An Attempt at Decorative Painting* (Philadelphia Museum of Art).[46]

Last Half of May Monet goes to London for twelve days, presumably to attend the wedding there of Octave Mirbeau and Alice Regnault on May 25. While in London, Monet is urged by Whistler to exhibit with the Society of British Artists, of which Whistler will soon become president.[47]

May 25–June 30 Twelve paintings by Monet (possibly cat. no. 67) are included in the Celebrated Paintings exhibition at the National Academy of Design, New York.[48]

June Sargent and Rodin are among many guests to visit Giverny. A Sargent portrait of Monet at work alongside Blanche Hoschedé in the studio boat may date from this summer. The 2,000 francs Sargent will pay Monet in August for a recent square-format winter landscape with a view of Bennecourt in the background is the highest price received by Monet for any work this year, when his art income will amount to 44,500 francs.[49]

Early Summer American painter Willard Metcalf, who has already visited Giverny a few times, returns with his fellow American painters Theodore Robinson and Theodore Wendel. With John Leslie Breck, Louis Ritter, Henry Fitch Taylor, and Canadian William Blair Bruce, the artists rent a large furnished house near the Seine and take meals at the Café Baudy. The café's proprietors, Angélina and Lucien Baudy, expand their premises into a hotel for a steady stream of artists who base themselves in Giverny during the vacation season.[50]

July–August Monet works on "figures out-of-doors the way I understand them, done like

landscapes. It is an old dream that always plagues me and I would love to carry it to realization one time." By early September, however, he reports that he has scraped off or torn almost every canvas started this summer. A large painting of Alice Hoschedé's daughters fishing from a moored rowboat (fig. no. 54) may have been begun or even finished this summer. The example of recent works by Morisot is apparently a major impetus for these figure paintings.[51]

September 18 Theodore Robinson, the first American to take lodging at the Hôtel Baudy, stays at the inn through January 4, 1888. While for the most part the influx of Americans this summer annoys Monet, he develops an especially close friendhip with Robinson, whose diary of his encounters and conversations with the French painter is perhaps the most valuable written record of Monet's life during this period.[52]

October–November Durand-Ruel's plans to stage a second Impressionist exhibition in New York are thwarted when rival American dealers protest that he should be forced to pay the then heavy customs duties on imported art works. The controversy delays this exhibition until May.[53]

November 25 Four paintings by Monet (see cat. no. 86) are shipped to London by Theo van Gogh for presentation in the Winter Exhibition of the Royal Society of British Artists. It is unknown whether Monet goes to London for the opening, although he writes that he was intending to paint "several views of the Thames in the fog."[54]

54. Claude Monet, In the "Norvégienne," 1887 and/or 1888. Oil on canvas; 98 × 131 cm, 38¼ × 51 in. Musée d'Orsay, Paris (RF 1944.20) [W 1151].

1888

January 12–18 Monet departs from Paris for the Mediterranean coast town of Antibes, expecting to return to Giverny in early March. He stays at the Château de la Pinède, a hotel popular with artists and recommended by Maupassant. He dislikes the other artist guests, especially the acclaimed Salon landscape painter Henri Joseph Harpignies and his students. Monet spends the first few days exploring the surrounding area, even hiking twenty-five kilometers from Monte Carlo to Nice.[55]

January 19–23 Describing the locale as "fairytale-like," Monet begins to work after hiring a porter. From a beach to the east of the fortified town, he paints views of Antibes silhouetted against snow-covered mountains (see cat. no. 87). A few days later, he learns that an artist has recently been jailed for painting Antibes, having contravened a law to prevent spying. Monet obtains permission from the War Ministry to continue working on this motif through the influence of his friend Castagnary, now director of the Fine Arts Ministry.[56]

Late January Continuing his efforts on behalf of ongoing Impressionist group shows, Monet remarks to Petit that Paul Helleu, Morisot, Renoir, and Whistler have agreed to participate in the dealer's next International Exhibition. Petit has hinted to Monet that his upcoming exhibition plans are uncertain. Referring to the same exhibition, Monet writes to Rodin that he has no idea when he will return to Paris and that to render sunlight in Antibes one would need gold and gemstones.

Monet encourages Alice Hoschedé to invite over the American painters (presumably Robinson and perhaps Breck, who also spends this winter in Giverny) to lift the family's spirits in his absence.[57]

February 1–10 "What I will bring back from here will be sweetness itself, white, pink, blue, all of it enveloped in this fairytale-like air," Monet reports from Antibes, comparing his efforts to "wrestling" and "search[ing] for the impossible." By now he has fourteen works under way. Eyestrain from working in steady sunlight prevents him from reading in the evenings. Although he buys a straw hat for protection from the sun, he becomes overfatigued trying to take full advantage of consistently splendid weather. Theo van Gogh asks to be the first to see the Antibes works.[58]

February 12 Monet writes to Geffroy that the sky is so blue that one "swims" in it. Boudin had used similar language to describe the sky in his December 2, 1856, diary entry.[59]

February 27–28 Sale in Paris of the Leroux collection, with eight paintings by Monet, each selling for between 1,000 and 2,055 francs: two to Chocquet, three each to Durand-Ruel and Boussod & Valadon. Concerned that this sale might depress his prices, Monet cables his dealers (Boussod & Valadon, Durand-Ruel, Petit, as well as Portier) in advance to protect their mutual market interests.[60]

February 29 Monet stops work on his views of Antibes, since the course of the sun has changed, altering the lighting. Marthe Hoschedé is apparently considering marriage to an American painter.[61]

March 4 Blanche Hoschedé intends to submit one of her own paintings to the Salon. Two of Breck's Giverny landscapes will be accepted.[62]

March 10–April 7 Monet writes to Helleu, Morisot, and Whistler, urging them to prepare for the Petit exhibition in April. Intermittent rain and wind frustrate Monet's work, although he begins to think about frames for the works in progress. But Petit now doubts that there can be a group exhibition this spring, and Monet learns on April 7 that he has canceled it.[63]

April 4 Although he may have lodged somewhere else in Giverny throughout the winter, Breck now takes a room at the Hôtel Baudy until the end of October.[64]

April 10–14 Monet informs both Durand-Ruel (about to return to New York, where he opens a branch gallery) and Theo van Gogh that he will sell his new works to the first to come to Giverny to do business.[65]

April 22 Having enjoyed splendid working conditions for more than a week, Monet packs the first crate of canvases for shipment back to Giverny from Antibes.[66]

April 24–28 Realizing the urgent need to exhibit and sell, Monet continues to plot with Renoir, Rodin, and Whistler about the options with Durand-Ruel and Petit. Renoir reserves the Durand-Ruel Gallery, Paris, for a group exhibition in mid-May. Although Monet had already decided against exhibiting with Durand-Ruel, he orders frames, to be ready for any eventuality.[67]

Early May Stopping in Paris on his way from Antibes to Giverny, Monet sees all his dealers. Provoked by Durand-Ruel's son Charles, who is supervising the gallery during his father's trip to America, Monet points out that without his permission none of his works can be included in any exhibition for which an entrance fee is charged. Petit offers to rent Monet his gallery for October and November. Whether or not the Durand-Ruel and Petit galleries are acting in concert during this period, Monet keeps Morisot, Rodin, and Whistler informed of his decisions, evidently with the understanding that together they can exert leverage with the dealers.[68]

May 20 Theodore Butler, in Giverny presumably for the first time, takes lodging at the Hôtel Baudy through early September.[69]

May 21–24 Monet goes to Paris for dinner with Whistler. Rodin offers Monet a gift, his choice of two works shown to him in photographs. Monet chooses the Helmet-Maker's Wife. It is probably around this time that Monet gives a Belle-Ile painting to the sculptor.[70]

May 25–June 25 Monet does not have works in the Impressionist group exhibition at the

Durand-Ruel Gallery, Paris, although over 120 works by Boudin, Caillebotte, Morisot, Pissarro, Renoir, Sisley, Whistler, and others are included.

May 27 Monet is back in Paris, staying at the Hôtel Garnier. He dines with Whistler and Mallarmé, whose French translation of Whistler's *Ten O'Clock*, an essay advocating art for art's sake, is about to be published.[71]

June 4 Boussod & Valadon buy ten Antibes paintings for 11,900 francs (possibly cat. no. 88), with a contractual agreement to share fifty percent of their retail markup with Monet. Monet assures them the right of first refusal of his new works. The gallery immediately exhibits (through July) the group at its 19, boulevard Montmartre, branch in two small unadorned mezzanine rooms. The response from colleagues, critics, and visitors is extremely positive. However, Félix Fénéon, champion of Seurat and the Neo-Impressionist commitment to scientific analysis of color, condemns the works as "brilliant vulgarity" and objects to the improvisatory bravura of Monet's method. Degas cynically considers Monet's paintings to be market-oriented.[72]

June 20 Monet confides to Geffroy how much he wants to prove that he can do something altogether different, but he feels that he cannot take up his figure paintings again, thanks to the "damned Americans" now in Giverny. Judging from their dated 1888 works, Breck and Wendel are both at work in the meadow where Monet intends to return to subjects begun the previous summer. Breck's undated *Mill Stream, Limetz* (private collection) so closely resembles a pair of 1888 works by Monet as to suggest that the artists painted at the motif in tandem.[73]

June 23 Publication in *La Cravache parisienne* of an article by G[eorges] J[eanniot] based on an interview in which Monet claims, contrary to fact, that he never retouches works in his studio. In spite of this inaccuracy, the article provides a valuable account of Monet's working technique, from his stenographic charcoal underdrawing on canvas to his speedy paint application during satisfactory light conditions. The author notes that after no more than an hour, the artist starts a new canvas of the same subject, thus creating serial variations.[74]

Early July Monet invites Durand-Ruel to Giverny in an attempt to mend their business relationship. Although no sales to Durand-Ruel are ultimately documented for this year, the dealer proposes to purchase eight works, which Monet needs to finish. It is agreed that Durand-Ruel should reach an understanding with Boussod & Valadon about shared access to the painter's new works.[75]

Mid-July Monet goes to London for three days, staying with Sargent.[76]

August 30 Despite the distrust resulting from the canceled International Exhibition earlier this year, Monet writes to Petit about a future project, probably the Monet–Rodin exhibition, which will become a serious topic of discussion in February 1889.[77]

September–October Prevented by bad weather during the summer from completing figure paintings, Monet begins the first five of his *Wheatstacks* paintings, plotting his compositions as notebook pencil sketches. He will return to the subject two seasons later. While haystacks and wheatstacks are staples of the nineteenth-century landscape repertoire by now, it is worth noting that Metcalf paints several works on this subject at Giverny around this time.[78]

October Having drawn a low number in the lottery in January, Jean Monet begins his military service in Le Havre.[79]

November Boussod & Valadon buy seven paintings for 9,700 francs (and rights to half of any profits). Monet adds finishing touches and delivers the works on December 31. Monet's total art income for 1888 amounts to 28,000 francs.[80]

1889

January Mallarmé asks Monet to provide an illustration to accompany "La Gloire" in a volume of his poems entitled *Le Tiroir de laque*. By December 1887 Mallarmé had already asked Morisot for an illustration (now lost) to accompany "Le Nenuphar blanc," the final poem in the collection. Monet is "charmed" by Morisot's "white water lily done with the famous three [colored] pencils," but he never provides the poet with any art work.[81]

February–March Sixteen of Monet's works (including recent Giverny figure paintings [see cat. nos. 89 and possibly 90], *Rain at Etretat* [cat. no. 80], and perhaps one of his first *Wheatstacks*) are exhibited at the Montmartre branch of Boussod & Valadon at the same time as works by Degas. In conjunction with this exhibition, a long interview with Monet appears in *Gil Blas* on March 3, in which the painter stresses that his chief artistic concern is the "envelope" of pulsating colored light, more than the solid physical facts of landscape. Geffroy (in *La Justice*, February 28) and Mirbeau (in *Le Figaro*, March 10) also publish eulogistic reviews, Mirbeau hyperbolically claiming that Monet is equal to the greatest painters of all time. His front-page essay stresses Monet's methodical, near-mathematical rigor.[82]

February Rodin becomes the first foreign artist elected a full member of Les XX, and Monet (who participated in their 1886 exhibi-

tion) is invited for the second time, exhibiting four works (possibly cat. no. 84) owned by Boussod & Valadon. Paul Gauguin, Pissarro, and Seurat are also represented in the society's sixth exhibition.[83]

Mid-February Geffroy takes Monet, poet and Art Nouveau architect Frantz Jourdain, and editor of *La Justice* Louis Mullem for a brief visit to poet Maurice Rollinat in the small hilltop village of Fresselines, overlooking the confluence of the two sources of the river Creuse in central France. Impressed by the rocky motifs in the area, Monet promises Rollinat that he will return for a month's work.[84]

Late February Petit offers his gallery to Monet and Rodin for an exhibition to be held at the time of the Universal Exposition, with the dealer taking admission fees, a percentage of any sales, and a work outright from each artist.[85]

March 6 Monet goes to Paris to discuss business with Rodin and Theo van Gogh. The same evening, Monet returns to Fresselines to begin a major painting campaign, lodging at the village inn. Throughout his stay, Monet frequently dines at Rollinat's and listens to him recite poems and play the piano. Monet expects (unrealistically) to finish at Fresselines quickly enough to be able to paint at nearby Crozat.[86]

March 12–14 Monet returns briefly to Paris to discuss plans for the ambitious Monet–Rodin exhibition scheduled at Georges Petit's gallery for June. Petit wants fifteen percent of sales proceeds, whereas Monet is offering ten percent. Mirbeau agrees to provide text about Monet for the catalogue.[87]

March 18–28 Back in Fresselines, Monet now has fourteen canvases under way, but rainy, windy, and sometimes snowy weather interrupts his promising start. He fears the appearance of spring greenery that will change the colors of his "somber and sinister" subjects.[88]

April 4 "Looking at my canvases, I am terrified to see them so somber; in addition several have no sky. This will be a lugubrious series," Monet writes. Only two skyless works are completed, but the concept of eliminating any horizon from his compositions will acquire considerable significance for Monet in subsequent years.[89]

April 5–11 As it crests, the river Creuse starts to change color and widen, forcing Monet to halt progress on works begun. Meanwhile the cold and rain have so badly chapped his hand that he needs to wear a glycerin glove day and night. Writing to Morisot, Monet compares the Creuse landscape in its savagery to Belle-Ile.[90]

April 12 Petit offers his gallery space to Monet and Rodin for three months beginning in early July in exchange for 8,000 francs' worth of

55. Monet's house and garden at Giverny, late 1880s/early 1890s (prior to a repainting of the shutters and the construction of a new chimney for improved heating).

work by each, ten percent of all sales, and fifty percent of entrance fees. The artists accept, although in the final arrangement, the opening date is moved forward to June 15, with the dealer requiring a 10,000 franc rental fee per artist and fifteen percent of sales.[91]

April–May Twenty Monet works, including some from the February Boussod & Valadon exhibition (see cat. nos. 30, 80, 84, 89, and 90), are presented in London at the Goupil Galleries, 116–117 New Bond Street. The catalogue preface is a translation of Mirbeau's March 10 *Le Figaro* article. Evidently no sales result from the exhibition, but press response is positive, and Monet is pleased that some critics compare his works favorably to Sargent's.[92]

April 13–30 Monet frets that the subsiding river has again changed color and that spring green tones have appeared, obliging him to modify works in progress. Lumbago leaves Monet bedridden on April 22, but two days later he is back at work between rainstorms, sometimes adding only three brushstrokes to a promising canvas before a change in the weather obliges him to stop. "It is so stupid to be thus at the mercy of the weather," he realizes, and wonders whether Gustave Flaubert, one of his favorite writers, would have written differently had he also been a painter.[93]

May 3–15 Most motifs have changed in the three weeks since weather has permitted Monet to visit them; some trees have been cut down and another has sprouted leaves. Monet offers the owner of this tree fifty francs for permission to cut the leaves off, and he hires men to lug ladders into the ravine on May 8 for the defoliation. While supervising the work, Monet has his hair cut by a barber summoned to the remote

site. His desperate moves save four of the five works under way there, although the sunlight on the river, which Monet compares to "sequins and diamonds," nearly blinds him.[94]

May 6 Opening of the Universal Exposition, symbolized by the new Eiffel Tower. Three paintings by Monet are included in a special exhibition chronicling a century of French art. His works are not included in another exhibition at the Universal Exposition of 1880s art where Rodin's works are featured. A highlight of the centenary exhibition is Manet's *Olympia* (fig. no. 9). Sargent apparently learns of an American's interest in acquiring the work for 20,000 francs from Manet's estate. This information prompts Monet to organize a subscription campaign to purchase the work for the French National Museums.[95]

May 12 Theodore Robinson takes lodging at Hôtel Baudy, Giverny, through December 12.[96]

Around May 18 Monet returns to Giverny.[97]

Late May–Mid-June Monet is preoccupied with work for the forthcoming Monet–Rodin exhibition: loan arrangements with collectors, paintings to be finished, and frames. Of the 156 works he intends to show, only 145 are finally included (see cat. nos. 9, 12, 15, 22, 26, 34, 35, 41, 46, 50, 54, 56, 57, 68, 80, 82, 85, 89, and possibly 24, 87, and 88); among these are four undated figurative compositions. There would have been visual interplay between the white-clothed figures in these works and Rodin's plasters and marbles. It is not known why Monet withholds several other of his most important pre-1889 figure paintings: for example the two *Studies of a Figure Out-of-Doors* (fig. nos. 49 and 50), *Young Women in a Boat* (cat. no. 93), and his 1866 *Women in the Garden* (fig. no. 14).[98]

June 15 Monet installs his paintings for Petit's exhibition in two tiers, without concern for chronological order, although the fourteen Creuse paintings are grouped together. Rodin's delay with installing his works frustrates Monet, who is concerned that the larger sculptures, such as the *Burghers of Calais* (fig. no. 51), may block views of his paintings.[99]

June 20 Boston painter Lilla Cabot Perry and her family take lodging at the Hôtel Baudy through October 29. They are with an American sculptor—presumably Paul Wayland Bartlett, who has been writing about Rodin—who has a letter of introduction to Monet. The Perrys will spend eight more summers at Giverny over the next twenty years.[100]

June 21–September 21 Exhibition at the Georges Petit Gallery of 145 paintings by Monet and 36 sculptures by Rodin. In his catalogue preface, Mirbeau stresses that Monet is self-taught and does not work in a conventional studio, but records the fairytale-like dream of light that envelops all things, employing unprecedented methods designed to capture "instantaneity," or roughly thirty-minute segments of nature. Noting that Monet uses sable brushes and seldom mixes colors on his palette, Mirbeau explains how the artist brings as many as ten canvases in progress to a given site, putting one aside to work on another when light conditions shift. Sometimes Monet devotes sixty sessions to the same half-hour "history," observed in detail day after day until fully realized.

Monet's half of the exhibition is given far less press than Rodin's. The most important article about Monet, written by Octave Maus, is published in *L'Art moderne*, Brussels. Maus stresses the series incorporated in this exhibition, noting five versions of one Creuse motif, three of another, and two closely related *Wheatstacks* paintings. He also points out the interest of American collectors in Monet's works.[101]

Mid-July Monet's mood is disagreeable throughout the Petit exhibition, despite considerable market interest in his work. The most significant client to visit Giverny is the American dealer James Sutton, partner in the American Art Association. Pissarro, perhaps exaggerating, claims in September 1893 that Sutton owns 120 Monets and has become a competitor to Durand-Ruel. A significant Sutton purchase in July 1889 would explain the speculative interest in Monet's works in the following months. Monet's personal account books for 1889–97 have not survived.[102]

July 22, 1889–February 1890 Monet corresponds with fellow artists, dealers, and collectors to obtain contributions toward the 20,000-franc purchase price of Manet's *Olympia* for donation to the French National Museums.[103]

September 13–14 Pissarro claims that an American has bought a Monet for a record 9,000 francs. The work in question, one of Monet's first *Wheatstacks* variations (Hill-Stead Museum, Farmington, Connecticut), was purchased from Monet by Boussod & Valadon for 2,500 francs (and immediately sold for 4,500 francs) just days before the opening of the Monet–Rodin exhibition, in which it is included. As this exhibition comes to an end, Boussod & Valadon buy it back from the owner, Mr. Oppenheim (who had never taken possession), for 6,500 francs and sell it to Alfred Pope for over 10,000 francs.[104]

October 9 On rainy days, Monet is at work on a painting of a figure in an interior setting. He claims that he has scraped out the considerable amount of work he has done recently.[105]

October Monet sends Mirbeau a Bordighera painting as a gift in thanks for his catalogue preface. Monet also promises a painting to Mallarmé as consolation for not providing the poet with the illustration he had requested in January.[106]

November 2 Prince Edmond de Polignac, who sells a painting that he had lent to the Monet–Rodin exhibition, writes to reassure Monet that its new owner is not a foreigner, as if that were exceptional around this time. From this same exhibition, Polignac had acquired the only large late-1880s figure painting sold by Monet before the 1920s (fig. no. 54).[107]

December 1889–January 1890 The debate over whether or not Manet's *Olympia* (fig. no. 9) should be accepted by the French National Museums is carried on in the press, nearly leading to a duel between Monet and Manet's old friend Antonin Proust.[108]

1890

February 7 Monet presents to Armand Fallières, Minister of Public Education and Fine Arts, a letter announcing the gift of Manet's *Olympia* to the French National Museums. In accordance with the regulation prohibiting any work from entering the Louvre until ten years after an artist's death, *Olympia* will go to the Luxembourg Museum, which is devoted to contemporary art. On March 13 the committee appointed by Fallières to consider the donation recommends that the painting be accepted by the Luxembourg, but without any guarantee that it will automatically enter the Louvre. It goes on view by November.[1]

April 3 American painter Mary Fairchild Mac-Monnies and sculptor Frederick MacMonnies make their first visit to Giverny, where they will settle in 1897.[2]

May 3–November 3 Theodore Robinson stays at the Hôtel Baudy, Giverny.[3]

56. Claude Monet, *The Boat*, probably 1890 or 1891. Oil on canvas; 146 × 133 cm, 57 × 52 in. Musée Marmottan, Paris (5082) [W 1154].

May 5 Monet goes to Paris to see Theo van Gogh and Rodin, and to visit the Salon with Geffroy. Concurrent with Monet's Paris visit, there is an exhibition of Japanese prints at the Ecole des Beaux-Arts, Paris (April 25–May 22).[4]

May 12 Monet writes to Caillebotte: "I congratulate [Renoir] for not wishing to be decorated; that could have been helpful for him, it is true, but he must succeed without it, it's more chic." But according to an 1892 entry in Robinson's diary, Monet and Renoir were both offered the Legion of Honor during the winter of 1891–92, and both refused it.[5]

June 8 Monet buys back unidentified landscape studies from Boussod & Valadon for 2,000 francs, perhaps to destroy them.[6]

June 22 Monet writes to Geffroy: "I have taken up things impossible to do: water with plants moving at the bottom [see cat no. 94 and fig. no. 56]. . . . It's wonderful to look at, but the desire to render it is maddening. After all, I always attack things like this." By mid-July poor weather curtails the project, and despite good weather for the rest of the summer, rheumatism hampers Monet's work.[7]

July 13 Morisot, her family, and Mallarmé visit Giverny and choose a painting as a gift for the poet.[8]

July 27 Geffroy brings Clemenceau to Giverny, where Monet is working on *Poppy Field* variations (see cat. no. 95).[9]

August 23 Publication in *Art et critique*, under the pseudonym Pierre Louis, of Maurice Denis's influential proposition: "Remember that a painting, before it might be a battle horse, a nude, or any anecdote whatsoever, is fundamentally a flat surface covered with colors arranged in a certain order."

September 27 Monet writes to Geffroy that the weather has been poor, and he can no longer think of figure paintings: "I persist at several landscapes and that is all, for as I go along, I have more and more difficulties and need more time to render finally what I want."[10]

September 28 Durand-Ruel visits Giverny and buys ten works, which Monet promises to complete soon for delivery.[11]

September 30 Monet and Caillebotte visit Mirbeau at Les Damps. "We will discuss gardening," Mirbeau had promised. "Since art and literature are a joke, there is only the earth."[12]

Around October 1890–January 1891 Monet is at work again on twenty-five more *Wheatstacks* during weather conditions that are ideal, especially for snow effects. He writes to Geffroy that he is after "instantaneity, above all the envelope, the same light diffused everywhere." According to one account, Monet pays a farmer to delay harvesting his crop so that he may finish his paintings. Blanche Hoschedé, who is painting and selling her own *Wheatstacks* compositions, plays the role of "porter" for the numerous canvases simultaneously under way.[13]

October 30 Monet is in Paris to meet with Durand-Ruel. He reserves some landscapes for purchase at Siegfried Bing's "Le Japon artistique" exhibition.[14]

57. John Leslie Breck, *Studies of an Autumn Day, No. 2*, 1891. Oil on canvas; 32.7 × 41.1 cm, 12⅞ × 16³⁄₁₆ in. Terra Foundation for the Arts, Daniel J. Terra Collection (1989.4.2).

58. John Leslie Breck, *Studies of an Autumn Day, No. 3*, 1891. Oil on canvas; 32.7 × 40.8 cm, 12⅞ × 16¹⁄₁₆ in. Terra Foundation for the Arts, Daniel J. Terra Collection (1989.4.3).

November 17 With the help of an advance from Durand-Ruel, Monet purchases his Giverny home and property, which he has rented since 1883, for 22,000 francs payable in four annual installments.[15]

December 3 The National Gallery of Norway in Oslo buys Monet's *Rain at Etretat* (cat. no. 80) from Boussod & Valadon, marking the first museum acquisition of one of Monet's works.

December 14 Monet refuses Durand-Ruel's suggestion to stage another group exhibition of Impressionist painters, urging instead exhibitions of single artists' recent works.[16]

1891

January 27 Monet goes to Paris to deliver a *Wheatstacks* painting to collector Paul Gallimard, asking him to tell anyone who inquires that he paid 5,000 francs for it. A week later, Boussod & Valadon buy two *Wheatstacks* and reserve a third.[17]

February Thirty-two works by Monet (see cat. no. 31) are presented together in an exhibition at the Union League Club in New York.

Mid-February Durand-Ruel comes to Giverny to buy recent works. Monet has decided to sell *Study of Rocks, The Creuse (Le Bloc)* (cat. no. 91) to Clemenceau, who had admired the painting on July 27, 1890, for whatever price he wants to pay. On a visit to Paris, Monet sees a work by Morisot for sale at Portier's gallery and asks to buy it; but learning of his interest, Morisot makes it a gift.[18]

March–April Although he had planned to be painting the cathedral and coal workers at Rouen (where his son Jean had begun to work for Monet's brother Léon), Monet remains in Giverny to oversee considerable work on the garden.[19]

March 7 Publication of "Claude Monet" by Mirbeau in *L'Art dans les deux mondes*, for which Monet reluctantly provides drawings to be reproduced as illustrations. Based on Mirbeau's discussions with Monet at Giverny the previous December, the article gives the first detailed account of Monet's garden (three seasonal plantings are described) and acclaims the new winter *Wheatstacks* series as "states of the planet's consciousness" and "the drama of the earth."[20]

March 19 Ernest Hoschedé dies in Paris with Alice Hoschedé at his side; he is buried at Giverny.[21]

April 2 Monet is in Paris for the monthly Impressionists dinner and delivers *Study of Rocks, The Creuse (Le Bloc)* to Clemenceau, whose efforts to prolong Jean Monet's military leave have failed.[22]

April 3–9 According to Pissarro, Parisian dealers all talk about a remarkable demand for Monet's *Wheatstacks* paintings on the part of Americans such as Sutton, who are willing to pay between 4,000 and 6,000 francs for them. About Monet's plan to have an all-*Wheatstacks* exhibition at Durand-Ruel's, Pissarro comments, "I do not know how it is that Monet is not annoyed by limiting himself to this repetition of the same subject; such are the terrible effects of success."[23]

April 6–November 20 Theodore Robinson stays at the Hôtel Baudy, Giverny.[24]

April 13 Monet orders shallow (profile) frames for his forthcoming exhibition at Durand-Ruel's, including white frames for two of the twelve paintings he will exhibit.[25]

May 4–16 Monet, in Paris from May 1, sees a flower show and installs a one-artist exhibition at the Durand-Ruel Gallery at 11, rue Le Peletier, Paris, with twenty-two works, including fifteen *Wheatstacks* (see cat. nos. 96, 97, 99, and 102), and a large pair of 1886 figure paintings (see fig. nos. 49 and 50) installed above them. Clemenceau is listed as a lender (cat. no. 91). Monet tells a visitor to the exhibition that "the full value [of one painting] is not apparent except by comparison [with the other paintings] in the succession of the series as a whole."

Geffroy provides the catalogue preface, comparing the colors to gems, fire, and blood, evoking mystery and fate. According to Geffroy, Monet wants to return to paint in London, Algeria, and Brittany, and to carry out campaigns in Switzerland and Norway, and also to visit the church at Mont-Saint-Michel, given his interest in the cathedrals of France as man-made promontories (at an unknown date, Monet makes notebook sketches of this last site). Writing to Bracquemond, Henri Béraldi summarizes the exhibition as "Fifteen stacks of straw. *The same*, taken at different hours of the day. There is the gray stack, the pink stack (six o'clock), the yellow stack (eleven o'clock), the blue stack (two o'clock), the violet stack (four o'clock), the red stack (eight o'clock in the evening), etc., etc."

59. Theodore Robinson, *Afternoon Shadows*, 1891. Oil on canvas; 46.4 × 55.6 cm, 18¼ × 21⅞ in. Museum of Art, Rhode Island School of Design, Providence, Gift of Gustav Radeke.

60. Edgar Degas, *Four Dancers*, date unknown (1890s). Oil on canvas; 151.1 × 180.2 cm, 59½ × 71 in. National Gallery of Art, Washington, D.C., Chester Dale Collection (1963.10.122).

Near unanimous praise for the exhibition comes from journalists, and, according to Pissarro, Monet's paintings sell out within days of the opening at prices of 3,000 to 4,000 francs. Durand-Ruel buys ten works, including seven *Wheatstacks* (at 2,500 francs each), on May 9, and asks Monet to retouch one of them after the exhibition.[26]

Spring Monet begins his *Poplars* series, traveling to a site two kilometers south of his home in his studio boat. No surviving works from this year correspond to the big, square "whirl" canvases of 1891 mentioned by Robinson in his diary on October 5, 1892, suggesting that Monet may have destroyed a group of paintings from this time. Robinson may, however, be referring to works such as *The Boat* (fig. no. 56).[27]

June A Japanese gardener comes to Giverny.[28]

June 16 Durand-Ruel and his family visit Giverny. He selects six paintings for Monet to finish and deliver. In 1891 Durand-Ruel buys 77,000 francs' worth of art from Monet, whose art income this year will total around 100,000 francs and will establish him as a wealthy man. In early July Monet confides: "It's a visit every week, either by a dealer or by a collector, and in the end I will soon have no more works in the studio."[29]

July 7 Monet takes three works to Petit's gallery in Paris to show to Chicago collector Bertha Honoré Palmer, who had bought five Monet paintings from Durand-Ruel on July 2 and will buy two more from him on July 8. Back in Giverny on July 8, Monet is visited by potential buyers the following two days.[30]

July 9–November 21 Breck stays at the Hôtel Baudy, Giverny, and paints a series of fifteen *Wheatstacks* paintings (see fig. nos. 57 and 58), apparently tracing the same drawing on each canvas and then recording a wide range of light effects. Breck will exhibit his variations on the wheatstack motif in 1893 in Boston. Perhaps with the market interest for Monet's *Wheatstacks* in mind, Robinson also addresses the motif (fig. no. 59), Sisley will start to paint the same subject later this year, and Degas will incorporate haystacks as theater scenery in the background of his ambitious painting *Four Dancers* (fig. no. 60), with his hallmark female figures in the foreground presented as pose variations on a single type.

Monet asks Breck and another American to stay away from Giverny because of their interest in Alice Hoschedé's daughters.[31]

July 14–October 20 Lilla Cabot Perry and her family stay at the Hôtel Baudy, Giverny.[32]

Mid-July Monet gives a painting to Pissarro, who pays back the 1,000 francs borrowed on May 1, when he needed medical attention for an abscessed eye. He hopes to send Monet a painting of his in exchange.[33]

July 28 Monet is busy painting and "arranging the house and the garden to my taste." Monet's accomplishments as a gardener have often been recognized, but his simultaneous efforts to decorate the interior of his home are not well known. A number of the most important descriptions of the home are incorporated below in the chronology, but precisely when Monet made changes to the interior decoration, the extent of his personal role in the decorations, and

the significance of this activity in the context of his career as a whole are unknown.[34]

August 2 Public auction of poplar trees bordering the river Epte at Limetz. Because Monet has been painting these very trees since spring, he offers to pay the lumber dealer to leave them standing until his work is completed. Perry reports: "In one of his *Poplars*, the [light] effect he captured lasted only seven minutes, or until the sunlight left a certain leaf, when he took out the next canvas and worked on that." Perry will also recall that while Monet was painting on the Epte in his boat one Sunday, he became so aggravated that he threw all his art supplies into the water. In September he asks Caillebotte to send him a larger, more stable boat by train. On October 8, 1891, Monet buys the small island, L'Ile aux Orties, where he keeps his boats.[35]

October 7 Butler returns to Giverny.[36]

October 16–20 Still struggling with his *Poplars*, Monet explains, "I am still striving for better or for worse with the wonderful motif of landscape that I had to do in all kinds of weather conditions in order to end up with just one that would represent no particular weather or season, that would be the distillation of a certain number of good intentions."[37]

October 20 Bertha and Potter Palmer buy two *Wheatstacks* paintings by Blanche Hoschedé, as well as some of the same motif by Monet that New York dealer Michael Knoedler had recently acquired from Monet.[38]

December 8–22 In London Monet sees Whistler, who earlier this year had sent him two lithographs via Mallarmé. Monet hopes to return to paint a London series during the winter. On December 9 Pissarro claims that Monet's London series is awaited with impatience.[39]

December 20 Death of Monet's half-sister, Marie, and subsequent redistribution of their father's estate to Monet and his brother.[40]

1892

January Monet delivers four *Poplars* paintings on January 6 to Boussod & Valadon, where the works are promptly placed on view. He delivers seven *Poplars* to Durand-Ruel on January 26–27. When Mirbeau sees them a few weeks later, he remarks that Monet "has attained the absolute beauty of great decoration."[41]

February 5 Monet goes to Rouen, where he begins work on his *Rouen Cathedral* series. He stays at the Hôtel d'Angleterre at 7–8, cours Boieldieu, and on February 12 arranges for temporary access to an empty apartment facing the cathedral. Mirbeau visits him in Rouen.[42]

February 13 On a weekend trip home, Monet falls ill and cannot return to Rouen until February 24. While in Giverny he finishes six more *Poplars* for his upcoming exhibition at the Durand-Ruel Gallery, Paris, intending to keep two or three of these for himself. He has already ordered frames. Mirbeau admires the new *Poplars* paintings in Paris on February 17.[43]

February 20 In *Art et critique*, Maurice Denis calls on wealthy industrialists to commission decorative ensembles from young painters.[44]

February 29–March 10 Fifteen paintings—installed by Monet on February 28—comprise an exhibition entitled "Monet, Series of Poplars on the Banks of the Epte" at the Durand-Ruel Gallery, Paris (see cat. no. 103). At the close of the exhibition, Monet asks Durand-Ruel to return five paintings as well as three special frames: one white, one oak, and one he describes as made of four trees (presumably fashioned of wood from four of the poplar trees felled after his series was finished). The other twelve frames are added to those kept in reserve at the dealer's. As was the case with the *Wheatstacks* exhibition, the variety of frame types is apparently at odds with any wish to present closely related works in a consistent decorative ensemble. Pissarro remarks upon the frames in a letter to Monet, in which he also comments enthusiastically about "three arrangements of *Poplars*, evening," implying that coloristically related works are installed adjacent to one another.

At the opening, Degas tells Monet of his plans for an exhibition of fantastical landscape paintings incorporating double images such as nudes transformed into clifftops.

61. Rouen Cathedral, photographed by Neurdein, c. 1890. Musée Marmottan, Paris. The disk above the main portal, represented in Monet's paintings of Rouen Cathedral, is here legible as a modern clockface.

Among the relatively few reviews, the most noteworthy is that published in April by Symbolist G. Albert Aurier in *Mercure de France*, characterizing the *Poplars* as a "glorious Mass of lights in a modern sun temple."[45]

Early March Immediately returning to Rouen after the opening of his exhibition in Paris, Monet now paints from the window of a lingerie store overlooking the cathedral. By midmonth he works on as many as nine canvases in a single day, starting at 8 A.M. and working until 6:30 P.M. According to Perry, he uses long, flexible brushes that are made to order. In the evenings, Monet sees his brother Léon (who lives in Déville, west of the city) and the collector François Depeaux, who immediately offers to buy two *Rouen Cathedral* paintings, one for himself and one for the Rouen Museum, although Monet declines this premature offer.[46]

March 22 Monet agrees to give Durand-Ruel first choice on the *Rouen Cathedral* paintings, although he does not want an exclusive contract with any dealer. Meanwhile, Monet learns that Theodore Butler is courting Suzanne Hoschedé, and he threatens to sell the house and move the family rather than endure a repetition of the previous summer. Monet comes back to Giverny occasionally, with one of many household servants picking him up at the Vernon train station.[47]

March 26 The Luxembourg Museum purchases Renoir's *Young Women at the Piano*. Determined to be worthy of this distinction, Renoir makes six versions of this one composition before he is satisfied, thus producing a sort of "series" of a single genre scene. The museum also hopes to acquire works by Degas and Monet around this same time.[48]

March 28–April 9 Exhibition of twenty-one works by Monet (see cat. nos. 43 and 57) held at the St. Botolph Club, Boston, organized by Desmond Fitzgerald, who lends five works and borrows others from Boston collectors.[49]

April The owner of the Rouen lingerie shop asks Monet to stop painting in the afternoons because his presence is upsetting to customers. Depeaux provides a screen so that both painter and clients have privacy; within the small space allotted him, however, Monet can never get more than a yard away from the canvas on which he is working. Despite satisfactory progress, Monet has a nightmare that the cathedral is falling on top of him.[50]

May 7 The Palmers meet Monet in Paris at the opening of the Renoir exhibition (to which Monet is a lender) at the Durand-Ruel Gallery. In the preceding weeks, the Palmers had purchased eight Renoirs from Durand-Ruel, paying 10,000–15,000 francs each for three of them.

62. Edgar Degas, *Landscape*, 1892. Monotype and pastel; 30 × 40 cm, 11¾ × 15¾ in. Museum of Fine Arts, Boston, Denman Waldo Ross Collection (09.295).

63. Edgar Degas, *Landscape*, 1892. Monotype and pastel; 25.4 × 34 cm, 10 × 13⅜ in. The Metropolitan Museum of Art, New York, Purchase, Mr. and Mrs. Richard J. Bernhard Gift (1972.636).

According to Robinson's diary, the Palmers buy a painting by Blanche Hoschedé and four *Rouen Cathedral* paintings. Such a sale seems highly unlikely at this early date; perhaps they reserved four paintings from the still-incomplete series. Only one *Rouen Cathedral* is documented as part of their early 1890s collection, and this work will be returned to the artist on March 29, 1893, for 12,000 francs' credit.

Monet's art sales for 1892 will amount to more than 100,000 francs.[51]

Early May Returning from America, Robinson stops at Rouen and, immediately upon his arrival in Giverny on May 23, visits Monet and sees the new *Rouen Cathedral* paintings. Monet explains, "I sought as always. I wanted to do architecture without any dashes, any lines." Writing to American painter J. Alden Weir, Robinson enthuses: "[The *Rouen Cathedral* paintings] are simply colossal. Never, I believe, has architecture been painted [like this] before, the most astonishing impression of the thing, a feeling of size, grandeur and decay . . . and not a line anywhere—yet there is a wonderful sense of construction and solidity. Isn't it curious, a man taking such material and making such magnificent use of it?"

Meanwhile, with the help of Mirbeau, Monet is attempting to hire a chief gardener, eventually choosing Félix Breuil, the son of the gardener who worked for Mirbeau's father. Monet's son Michel and Jean-Pierre Hoschedé are compiling a book about the plants of Vernon.[52]

June 3 Monet tells Robinson, referring to an 1885 Etretat painting owned by Sargent, that he regrets his inability to work as he had before. Robinson writes in his diary: "At that time [in the 1880s] anything that pleased him, no matter how transitory, he painted, regardless of the inability to go further than one painting. Now it is only a long entwined effort that satisfies him, and it must be an important motif, one that is sufficiently *entraînant* [captivating]. 'Obviously one loses on the one hand if one gains on the other. One cannot have everything. If what I am doing no longer has the charm of youth I hope that there are more successful qualities so that one could live longer with one of these paintings.' He agreed with me that it was a pity one could not always paint freely, all sorts of things, without thinking too much of their importance."

This summer Monet adds one or two Jongkind watercolors to his collection.[53]

June 10 Butler, Ferdinand Deconchy, and Robinson dine with the Monets and Hoschedés in the Giverny garden. After dinner the party tours the garden paths with Chinese lanterns, to appreciate night-blooming flowers.[54]

June–July Busy finishing canvases that have been selected by buyers, rather than starting new works, Monet agrees to lend Pissarro 15,000 francs so that he can buy a house at Eragny; the loan is repaid in 1896. Monet also asks Pissarro to sell him *Peasants Putting Up Pea Stakes* (private collection), an 1891 work included in Durand-Ruel's February 1892 Pissarro exhibition. Pissarro hopes Monet will accept it as a gift, although Monet has offered to pay the market price.[55]

July 3 Dining at Giverny, Robinson learns that a figure painting by Monet has just been acquired by the Japanese dealer Tadamasa Hayashi, who, since the beginning of the 1880s, has been one of the most active Asian art dealers in Paris.[56]

July 7 Sara Hallowell, Chicago art agent, visits Giverny. Two days later, she writes to Potter Palmer: "The other day [Isidore] Montaignac secured three of [Monet's] pictures—not direct from him—and sent to me to come see them. . . . I could not go until the next day when I found all three had been sold immediately, on the day on which Montaignac received them. These were sold respectively for 7,000, 6,500, and 6,000 francs. Both Durand-Ruel and Montaignac tell me they find Monet absurd in his prices now, asking *them* even more than he did you when you visited his studio, so now the dealers are scouring Paris for his pictures."[57]

July 12 Monet refuses a commission from American artist H. Siddons Mowbray and his wife to undertake a large decorative project, because the size "frightens" him.[58]

July 16 Civil marriage at Giverny of Monet and Alice Hoschedé, with Caillebotte, Helleu, and Léon Monet among the witnesses.[59]

July 20 Marriage of Suzanne Hoschedé and Theodore Butler, followed by lunch in Monet's studio. Theodore Robinson makes a painting of the occasion (Musée Américain, Giverny). After a honeymoon, the Butlers take up temporary residence at the nearby Maison Baptiste, awaiting the construction of a new house into which they will move in the fall of 1895.[60]

Late July–Early August The Monets visit the summer home of Léon Monet at Petites-Dalles on a tour of the Normandy coast. Referring to two works brought back from this trip, Monet tells Robinson that he has "quite lost the power of doing a thing at once and letting it go at that—as he did twenty-five years ago—now he wants to feel that he has time to keep at a thing for a certain space of time."[61]

September 5 Robinson dines with Monet, who is dressed "in his ruffles and dark blue clothes." Monet is depressed, not having worked for four months and unwilling to travel while construction of his greenhouse is under way. Monet speaks with admiration of Turner's *Rain, Steam, and Speed* (National Gallery, London) and of his watercolor studies from nature. Having just returned from London, Pissarro has recently visited Giverny.[62]

October 5 Robinson writes in his diary that Monet's big, square "whirl" series of 1891 demonstrates Monet's tendency to overwork paintings. The reference to this series and to other unrecorded works suggests that Monet later destroyed a group of paintings from 1890–93. A few days earlier, Monet had begun and destroyed a painting of sunflowers and green grass. A reference in Robinson's diary suggests that Cassatt, then working on her decorative mural (now lost) for the World's Columbian Exposition in Chicago, may have been in Giverny around this time.[63]

November According to Perry, Monet keeps a vigil in his newly completed greenhouse, joined by his wife and stepdaughters, throughout the first night after the heating system is installed, fearful for the gloxinias that it might malfunction.[64]

November 6 Pierre Lagarde is elected to paint murals for the Paris City Hall, replacing Jules Breton. Monet is proposed to the selection committee by Rodin, but he receives only four votes to Lagarde's ten.[65]

November 7–18 Exhibition of between twenty-four and twenty-six closely related Degas landscapes rendered in pastel over monotype at the Durand-Ruel Gallery, Paris (see fig. nos. 62 and 63). This, the only one-artist exhibition that Degas ever sanctioned, appears to be a response to Monet's recent exhibition of landscapes in series. Degas may have wished to stress his own ongoing commitment to seriality, which he had begun to explore as early as 1886, when he presented a group of nudes at the Impressionist exhibition. Alternatively, Degas's exhibition may have been a response to comments by Georges Lecomte, who dismissed landscape in Degas's works as "accessory decor for mounted jockeys" in *L'Art impressionniste d'après la collection Durand-Ruel*, published earlier this year. Lecomte also offered an important appreciation of the doors decorated with Monet still lifes for Durand-Ruel (see fig no. 42).

During the early 1890s, Caillebotte works on a set of decorative door panels with orchid motifs for his dining room at Petit Gennevilliers (fig. no. 64); they recall the still lifes Monet painted for Durand-Ruel's sitting-room doors in the 1880s (see cat. nos. 72, 73, and 74).[66]

64. Gustave Caillebotte's decorative door panels representing the orchids in his greenhouse, probably painted in the early 1890s, for his dining room at Petit Gennevilliers.

December 2 Dining with Robinson in Le Havre, Jacques Hoschedé estimates that Monet's current six-month hiatus is the longest the artist has ever gone without painting.[67]

December 21 The Monets go to Paris for a few days. At Durand-Ruel's gallery, Monet sees Pissarro's 1883 paintings of Rouen Cathedral and some recent paintings, including a small series of views of Mirbeau's garden and views of Kew Gardens and Charing Cross Bridge in London. He also sees Geffroy.[68]

1893

January–Mid-February During severely cold weather, Monet paints snowscapes and ice floes on the Seine, as he had done in the winter of 1879–80.[69]

February 1–2 Monet sees Pissarro at the Utamaro–Hiroshige exhibition organized by Bing at the Durand-Ruel Gallery, Paris.[70]

February 5 Monet purchases land across the railroad track along the south border of his garden (four trains pass daily). He immediately begins planning his water garden on this new plot.[71]

February 15–March 15 Monet returns to the Hôtel d'Angleterre in Rouen to continue work on his *Rouen Cathedral* series. Although he is no longer able to paint from the lingerie shop, he finds yet another nearby workplace. Depeaux

arranges for the same porter to be on hand for Monet's arrival to deploy easels and canvases to different sites and to carry them back to the hotel at the end of the day. Monet visits the Botanical Gardens in Rouen on February 16 to inspect the greenhouses. He returns to Giverny on Sundays to spend time with his family and to review the extensive work under way on his gardens. In Giverny, Butler paints trains at different times of day; the present whereabouts of these paintings are unknown.[72]

March 17 Monet petitions the Eure district commissioner for permission to dig channels tapping into a branch of the river Epte (which borders his new plot) to irrigate his garden pool. He also requests permission to construct two light wooden bridges from his property to the other side of the river, where he has rented land. Civil engineers inspecting the site raise questions that aggravate Monet, who by March 20 wants nothing more to do with engineers or digging. Vowing to drop the whole project, Monet instructs Alice Monet to "throw the water plants into the river; they will grow there. . . . Shit on the Giverny natives, the engineers." Nevertheless, Monet submits a second petition to the commissioner on March 24. In April Giverny neighbors again raise objections.[73]

Second Half of March–Early April Good weather allows Monet to work to exhaustion, making progress on a record fourteen canvases in one day. But he tells Geffroy that "anyone who claims to have finished a painting is a terrible braggart; to finish meaning complete, perfect." Monet notices that sunlight no longer falls obliquely across the cathedral's façade as it had in February. Working through April 12, Monet becomes characteristically dissatisfied: "It's a crust intoxicated with colors and that's all, but it's not painting."[74]

April 24 Birth of James (Jimmy) Butler, son of Suzanne Hoschedé Butler and Theodore Butler.

May 1 President Grover Cleveland opens the World's Columbian Exposition in Chicago, which will be attended by twenty-three million visitors. The official French exhibition installed in the Art Palace includes no works by Impressionist painters but, thanks to the Palmers, these artists are well represented in the same building as part of a loan collection of works from private American collections. Four Monets are in this section (see cat. nos. 36 and 44).[75]

July 17 In a letter to the Eure district commissioner, Monet belittles the municipal council members and others who oppose his plan to divert a branch of the Epte for his water garden on the grounds that his plants might poison the river. He explains that his goal is simply to cultivate motifs to paint, such as water lilies, reeds, and irises. Ten days later he receives the permits.[76]

65. Monet in his yellow dining room at Giverny, decorated with Japanese prints; date of photograph unknown.

66. View, looking east, of the Japanese bridge in Monet's garden at Giverny, probably 1893.

August 23 Monet requests a 5,000-franc advance from Durand-Ruel, presumably to meet the expenses associated with enlarging his garden. On October 12 the dealer buys four paintings, and his son Joseph takes snapshots. Again Monet needs 5,000 francs. His art income for 1893 will exceed 60,000 francs.[77]

October 30 Monet shows twenty-six *Rouen Cathedral* paintings to Morisot and her daughter Julie Manet. The teenager notes that, since their last visit, Monet has constructed a new room for himself above his studio. Installed on

its white walls are works by Monet's associates. Alice Monet's room is blue; those of Blanche and Germaine are violet. The living room is violet and is decorated with Japanese prints, as is the yellow dining room (fig. no. 65). Chrysanthemums are growing in the greenhouse. The Japanese bridge spans the new pond (fig. no. 66). Julie Manet does not note in her diary that the exterior of the house has also been transformed. The shutters are now painted green, resulting in a green and pink exterior similar to that of the second house Monet rented in Argenteuil in 1874–75.[78]

1894

January 24 Having received architectural advice from Louis Bonnier, the brother-in-law of his painter friend Deconchy, Monet reports that he intends to construct a new kitchen at Giverny and eventually to extend the west portion of his house to accommodate a studio. Bonnier will come to Giverny in May.[79]

February–March In the studio at Giverny, Monet brings his *Rouen Cathedral* paintings to resolution for exhibition.[80]

February 21 Death of Gustave Caillebotte. Monet goes to Paris for the funeral on February 26.[81]

March 19 Auction of Théodore Duret's collection, including six paintings by Monet, at the Georges Petit Gallery, Paris. These include two large decorative panels commissioned in 1876 for the Hoschedé's country house. Given the enormous current interest in decorative painting, the reappearance of these works marks Monet as a precursor of Edouard Vuillard and his associates. While in Paris for this sale, Monet discusses Caillebotte's bequest with Renoir, an executor of the estate.[82]

March 20 The French National Museums accept the entire group of Impressionist paintings in the Caillebotte bequest, but without guaranteeing their eventual transfer to the Louvre. Given the Luxembourg Museum's policy of limiting the number of works on display by a single artist to three, however, only part of the collection can be exhibited in Paris. It is proposed to send the remainder to annex museums until more gallery space becomes available.[83]

Late March Durand-Ruel sends Monet a Caillebotte flower painting left to him as a keepsake and Cézanne's *Geraniums and Apples* (Metropolitan Museum of Art, New York), a gift from Helleu. Monet adds to his collection on April 20, when Henri de Toulouse-Lautrec sends him his *Yvette Guilbert* poster.[84]

March–May Monet is hard at work on new subjects, including a small series of poplar trees observed across a meadow (see cat. no. 104) and riverscapes painted at Port-Villez from his studio boat. He works from 4 to 9 A.M. Stressing the parity between landscape and its mirror reflection on the river's surface, these Port-Villez paintings extend an idea that Monet had explored when he first arrived at Giverny in 1883. A group of six paintings of the church dominating the Vernon skyline, repeated upside-down as a reflection in the river (see cat. no. 106), likewise harks back to 1883 works, which themselves draw upon experiments initiated at Vétheuil in 1880. Both groups are apparently intended for a planned mid-May exhibition at the Durand-Ruel Gallery, Paris.[85]

67. J.M.W. Turner, *Landscape with a River and a Bay in the Distance*, c. 1840/50. Oil on canvas; 94 × 123 cm, 37 × 48½ in. Musée du Louvre, Paris (RF 1967.2).

April 29 Visiting Giverny to discuss the upcoming exhibition and to advance 5,000 francs to Monet, Durand-Ruel is shocked by Monet's proposal that his *Rouen Cathedral* paintings should sell for 15,000 francs apiece.[86]

May Monet challenges Durand-Ruel by indicating that he can contact other dealers and collectors who already have expressed interest in the *Rouen Cathedral* paintings, and in this way escape the pressure of an exhibition deadline. Not wanting to lose the opportunity to show and sell the paintings himself, Durand-Ruel agrees to postpone the exhibition, scheduled to open in a few weeks, for a year. Durand-Ruel complains about the high prices Monet is asking for his *Rouen Cathedral* paintings and explains to the artist that because recently active buyers (like the Palmers) are now trying to sell their paintings back, the dealer is using his capital to prop up an artificially inflated market for Monet's work. Monet responds by suggesting the possibility of an autumn 1894 exhibition, with the understanding that he will not allow the best *Rouen Cathedral* paintings to be sold for a price less than what he is asking, but he could accept lower prices for the others.

Geffroy's most recent collection of *La Vie artistique* essays, published this month, amounts to propagandistic enthusiasm for Monet, to whom it is dedicated. Urging Geffroy to visit, Monet tells him that the irises are in bloom, which suggests that planting of the water garden is under way.[87]

June 1 Monet goes to Paris to help Renoir install the memorial exhibition of Caillebotte's work held at the Durand-Ruel Gallery, Paris, from June 4 to June 16.[88]

June Two late paintings by Turner are included in an exhibition in Paris of English paintings (see fig. no. 67). Fairytale-like coastal views that Monet will paint in 1896–97 (see cat. no. 110) are similar in spirit to such late Turner paintings.[89]

July 10–August A work by Butler is included, with works by Pierre Bonnard, Denis, and other Nabis, in the Seventh Exhibition of Impressionists and Symbolists at Le Barc de Bouteville Gallery, Paris. Butler also participates in this group's eighth exhibition, held from November to December.

August–September Monet invites Maurice Joyant, who had left Boussod & Valadon in October 1893 to start his own dealership with Michel Manzi, to Giverny to see the *Rouen Cathedral* paintings. Joyant is acting on behalf of the collector Isaac de Camondo, who will buy four of them by the end of the year. Camondo (who also has a fine Asian art collection) had expressed his intention of eventually donating his collection to the Louvre. On September 10 Pierre Valadon comes to Giverny on behalf of Montaignac, Durand-Ruel, and his own interests, proposing a bulk purchase of *Rouen Cathedral* paintings at a unit price far below that set by Monet. Monet agrees to a reduction in the price per canvas from 15,000 to 12,000 francs.[90]

September Two works by Monet are included in the Eleventh Annual Exhibition of the St. Louis Exposition and Music Hall Association.

Monet will also have paintings in this exhibition in 1895–97.

October 11 Birth at Giverny of Alice (Lily) Butler, second child of Suzanne and Theodore Butler. Suzanne becomes seriously ill afterward and eventually is paralyzed. Consequently, both children receive a great deal of care from the Monets.

Late October Pissarro asks to come to Giverny to see the *Rouen Cathedral* paintings. "All Paris is talking about the price Monet is asking for his *Cathedrals*, a whole series, which Durand wants to treat himself to, but Monet is asking 15,000 francs for each."[91]

November 7–30 Cézanne stays at the Hôtel Baudy, Giverny. Cassatt has a meal with him at the hotel. Monet is at work on three paintings of a farmer's field, and Cézanne will later recall: "[Monet] is a great lord who treats himself to the haystacks that he likes. If he likes a little field, he buys it. With a big flunky and some dogs that keep guard so that no one comes to disturb him. That's what I need." By now Monet owns at least two paintings by Cézanne.[92]

November 28 Geffroy returns to Giverny, this time with Clemenceau, Mirbeau, and Rodin, to meet Cézanne and to see the *Rouen Cathedral* paintings before Monet delivers those purchased by Camondo.[93]

December 17–20 Auction at the Hôtel Drouot, Paris, of Clemenceau's large collection of Japanese art.

1895

Sometime this year, the Union League Club of Chicago buys a Monet Argenteuil painting.

January 6–12 Monet makes his first painting of the arched bridge spanning his new water garden, covered in snow.[1]

January 12–24 Exhibition at the Durand-Ruel Gallery, New York, of forty works by Monet (see cat. nos. 28, 75, 76, 95, and 100).

January 17 French National Museums officials meet with Caillebotte's brother Martial and Renoir, who, since March 20, 1894, have become increasingly opposed to the idea of exiling roughly half of the works in the bequest to museums outside of Paris, which would contravene the specific provision in Caillebotte's will that the works not be sent to the "attic or provinces." A decision is finally made to accept only those paintings that can be hung at the Luxembourg Museum and to release the remaining works to Caillebotte's heir, Martial.[2]

January 28–29 Monet goes to Paris and sees Renoir (probably about the Caillebotte bequest) before departing by train for Oslo (then called Christiana), Norway.[3]

68. Claude Monet, *Mount Kolsaas*, 1895. Oil on canvas; 65 × 100 cm, 25⁹⁄₁₆ × 39⅜ in. Courtesy of Sotheby's [W 1408].

69. Monet at Giverny, photographed by Margaret Perry (daughter of the American painter Lilla Cabot Perry), September 28, 1895.

February 1–8 Fulfilling an ambition expressed in 1891, Monet arrives in Oslo. Monet's stepson Jacques Hoschedé, who is in the shipping business and married to Norwegian Inge Jorgensen, successfully discourages local artists from staging a hero's reception at the station and installs Monet in a bed-and-breakfast after his long, difficult journey. From February 5–8 Jacques takes Monet by horse-drawn sleigh on a mountain tour. The daytime temperatures of minus 20–30 degrees Celsius are tolerable in bearskins.[4]

February 4–16 Exhibition at the St. Botolph Club, Boston, of twenty-seven works by Monet (see cat. nos. 76, 95, and 100).

February 10–13 On walks and train trips with Jacques, Monet explores the Oslo area, looking for motifs that can be reached without skis and observed from under shelters.[5]

February 14 Monet visits an artists' colony in the farm village of Björnegaard, outside the fjordside town of Sandvika, fifteen kilometers southwest of Oslo. Hermann Joachim Bang, a Danish writer in residence, speaks French. Monet takes a room there on February 19 and begins to paint. As "porter," Jacques shovels paths to the sites where Monet chooses to set up his easel. The painter is bothered by the blinding snow-reflected sunlight and adulatory visitors.[6]

February 26–March 1 When he has eight canvases under way, Monet writes to Geffroy: "I painted part of the day today, while it was snowing continually: you would have laughed to see me entirely white, my beard covered

in icy stalactites." Monet has begun to paint Mount Kolsaas (see fig. no. 68) and the snow-covered town of Sandvika (see cat. no. 107), intrigued by the resemblance of these Norwegian motifs to those celebrated in Japanese woodblock prints.[7]

February 28 Having consulted with the artists, Luxembourg Museum curator Léonce Bénédite chooses forty of the works bequeathed by Caillebotte for display in Paris. Of the sixteen paintings by Monet that are part of the collection, he selects eight (cat. no. 54 is among those not accepted).[8]

March 2 Death of Morisot.[9]

Early March Monet postpones the opening of his forthcoming Durand-Ruel exhibition for two weeks, until mid-May, realizing that he will need more time in Norway. He follows a demanding routine, getting up at 6 A.M., starting work at 8 A.M., breaking from 1:30 until 3 P.M., and continuing to paint until 7 P.M.[10]

March 26 Monet returns to Oslo and stays at the Grand Hotel. He takes a fjord cruise on an ice cutter.[11]

March 29 Prince Eugen of Sweden visits Monet and sees a *Rouen Cathedral* painting that the artist has brought with him to Norway apparently to finish.[12]

April 1 Monet leaves Oslo, traveling by train to Giverny.[13]

April 4 In an article about Monet in the Oslo newspaper *Dagbladet*, Monet is quoted from interviews: "The motif is something secondary

for me; what I want to render is what is between the motif and me."[14]

April–June At Cézanne's request, Geffroy poses seated in his home office for a portrait (Musée du Louvre, Paris). Monet lunches with them on April 31.[15]

April 23 Monet goes to Paris with some of the paintings to be included in his Durand-Ruel exhibition scheduled to open May 10. Helleu helps him find frames.[16]

April 25–26 Durand-Ruel pays 20,000 francs for one of the nine Monets offered at an American Art Association auction of works owned by Sutton.[17]

May 10–31 Exhibition of paintings by Monet at the Durand-Ruel Gallery, Paris. The exhibition consists of forty-nine works, according to the last-minute catalogue (see cat. nos. 104, 106, and 107); at least two additional works are not in the catalogue. In the first room are eight paintings of the church at Vernon (only six survive, suggesting the possibility that the artist destroys two of them subsequent to this exhibition); in the following two rooms, there are twenty *Rouen Cathedral* paintings (all dated "1894"). Monet also presents eight Norway paintings, although he has not had the chance to elaborate these in his now characteristic fashion, and apparently they are not for sale. Monet provides frames for most of the works, replacing all but two of the lenders' frames. These frames may be the same ones used in his 1891 and 1892 exhibitions of works in series, but whether or not they are uniform in format or color remains unknown.

Boudin, Cézanne, Degas, Pissarro, and Renoir are amazed by the virtuoso painting technique. The iridescent and richly metaphoric colors, along with the density of the impasto surfaces, intrigue critics in their mostly enthusiastic accounts of the exhibition. Curiously, some wide-circulation newspapers fail to cover the exhibition.[18]

May 20 In his nearly bankrupt newspaper *La Justice*, Clemenceau publishes a full-front-page review of Monet's exhibition, expressing the wish that the paintings had been installed in chronological sequence so that a viewer could fully appreciate the gradual ebb and flow of light. He calls upon the president of France, Félix Faure, or some millionaire to buy them all and thus keep the series together: "Why has it not occurred to you to go and look at the work of one of your countrymen on whose account France will be celebrated throughout the world long after your names will have fallen into oblivion? . . . Perhaps you might consider endowing [France] with these twenty paintings that together represent . . . a revolution without a gunshot." Reporting a rumor that the State is contemplating a purchase, Pissarro echoes Clemenceau's opinion: "[Monet's] *Cathedrals* will be dispersed this way and that and above all they should be seen as an ensemble."[19]

May 24 Monet writes to Geffroy: "I just spent nearly eight lazy days, looking at the water, the flowers, the sky." He adds, "I have to come to Paris next week, probably for a few days [to deinstall his exhibition]. At that time we can see about realizing the arrangement that Clemenceau dreamed about. It is the very least that I could provide this pleasure for him after the admirable article that he did." On May 30 Monet perhaps reinstalls the *Rouen Cathedral* galleries, since the exhibition is extended until June 8.[20]

May 26 Over Monet's objections, the Giverny municipal council votes in favor of construction of a starch factory. Offering to pay a lump sum (5,500 francs) to offset any losses in rental revenues to the factory, the artist wages opposition at the district and national level. His offer is finally accepted on February 9, 1896.[21]

June 14–23 After consulting a doctor about disabling dizzy spells, Monet returns to Argelès-de-Bigorre in the Hautes-Pyrénées. He had been there with Alice and chronically ill Suzanne Butler following the opening of his exhibition in May. On June 19 the group moves on to Salies-de-Béarn.[22]

September At Giverny, art historian Bernard Berenson is "taken off his feet" upon viewing Monet's *Rouen Cathedral* paintings. Later this month, Monet receives a gift of two heavy cases of perennial plants from New York collector Horace Havemeyer.[23]

70. Monet's house at Giverny, photographed by a member of the Perry family sometime between 1893 and 1897.

71. Claude Monet, *Chrysanthemums*, 1896–97. Oil on canvas; 89 × 30 cm, 35 × 11¹³⁄₁₆ in. Courtesy of Sotheby's [W 1497].

November 17–18 Monet takes Suzanne Butler to Paris for medical help.[24]

Mid-November Comprehensive Cézanne exhibition, with around 150 unsigned and undated works presented in rotating groups of about fifty works each, at the Ambroise Vollard Gallery at 39, rue Lafitte, Paris. Vollard, who had opened this gallery in 1894, had not met Cézanne until now. Degas, Pissarro, and Renoir all acquire works, and Monet apparently buys three.[25]

November 23–24 Suspicious that Durand-Ruel may be conspiring with fellow dealers to discourage collectors from purchasing *Rouen Cathedral* paintings, Monet flatly refuses his request to take works to the United States on consignment. Monet informs Durand-Ruel that Sutton buys ten *Rouen Cathedral* works on a November 24 visit to Giverny, although in fact Sutton buys only four or five.[26]

December 26 Opening of Bing's L'Art Nouveau Gallery at the corner of rue de Provence and rue Chaucat, Paris, in a starkly modern building designed by Bonnier. Over the rue Chaucat door to the Japanese section of the gallery is a stained-glass window by Louis Comfort Tiffany based on a Toulouse-Lautrec design. The window depicts an episode from the 1892 ballet *Papa Chrysanthemum* in which a Western bride in Japan dances on water lily pads. While Bing exhibits all manner of artists, from Cassatt and Rodin to Emile Gallé, his great innovation, as Geffroy points out in a January 13, 1896, review in *Le Journal*, is "a series of rooms—dining room, smoking room, study, boudoir, waiting room—all these rooms furnished and decorated by an artist [Henry Van de Velde, Charles Conder, Denis, Albert Besnard, Vuillard]. . . . It is the interesting demonstration of the experience of days of old, attempted by artists of today, knowingly and ingeniously resolved; to mix art and life environment."[27]

1896

January–March Pissarro paints serial variations of smoke-filled river views from a room at the Hôtel de Paris, Rouen. These cityscapes, some of which are included in a one-artist exhibition at Durand-Ruel's gallery in Paris beginning on April 15, feature ships, bridges, and overcast weather, as will Monet's 1899–1904 views of London.

February 8 Monet expresses interest in acquiring 1830–31 flower prints by Hokusai, adding to those of irises, chrysanthemums, peonies, and convolvuli already in his collection.[28]

February 9–29 Stopping at Le Havre, Monet returns to Pourville on the Normandy coast for a vacation followed by a work campaign. He ex-

72. View, looking east, of the Japanese bridge, photographed by a member of the Perry family, around 1896.

tends ideas he had developed during a long stay there in 1882, although he chooses less distant motifs. He works at sheltered sites to avoid winter winds.[29]

February 26 Official acceptance of the forty works from Caillebotte's estate to enter the Luxembourg Museum.[30]

March 2–5 Monet goes to Paris to help Degas, Mallarmé, and Renoir install the Morisot memorial exhibition at the Durand-Ruel Gallery. Fulfilling Morisot's wish that he choose a keepsake, Monet selects *Julie Manet with her Greyhound* of 1893 (Musée Marmottan, Paris).[31]

March 6–Around April 2 In Pourville, Monet uses a beach house as a shelter but is unable to paint much because of bad weather. Meanwhile, Suzanne Butler finally returns to Giverny from Paris.[32]

March 9 Opening at the American Art Galleries, Madison Square South, New York, of "Marvelous Paintings of Cathedral Rouen by Claude Monet," featuring fourteen *Rouen Cathedral* works (see cat. no. 105).[33]

April 2 Death of Theodore Robinson in New York.

Summer Monet begins his *Mornings on the Seine* series working in his studio boat. Unfavorable weather obliges the artist to postpone development of the full series until the following year. Shown these paintings while visiting the Perrys in Giverny, American painter Cecelia Beaux notes the dramatic change in Monet's technique now from thick impasto brushwork to flat tonal painting.[34]

September 8 In order to continue his series of cityscapes, Pissarro checks into the Hôtel d'Angleterre in Rouen, taking the same room with a wonderful view of the port that Monet had occupied during his 1892–93 campaigns there.[35]

November Monet paints flowers (see fig. no. 71).[36]

November 5, 1896–January 1, 1897 Three works by Monet are included in the First International Exhibition at the Carnegie Institute, Pittsburgh. Works by Monet will be included in exhibitions in 1897–1903, 1907–14, 1916, and 1919–27.[37]

December 9 The National Gallery, Berlin, purchases an 1880 Vétheuil painting from Durand-Ruel. This is one of six works by Monet in an exhibition held there during the previous month or two. A Monet painting of Argenteuil is donated to the museum in 1899.[38]

1897

Around January 18 Monet returns to Pourville to continue with works begun the previous year, even though the beach house he had used in March as a shelter is unavailable.[39]

Mid-January The Monets are sued by a Mr. Guérin over 1877 art transactions with the dealer Legrand.[40]

January 28–29 Monet visits the new annex to the Luxembourg Museum constructed for the Caillebotte bequest. He suggests in vain

73. Portrait of Monet by an unknown photographer, taken before June 16, 1898.

that Cézanne's *L'Estaque* be moved to one of the better places given to his own works.[41]

February 1–2 At the auction of the Vever collection at the Georges Petit Gallery, Paris, one of Monet's 1874 Argenteuil paintings (cat. no. 37) is sold for 21,500 francs.[42]

February–March Monet needs to work quickly on clifftop motifs at Pourville when a group of sportspeople rent the land for shooting ranges. Fourteen paintings in progress (see cat. no. 109) depict one of Monet's favorite motifs since 1882: the glacial gorge of the Petit Ailly river in Varengeville, topped by a Napoleonic coast guard's post (see cat. no. 67). At another site, Monet has to stop people from burning dry grass while his work is under way. A tempest prevents him from painting during the first days of March, and wind becomes a major adversary later in the month. Sometimes he plays golf in the mornings.[43]

February 9 First public presentation at the Luxembourg Museum of works from the Caillebotte bequest, augmented by Manet's *Olympia* (fig. no. 9), Renoir's *Young Women at the Piano,* and Morisot's *Young Woman in a Ball Dress,* acquired by the State in 1894. Among Monet's works in the bequest, *The Lunch (Decorative Panel)* (fig. no. 28), which has not been exhibited since 1876, must seem particularly modern to Vuillard and his colleagues, who have only recently produced comparable decorative works. This first public presentation of Impressionist paintings in a French museum unleashes a storm of conservative protest.[44]

April 22–October 31 Two paintings by Monet are in the second Venice International Exhibition. His paintings will also be included in this exhibition in 1903, 1905, and 1922.[45]

May 1–September 30 Three Monet paintings are included at the International Exhibition in Dresden. Monet will also be represented at this exhibition in 1901, 1904, and 1926.

Early May Rodin sends Monet a gift of a drawing of Salomé on May 2. On May 3 or 4 Monet is in Paris and meets Rodin near his plaster statue of Victor Hugo, currently installed at the Salon de la Société nationale, which had opened on April 22.[46]

May 15–October Three works by Monet are included in the International Art Exhibition in Stockholm.[47]

June 9–10 Civil and church weddings of Jean Monet and Blanche Hoschedé take place in Giverny.[48]

August Maurice Guillemot, sent by *Le Figaro* to interview Monet, sets off at 3:30 A.M. to accompany the artist while he works on paintings in the *Mornings on the Seine* series (see cat. no. 108). One of Monet's gardeners accompanies him to handle the fourteen numbered canvases in progress, putting one aside for another as Monet responds to changing light conditions. Referring to the *Mornings on the Seine* paintings, which he hopes to exhibit in 1898, Monet tells Guillemot, "I would like to prevent anyone from seeing how it is done." Before lunchtime, Guillemot gets a tour of Monet's home: the "studio" with three rows of his own paintings on the walls; the pale yellow dining room with violet doors, where Monet displays his collection of Japanese prints (see fig. no. 65); the staircase decorated with posters by Jules Chéret; and the bedroom, where paintings by his Impressionist colleagues are installed.

Monet explains to Guillemot that he is making studies of his water garden for murals that will decorate a circular room. Monet mentions a large study for this same decorative scheme in an August 3 letter to Geffroy, who had just sent him a copy of his new book, *Pays d'Ouest,* which includes anecdotes of their 1886 meeting at Belle-Ile-en-Mer. Monet comments that the gardens take "all the money I earn."[49]

November 8–20 Exhibition of forty-seven works by Theodore Butler at Vollard's gallery, Paris.[50]

December 3 Monet writes to congratulate Zola for his recent articles supporting the innocence of Captain Dreyfus, whose conviction in late 1894 for espionage had become a scandal implicating top military and government officials.[51]

1898

January 13 Zola's "J'accuse," in support of Dreyfus, is published in Clemenceau's *Aurore.* Monet again writes to congratulate Zola, volunteering his name for inclusion in a list of supporters published by the newspaper on January 18. However, Monet does not go to Paris for Zola's trial in February, when the writer is found guilty of libel.[52]

March 23 Monet goes to Paris for the day, evidently to discuss the forthcoming Petit exhibition of around fifty works. In partnership with Montaignac, Petit has chosen eight unframed works to buy for 44,000 francs. In addition, Monet will concede one unframed painting as a rental fee for the gallery. His frames cost 200 francs each. Shipping costs are the responsibility of the dealers.[53]

May A plaster version of Rodin's *Balzac* exhibited at the Salon de la Société nationale is refused as "unfinished" by the Société des gens de lettres, who had commissioned it in July 1891 and complained about the artist's slow progress in 1894. Responding to the press controversy, Monet contributes 500 francs to a subscription to buy the work, but Rodin reimburses subscribers, not wishing to sell.[54]

May 9–June 10 Cézanne exhibition at Vollard's gallery.

June An exhibition at the Durand-Ruel Gallery, Paris, includes a room of works by Monet, as well as rooms of works by Pissarro, Pierre Puvis de Chavannes, Renoir, and Sisley.[55]

June 2–July One-artist exhibition of sixty-one works by Monet (see cat. nos. 108, 109, and 110) presented at the Georges Petit Gallery, Paris. These comprise several series, each related group—*Rouen Cathedral* paintings, Norway subjects, Pourville subjects, *Mornings on the Seine* paintings, and *Chrysanthemums*—installed on its own panel in the large room. Press coverage stresses how Monet has abandoned the brutal manner of his classic Impressionist period for subtly transparent atmospheric effects. Renoir finds the exhibition "empty."[56]

June 16 *Le Gaulois* issues a special supplement devoted to Monet, including a photograph of the artist (fig. no. 73) and an anthology of enthusiastic critical support from 1889 to the present. This same supplement is republished in a slightly smaller format on June 23 by *Moniteur des arts.*[57]

Summer Monet burns paintings with which he is dissatisfied.[58]

September 25 Monet has received a business proposition from Paul Cassirer, whose Berlin gallery is a showcase for modern art. Monet's

74. James (Jimmy) Butler, the son of Theodore Butler and Suzanne Hoschedé Butler, sitting on a daybed in Monet's house, around 1898–99.

75. View, looking west, of the exterior of Monet's second studio and greenhouse; date of photograph unknown.

works will be exhibited there once a year in 1900–05, 1908–14, and 1925.[59]

November 10–15 Monet suddenly goes to London because Michel Monet, who is living there, has fallen ill.[60]

November 20 Durand-Ruel goes to Giverny and buys eight paintings, including a *Rouen Cathedral*. Monet's art sales this year will be slightly above 170,000 francs.[61]

1899

January–February Twelve works by Monet (see cat. no. 87) are included in an exhibition of French art presented first in St. Petersburg, Russia, and then (in March) in Moscow.[62]

January Twenty-two works by Monet are presented at the Lotus Club, New York (see cat. nos. 31, 33, 59, 70, and 71). In the valuable pamphlet published for the occasion, William H. Fuller reports that the *Rouen Cathedral* paintings are Monet's personal favorites. In interviews with Fuller, Monet had pointed out that early in his career he had completed works in one session, "but now, I am more exacting, and it takes a long time for me to finish a picture."[63]

Late January Six works by Monet (see cat. nos. 63 and 83) are among twenty Impressionist paintings sent by Durand-Ruel for an exhibition at the Kunstsalon Ernst Arnold, Dresden.[64]

January 29 Death of Sisley at Moret-sur-Loing. On January 21 Sisley, on his deathbed, had asked Monet to come see him. At Sisley's funeral in Moret on February 1, Monet and Alice are among the few mourners, along with Pissarro and Renoir. After the funeral, Monet

promises Sisley's children that he will arrange a benefit sale for them and will ensure that a memorial exhibition is organized. Referring to a Sisley painting of a flood as a "masterpiece," Monet writes to Geffroy, "[Sisley] is a truly great artist . . . and I believe he is as great a master as any who has ever lived."[65]

February 6 Death of Suzanne Butler in Giverny at age thirty.[66]

February 6–23 Twenty-eight works (see cat. nos. 43, 57, and 103) are presented as "A Loan Exhibition of Pictures by Claude Monet" at the St. Botolph Club, Boston.[67]

February 16–March 8 Eighteen Monet paintings (see cat. no. 88), including two 1860s Salon figure paintings, *Camille in a Green Dress* (fig. no. 13) and *The Lunch* (fig. no. 15), are in a group exhibition at the Georges Petit Gallery, Paris. Monet, who attends the opening, lends a painting by Sisley to the show.[68]

April 6 or 10–May The Durand-Ruel Gallery, Paris, presents an exhibition of thirty-six Monets (see cat. no. 32) and works by Pissarro, Renoir, and Sisley, while simultaneously presenting a Corot retrospective.[69]

May 1 Benefit auction for Sisley's children held at the Georges Petit Gallery, Paris, thanks largely to Monet's efforts. He donates *Sandvika, Norway* (cat. no. 107) to the benefit, the first of the Norway works to be offered for sale. The auction disperses the contents of Sisley's studio. Purchasing a painting for himself, Monet keeps the bidding active.[70]

May 4–5 At the sale of the Doria collection held in his Paris gallery, Petit, acting for Monet, buys *Melting Snow, Fontainebleau* (Museum of

Modern Art, New York) by Cézanne (who is in Paris at this time, painting a portrait of Vollard) for 6,750 francs, the highest price yet paid for a Cézanne. Monet also buys an early Impressionist painting of a steamboat by Morisot at the same sale and expresses interest in one or two small early paintings by Corot.[71]

May 10 Monet writes to Geffroy that he has just installed his own works of all periods in his studio.[72]

July 1 and 3–4 Sale at the Georges Petit Gallery, Paris, of Victor Chocquet's collection, including ten paintings and three pastels by Monet (see cat. nos. 8 and 33). On Monet's advice, Camondo buys an 1873 Cézanne work, *House of the Hanged Man* (Musée d'Orsay, Paris). Monet also convinces Durand-Ruel to buy many works by Cézanne at this sale. Degas buys several works by Delacroix for his collection, which he intends to become a private museum.[73]

July 5 Monet writes to Geffroy that he has not worked for eighteen months.[74]

July 26 Monet thanks the dentist and collector Georges Viau for paintings that he has sent; his letter suggests a trade between them. Viau acquires nine Monets, including a *Poplars*, around this time.[75]

July–Early September Returning to a compositional idea first investigated around 1895, before the planting of water lilies, Monet paints a series of as many as twelve paintings showing the Japanese bridge spanning his water lily pool (see cat. no. 113). Nine of these are nearly square in format. A snapshot taken by a Durand-Ruel family member in July 1900 documents

76. Claude Monet, *Waterloo Bridge, Sun in the Fog*, 1899–1905. Oil on canvas; 73 × 100 cm, 28¾ × 39⅜ in. National Gallery of Canada, Ottawa (817) [W 1573].

77. Claude Monet, *Charing Cross Bridge, Smoke in the Fog, Impression*, 1899–1902. Oil on canvas; 73 × 92 cm, 28½ × 36¼ in. Musée Marmottan, Paris (5001) [W 1535].

the motif from the vantage point of the garden's entrance, which Monet used for these paintings. Another snapshot shows Monet at work there next to a tent.[76]

August 5 Monet asks the architect Bonnier to suggest the name of someone to review an outstanding bill, probably for construction of a building, erected on the northwest corner of his plot (fig. no. 75). The ground floor serves as a garage, darkroom, and gardener's storage area. A staircase decorated with Japanese prints leads to a large, square room with two bay windows, one looking north out onto the road, the other looking south toward the greenhouse and garden. While Monet uses this "second" studio to finish works, it is primarily a grand showroom for the constant stream of visitors hoping to purchase paintings directly from him. The upper floor also has guest rooms.[77]

September 15 Monet and Alice are in Le Havre to see off Theodore Butler, his two children, and their aunt Marthe Hoschedé, who are bound for New York. The Monets, with Germaine Hoschedé, continue on to London. They visit Michel Monet and stay in a seventh-floor suite at the Savoy Hotel during their six-week working vacation. Around this time, Butler paints several views of bridges and ships in New York harbor that parallel Monet's new *Thames* views.[78]

October 17 Monet informs Durand-Ruel that he has started some views of the Thames from his hotel window.[79]

Around October 25 The Monets leave London for Saint-Servan in order to visit Jacques Hoschedé, who has moved there from Oslo and is still in the shipping business.[80]

November 5 Durand-Ruel visits Giverny and reserves, at 6,000 to 6,500 francs each, seven *Water Lily Pond* paintings and eleven *Views of the Thames*, although none of the latter group is finished. The fact that Monet dates only six *Thames* paintings to 1899 suggests that he continued to develop most of his first versions of the subject after returning to London in early 1900. Indeed, in his account notebook, Monet scratches out the eleven *Thames* paintings reserved by Durand-Ruel. His art sales for 1899 will total 227,400 francs.[81]

November 25 Monet writes to Durand-Ruel asking for an advance of 30,000 francs to pay contractors. Monet also agrees to paint six decorative overdoor panels if the dealer provides him with dimensions, but nothing comes of this project. Monet is ill with hepatitis.[82]

Early December The Monets go to Paris, where they sit for photographs by Paul Nadar (son of the great caricaturist and portrait photographer), to whom Monet has promised to send an early pastel.[83]

Mid-December Monet paints icescapes at Giverny.[84]

December 23 Curiously, Clemenceau writes to thank Monet for the gift of a unique Creuse composition, *Study of Rocks, The Creuse (Le Bloc)* (cat. no. 91), although he had been identified as the owner of this work when it was exhibited in May 1891.[85]

December 25 Monet writes to Durand-Ruel that Sisley's son Pierre will go to Paris with several works on paper (a pastel and drawing by Renoir, a pastel by Jongkind, a sketch by Fantin-Latour, and a torn pastel by Sisley). Included in the group is one of Monet's own pastels that

needs to be quickly matted, framed with a simple wood filet, and glazed, since Monet intends to make a gift of it to Paul Nadar.[86]

1900

At some point during this year, a Monet Argenteuil painting is given to the Liège Museum.

January Monet learns that the organizers of the forthcoming Universal Exposition in Paris hope to include some of his works in the contemporary art section. With Durand-Ruel and colleagues such as Pissarro, Monet hopes to use his leverage to demand a well-installed display of paintings by the principal Impressionists.[1]

Mid-January Clemenceau and Geffroy visit Giverny, and Monet gives Geffroy a painting of Belle-Ile, where the two had first met in 1886.[2]

January 21 Durand-Ruel comes to Giverny and buys (at 6,000 francs each) eight more recently "finished" paintings from the late 1890s.[3]

January–February Renoir exhibition at the Bernheim-Jeune Gallery, Paris. Although Monet refuses to lend to this exhibition, he apparently buys a figure painting from it.[4]

January 30 Monet purchases Renoir's 1881 *Mosque (Arabian Festival)* (Musée d'Orsay, Paris) from Durand-Ruel for 10,000 francs.[5]

February 9 Monet arrives in London for a two-month work campaign, taking a suite at the Savoy Hotel on the floor below the one he had occupied the previous autumn, which is now reserved for soldiers wounded in the Boer War. A huge bouquet of flowers awaits him, sent by Sargent's friend Mrs. Charles (Mary) Hunter,

78. Interior of Monet's second studio, photographed by Joseph Durand-Ruel, July 1900.

79. Monet seated in his car, possibly the Panhard-Levassor he purchased in December 1900. The roads in Giverny were paved in June 1907.

who has evidently made arrangements with her friend Dr. Joseph Frank Payne for Monet to paint in a large reception room of St. Thomas' Hospital, which has a terrace view of the Houses of Parliament across the river. Sargent, Mrs. Hunter, and Dr. Payne keep Monet's evening social schedule full. Michel Monet, who still lives in London, lunches with the artist.[6]

February 11–12 Monet begins work. In his hotel room in the mornings, Monet paints the views from his window: Waterloo Bridge to his left (see fig. no. 76) and Charing Cross Bridge to his right (see fig. no. 77). Late afternoons (except Sundays) he goes to St. Thomas' Hospital to paint the Houses of Parliament with sunset effects (see cat. nos. 120, 121, 122, and 124). By early March he has fifty canvases under way.[7]

February 25–27 Clemenceau and Geffroy visit Monet in London. During the course of the visit, Monet acquires a drawing by Jean-Louis Forain for his collection. Clemenceau helps Monet obtain permission to paint in the Tower of London, although the artist does not in fact undertake any work there.[8]

March Exhibition of paintings by Butler at the Durand-Ruel Gallery, New York. Monet had arranged for this exhibition, which was a disappointment, in the hope that afterwards Butler would return to France with Alice Monet's daughter and grandchildren.[9]

Late March Monet has sixty-five paintings under way, but he has begun to edit out ones that are not "London" enough. To do justice to the *Houses of Parliament* paintings, which he considers as potentially interesting as his *Rouen Cathedral* series, Monet realizes that he will need to return to London the following year. Among his visitors are Irish novelist and art critic George Moore, Rouen collector François Depeaux, and Sargent.

Monet prepares to leave London, contacting Baron d'Estournelles de Constant for help getting his paintings through customs, paying an enormous art supplies bill, and packing eighty paintings into eight cases.[10]

Probably April 5 Monet arrives in Dieppe, en route to Rouen where Alice awaits him at the home of Jean and Blanche Monet. Together Monet and Alice go on to Le Havre to await Butler, his two children, and Marthe Hoschedé, who are disembarking from their Atlantic crossing.[11]

April The Durand-Ruel Gallery, New York, presents a Monet–Renoir exhibition, with twenty-six works by Monet.

April 19 Monet sends off eleven paintings recently chosen by Durand-Ruel at 6,000 to 6,500 francs each.[12]

May 1 Opening of the fine arts section of the Universal Exposition, Paris, which includes a gallery of Impressionism at the Grand Palais, with fourteen works by Monet (see cat. nos. 50 and 87), the best represented member of the group. Art historian André Michel, the reviewer for the Universal Exposition art section, writes in the *Gazette des Beaux-Arts* in November: "If I were a millionaire—or Fine Arts minister—I would ask Mr. Claude Monet to decorate a vast festive hall in a public place for me." At this exposition are three prominent horticultural displays of water lilies.[13]

Spring Monet is obsessed with paintings of his water garden begun the previous summer. He writes to Julie Manet on May 29 that he is too hard at work in his garden to attend her wedding: "I curse the painter that prevents me from coming."

On June 1 Monet does not attend the opening of a Rodin retrospective at the Pavillon de l'Alma on the Cours-la-Reine because he does not want to halt his progress on these paintings of the garden.[14]

Summer Boston collector Desmond Fitzgerald comes to Giverny for lunch and later describes the sixty-year-old Monet: "The ordinary [English] gentleman's dress was somewhat modified by little distinctive differences. The shirt was ruffled at the collar and breast and cuffs, and the trousers were fitted close to the leg from the knee to the ankle, and buttoned to prevent, perhaps, the flapping about of the cloth."[15]

July Durand-Ruel's sons come to Giverny and take snapshots documenting recent works (already in frames), some of which Monet subsequently destroys (see fig. no. 78).[16]

August 21–23 Monet writes to Durand-Ruel and Geffroy that he nearly lost an eye about a month ago while playing with the children and has been unable to work.[17]

October 31 Wedding at Giverny of Marthe Hoschedé and Theodore Butler.[18]

November Pissarro, who for the past year had been painting a series of views of Paris from an apartment overlooking the Tuileries Gardens, now begins a series of views of the Seine. Although only a few paintings from these urban series are exhibited in Pissarro's lifetime (some Paris scenes are shown in February 1902), they are executed precisely while Monet is undertaking a comparable project in London, amounting to a final dialogue between the two longtime colleagues. While extending this series of Paris

80. Claude Monet, *Central Pathway through the Garden at Giverny*, 1902. Oil on canvas; 89 × 92 cm, 35 × 36¼ in. Kunsthistorisches Museum, Vienna (MG 207) [W 1650].

views from a hotel room in the fall of 1903, Pissarro is taken to the hospital, where he will die on November 30.[19]

November 22–December 15 Exhibition of twenty-six recent paintings (see cat. nos. 113 and possibly 112) by Monet at the Durand-Ruel Gallery at 16, rue Lafitte, Paris. A dozen of these are paintings of his water lily garden spanned by the Japanese bridge. Monet is heralded by critics as a poet on the level of Victor Hugo.[20]

November 27 Publication of François Thiébault-Sisson's interview with Monet (conducted in Paris after the Durand-Ruel exhibition opening) in *Le Temps* provides a milestone account of Monet's life and career up until 1870.

Late November–Early December Monet sells three *Japanese Bridge* paintings (see cat. no. 114) to dealer Léonce Rosenberg and one to Russian collector Sergei Shchukin for 10,000 francs. Durand-Ruel, who had been buying works from Monet for 6,500 francs and selling them for 15,000 francs, becomes upset that Monet is underselling him. Better informed of his dealer's current profit margin, Monet raises his prices.[21]

Late December Joseph (Josse) Bernheim-Jeune and Gaston Bernheim de Villers, sons of Courbet's paint supplier, Alexandre Bernheim, begin business dealings with Monet, trading a Creuse painting back to him in partial payment for two other works and tempting him with a trade against an automobile. The latter offer comes too late, however: on December 28 Monet informs them that he has just bought a new

Panhard-Levassor (see fig. no. 79) for himself, in which he plans to return to the Mediterranean. His art income for 1900 amounts to 213,000 francs.[22]

1901

January 8–27 The Art Institute of Chicago presents a Monet painting for the first time: *The Beach at Fécamp* (private collection) is included in a loan exhibition.

January 23 Monet departs for London for the third consecutive year, with cases of canvases in progress, arriving on January 24 and taking the same rooms at the Savoy Hotel that he had occupied the previous year. The next day, Monet and Sargent go to the Hanover Gallery to see an exhibition of Impressionist paintings organized there by Durand-Ruel, including nine paintings by Monet. Sargent and Moore (who wants Monet to sketch his portrait) are Monet's regular dining companions during this stay, and Mary Hunter again invites Monet to dinners. Michel is now doing military service in Rouen.[23]

January 29 Delayed in customs, the cases of unfinished canvases arrive in London. While awaiting them, Monet reads Delacroix (probably the excerpts from his *Journal*, which were published in three volumes from 1893 to 1895). He also begins to make pastels of Thames motifs from his hotel room. Excepting a single pastel made in Norway in 1895 (private collection), Monet has not worked in this medium since his 1885 Etretat campaign.[24]

February 2 Monet and Sargent watch the state funeral of Queen Victoria. Monet meets the American novelist Henry James.[25]

February 3 Starting at 6 A.M. to render the Thames turned gold by the rising sun, Monet has four canvases of Waterloo Bridge under way from his hotel room window; the number jumps to twelve the next day.[26]

February 4 Monet returns to St. Thomas' Hospital to take up his *Houses of Parliament* paintings, working there during the late afternoons to capture the fairytale-like fireball sunsets (see cat. no. 122).[27]

February 9 Denying Durand-Ruel's request for a *Japanese Bridge* painting, Monet explains that he needs to keep it as a guide for finishing a related work in Giverny.[28]

Mid-February London fog sets in for two weeks. On February 21 Monet writes to Alice that he plans to exchange his return ticket for a later date, despite the fact that he is out of chocolate tongues and eau de prune.[29]

March 4 Monet begins a group of paintings of Leicester Square by night from a window of a small room at the Green Room, a club on St. Martin's Street. Sargent and Asher Wertheimer had helped Monet make arrangements to work there.[30]

March 9–10 Monet falls ill with pleurisy and is under the care of two doctors for the rest of the month. He is unable to paint, although he makes several pastels.[31]

April Monet returns to Giverny from London. He is eager to show his new London paintings to Durand-Ruel and Geffroy. On May 7 Pissarro reports the exaggerated rumor that the dealer has bought 100,000 francs' worth of paintings from Monet.[32]

May 10 In order to enlarge his water garden, Monet buys land on the south side of the river Ru for 1,200 francs.[33]

June 5 Durand-Ruel visits Giverny and urges Monet to make paintings of the central walkway leading through his garden to the house.[34]

Summer Arsène Alexandre comes to Giverny to interview Monet for an article published in *Le Figaro* on August 9, in which he acclaims Monet as a master gardener. About the water garden, now ten years old, he writes: "When the sunlight plays upon the water, it resembles —damascened as it is with the water lilies' great round leaves, and encrusted with the precious stones of their flowers—the masterwork of a goldsmith who has melded alloys of the most magical metals."[35]

July–Autumn Monet rents a house in Lavacourt. From his balcony overlooking the river, he paints a series of pictures of the village of

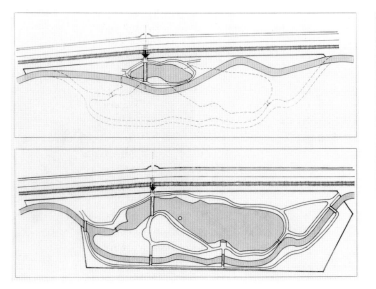

81. *Top:* a diagram of the pond that Monet constructed in 1892, prior to the extensive enlargement carried out in 1902. *Bottom:* the pond as enlarged in 1902 and modified in contour in 1910.

82. Monet at work near the water lily pond, probably summer 1904.

83. View of the enlarged water lily pond, looking west toward the Japanese bridge, around 1902/04. By 1905 Monet had added a wisteria trellis to the bridge.

1902

The Lyons Museum and the Petit Palais Museum, Paris, acquire paintings by Monet during this year.

January 21 Monet writes to the Giverny municipal council for permission to construct a trellis to shelter his gardens from the railroad that cuts through them.[40]

February 9 Monet buys a painting by Cézanne from Vollard.[41]

February 10 Alice worries that the construction of the new water lily pond (see fig. no. 81) will unnerve Monet, who has decided not to go see the exhibition of his works at the Bernheim-Jeune Gallery. The ambitious excavation entails digging and hauling tons of earth in order to make a new bed for the river Ru along the southern border of his property, thus clearing enough space roughly to triple the size of the water lily pond, extending it eastward. A small, man-made island is added to the enlarged pond, and four bridges are constructed across the diverted river. The vistas from paths around the enlarged pond will be Monet's nearly exclusive subjects for the rest of his life.[42]

February 11–25 The Durand-Ruel Gallery, New York, presents an exhibition of thirty-eight works by Monet (see cat. nos. 55 and 75), including the first London painting to go on public view.[43]

February 15–28 Around a dozen new Vétheuil paintings, nearly square in format, are included in "Recent Works by Camille Pissarro and a New Series by Claude Monet" at the Bernheim-Jeune Gallery at 8, rue Lafitte, Paris (see cat. nos. 115 and possibly 116). Monet provides his own frames, which will all be returned to him

Vétheuil, with its dominating church tower (see cat. nos. 115 and 116). He had first become obsessed with the motif when he lived there from 1878 to 1880 (see cat. no. 60). Monet makes the trip from Giverny to Lavacourt daily by car, often joined by Alice, Germaine, the Butlers, and family friends such as Sisley's daughter, Jeanne-Adèle. They furnish a second house and studio, even bringing rowboats so the family can enjoy country picnic outings while Monet spends the afternoons painting.[36]

August 13 Monet petitions for permission to divert more water from the river Ru as part of his plan to expand his water garden. Three months later, the Giverny municipal council

grants approval, providing that Monet install regulating sluices.[37]

November 19 Monet sends a shipment of paintings to Durand-Ruel, including four London paintings, still wet. He explains that he needs to ask more for paintings from his previous series because so few examples are left. Meanwhile, he is finishing his Vétheuil paintings for the Bernheim brothers. His art sales for 1901 will amount to 127,500 francs.[38]

November 29 The Bernheim brothers buy a *Rouen Cathedral* painting for Monet at the sale of the Lazare Weiller collection at the Hôtel Drouot, Paris.[39]

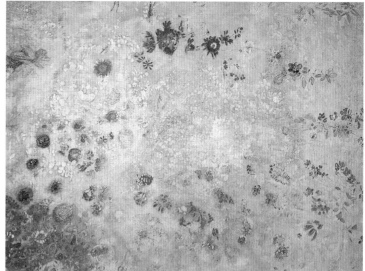

84. Snapshot, apparently by Monet or his son Michel, showing the artist's shadow on the water lily pond, usually dated around 1905.

85. Odilon Redon, *Decorative Panel*, c. 1902. Distemper on canvas; 185.8 × 256 cm, 73⅛ × 88⁹⁄₁₆ in. Rijksmuseum Twenthe, Enschede, The Netherlands.

at the end of the exhibition because, as Monet realizes, collectors generally do not want frames like his.[44]

February 26–27 Monet plants water lilies in the enlarged pond (see fig. no. 83).[45]

September 27 Monet agrees to let Thiébault-Sisson interview him again.[46]

October 24 Monet sends off two *Rouen Cathedral* paintings purchased by Durand-Ruel for 25,000 francs, bringing Monet's art sales for the year to 105,000 francs. Monet promises Durand-Ruel that he will work on paintings of the central pathway leading through the garden to his house (see fig. no. 80).[47]

November 12 Church wedding at Giverny of Germaine Hoschedé and Albert Salerou, a young lawyer whom she had met in February while visiting the Deconchys in Cagnes.[48]

Winter 1902–03 Monet finishes as many of his "delicate" London paintings as possible, in the hope of exhibiting them with Durand-Ruel in May 1903. Monet refuses to sell any more until all are finished.[49]

86. Claude Monet, *Water Lilies*, 1905. Oil on canvas; 89.5 × 100.3 cm, 35¼ × 39½ in. Museum of Fine Arts, Boston, Gift of Edward Jackson Holmes (39.804) [W 1671].

1903

Mid-February With interest from an endowment established by Mrs. Elizabeth Hammond Stickney, The Art Institute of Chicago acquires the 1896 painting *Bad Weather, Pourville* from Durand-Ruel for $2,900. This work (sold in 1930 for $2,400 and now in a private collection) is the first by Monet acquired by any American museum.

February 28 Learning that Depeaux is considering selling *The Turkeys (Decorative Panel)* (cat. no. 46), Monet attempts to buy it back through Durand-Ruel.[50]

March 12–16 Similar in spirit to Monet's water lily paintings now under way, a group of Symbolist flower still lifes by Redon is exhibited in a one-artist exhibition at the Durand-Ruel Gallery, Paris. At this exhibition Redon shows for the first time a large decorative panel (fig. no. 85) comparable to works Monet will undertake ten years later.[51]

April 2–25 Seven works by Monet (see cat. no. 45) are included in an Impressionist exhibition at the Bernheim-Jeune Gallery, Paris.[52]

April 10–May 10 Discouraged with the past month's work in the studio in Giverny on the London paintings, Monet writes to Geffroy that

he has destroyed some and fears that he may destroy them all: "My mistake was to want to retouch them." Monet informs Durand-Ruel on May 10 that he needs to hide his London paintings and is ready to return all cash advances on them. By now quite familiar with Monet's self-critical moods, the dealer is content to select other works for the time being. In November Monet asks his dealer about exhibition plans for the London paintings.[53]

Summer Despite unfavorable weather, Monet begins his first *Water Lilies* paintings (see cat. nos. 125 and 126) at his enlarged pond, describing them as "studies to bear fruit later."[54]

November 13 Death of Pissarro in Paris. Monet attends the funeral on November 15.[55]

December 12 Wedding at Giverny of Jean-Pierre Hoschedé and Geneviève Costadau.[56]

1904

March Publication in London of *Impressionist Painting*, dedicated to Monet, by Wynford Dewhurst, an Impressionist painter himself.[57]

April 7–30 Pissarro memorial exhibition at the Durand-Ruel Gallery, Paris, includes two works lent by Monet, who helped in its organization.[58]

April 8 Monet agrees to serve on the committee to acquire the enlarged version of Rodin's *Thinker* for the City of Paris, contributing 200 francs.[59]

Late April–Early May Durand-Ruel comes to Giverny on April 22 or 23 to help select London paintings for the forthcoming exhibition. Sending the paintings to Paris on April 28, Monet admits that he almost decided again to call off the exhibition. At Durand-Ruel's request, Monet asks Mirbeau to write the catalogue preface.[60]

May 9–June 4 Exhibition at the Durand-Ruel Gallery, Paris, of thirty-seven of Monet's *Views of the Thames* (see cat. nos. 118, 119, 121, and 123). The dealer purchases eighteen of the paintings at the outset of the exhibition for 10,000 to 11,000 francs each, the *Houses of Parliament* being the more expensive. Despite widespread knowledge that these paintings are as much studio works as on-the-spot Impressionist renderings, the exhibition is the most successful of Monet's career thus far. On May 19 the Paris edition of the *New York Herald* claims with exaggeration that nine paintings are already sold at 20,000 francs apiece. A London publisher expresses interest in an illustrated book of the exhibition. In an apparently unrelated effort, the commercial photographer Druet photographs the works and publishes them as an album. The exhibition is extended until June 7, when Monet returns to Paris to see it one last time. Durand-Ruel tells purchasers that the *Views of the Thames* are sold unframed, because Monet refuses to release his own frames.[61]

June Montaignac comes to Giverny and buys two paintings on behalf of Sutton. This sale will help bring Monet's art income for 1904 to 271,000 francs and marks the first purchase of a *Water Lilies* painting (cat. no. 125).[62]

Late June Monet gets a speeding ticket.[63]

July–August Monet writes to Durand-Ruel that he has been completely absorbed with work for two months, presumably on his *Water Lilies* paintings. The dealer wants to discuss the (ulti-

87. Monet standing beside the water lily pond, summer 1905.

mately unrealized) possibility of showing the London paintings in London.[64]

September? Exhibition of thirteen of Monet's London paintings (see cat. nos. 118 and 119) at the Cassirer Gallery in Berlin.[65]

October 8–28 Monet, Alice, and Michel, with their chauffeur, drive through Tours and Bordeaux and arrive in Biarritz on October 11. There they board a train to Madrid, arriving October 14, and meet Durand-Ruel. After three days admiring the works of Diego Velázquez in the museums of Madrid, they go to Toledo, which reminds Monet of North Africa. He admires paintings by El Greco. Leaving Madrid on October 20, they retrace their route home.[66]

October 15–November 15 Salon d'Automne, Paris, includes special exhibitions devoted to Cézanne, Puvis de Chavannes, Redon, and Renoir.

December 7–9 Monet returns to London for two days to look for an appropriate place to hold an exhibition of his London paintings. Perhaps he now begins to negotiate with the Dowdeswell & Dowdeswell Gallery for a spring 1905 exhibition. Meanwhile, Durand-Ruel agrees to exclude any London paintings from the group exhibition he is planning in London for January 1905.[67]

1905

January 14 Monet writes to Durand-Ruel that he is at work on London paintings for a never-

realized exhibition in London. He hopes the new versions will be as good as the previous ones, if not better.[1]

January–February A large Impressionist exhibition organized by Durand-Ruel at the Grafton Galleries, London, includes fifty-five paintings by Monet (see cat. nos. 32, 40, and 87).[2]

February 10–13 When painter Sir William Rothenstein visits the London Impressionist exhibition with Sargent's American poet friend L. A. Harrison, the two claim that Monet painted his *Rouen Cathedral* paintings from photographs (see fig. no. 61) rather than on the spot, and Harrison maintains that Monet had asked him for photographs of the bridges of London and the Houses of Parliament as aids for his recent London paintings. Insisting that the issue is of no importance, Monet admits to Durand-Ruel that Sargent had asked Harrison to get a photograph of the Houses of Parliament for him, although it served no purpose. Nevertheless, the incident apparently stalls (and eventually halts) Monet's plans to present an exhibition of London paintings in London.[3]

March "Loan Collection of Paintings by Claude Monet and 11 Sculptures by Rodin" is exhibited at Copley Hall, Boston (see cat. nos. 15, 36, 43, 55, 57, 71, 77, 96, 97, 103, 107, 118, and 119). With ninety-five works (including seven recent London paintings), this is the largest Monet exhibition since the 1889 Monet–Rodin show in Paris. In the catalogue, Desmond Fitzgerald points out that one New York collection (presumably Sutton's) contains fifty Monet paintings and another (presumably the Havemeyers') contains twenty-five, as does a Chicago collection (that of Mrs. Potter Palmer, who lends seven paintings to this exhibition).[4]

April–May The Grossherzogliches Museum, Weimar, presents a Monet retrospective with twenty-six paintings (see cat. nos. 32, 65, and 121) and acquires a *Rouen Cathedral* painting.[5]

April 4 With the understanding that the works will be donated to the National Gallery of Ireland, Dublin, Durand-Ruel sells two Monet paintings to the museum's director, Sir Hugh Percy Lane. *Waterloo Bridge* enters the museum in 1908.[6]

Summer? Louis Vauxcelles (the pseudonym of Louis Mayer) comes to Giverny with the German painter Felix Borchardt to gather material for Vauxcelles's article "An Afternoon with Claude Monet," published in *L'Art et les artistes* in December. They notice "a butler in full regalia" setting a table on the terrace, while a gardener in a boat is cleaning dead leaves from the water lily pond. They see *Water Lilies* paintings in the second studio and discuss other artists, such as Vuillard, whom Monet admires. The

88. Portrait photograph of Monet, taken by Baron Adolphe de Meyer, October 27, 1905.

article is illustrated with photographs by Ernest Bulloz, including the first published views of Monet's garden (see fig. no. 87). One of these indicates that Monet had added a trellis over his Japanese bridge in order to cultivate wisteria.[7]

July 3 In response to a question raised by a Detroit journalist, Monet explains that his palette contains only six colors: lead white, cadmium yellow, vermilion, deep red, cobalt blue, and emerald green.[8]

September Durand-Ruel comes to Giverny to select fourteen more London paintings, which Monet delivers in late October, except for one *Waterloo Bridge* retained so that he can make a similar one, also for Durand-Ruel. Mostly thanks to this single transaction, Monet's art income for 1905 will total 222,500 francs.[9]

October 18–November 25 The bold colors and stenographic brushstrokes in works by Henri Matisse, André Derain, and their colleagues, now dubbed Fauves ("wild beasts"), create a scandal at the Salon d'Automne. Vuillard exhibits six of his 1890s decorative panels, including an 1896 library ensemble for the cardiologist Louis-Henri Vasquez.

October 27 Joseph Durand-Ruel comes to Giverny with photographer Baron Adolphe de Meyer, who takes informal portraits of Monet (see fig. no. 88).[10]

Late November Monet refuses a request to donate paintings to the Petit Palais Museum, Paris.[11]

December Thirteen works by Monet are included in the "Opening Season 1905–1906" exhibition at the Toledo (Ohio) Museum of Art.[12]

1905–06 In his *Promenades philosophiques*, published in 1905, poet, critic, and Symbolist novelist Rémy de Gourmont devotes a chapter to Monet, designating him as perhaps "the greatest painter ever," equal in genius to Victor Hugo. Monet is also lavishly acclaimed in other books now: Geffroy, *La Peinture en France de 1850 à 1900*; Duret, *L'Histoire des peintres impressionnistes*; and André Fontainas, *L'Histoire de la peinture française au XIXe siècle*.[13]

1906

February 17–April 15 Three works by Monet are included in the International Art Exhibition at the Kunsthalle, Bremen, resulting in the museum's acquisition of *Camille in a Green Dress* (fig. no. 13). Paintings by Monet will be included in this exhibition in 1910 and 1914.[14]

Late February–Early March Monet oversees planting of bamboo around the water garden and eagerly awaits spring weather to begin painting there. When he does not work, Alice reminds him how hard the crippled Renoir is working.[15]

February 28–March 15 Exhibition of Redon's floral still lifes at the Durand-Ruel Gallery, Paris, includes more large decorative panels.[16]

March 8 Two 1880s Monet paintings are acquired by the Museum of Fine Arts, Boston. These are the first two of thirty-nine works by Monet in the museum's collection today.

March 11 Monet sells six paintings (including five London paintings) to Durand-Ruel and the Bernheims, who are acting as partners, for 70,000 francs. This is Monet's only sale for this year.[17]

March 19–31 Seventeen works by Monet from the Faure collection are exhibited at the Durand-Ruel Gallery, Paris (see cat. nos. 22 and 41). Most of these same works are subsequently exhibited from September 1906 to January 1907 at galleries in Berlin, Munich, and Stuttgart.[18]

April 1 The twenty-one-year-old Prince de Wagram (who already owns around fifty works apiece by Monet and Renoir) comes to Giverny in his 120-horsepower Itala with the Bernheims' cousin Essel.[19]

May 31–June 1 Fifteen works by Monet are sold along with other works in the Depeaux collection at the Georges Petit Gallery, Paris. *The Turkeys (Decorative Panel)* (cat. no. 46) fetches the highest price (20,000 francs) for a Monet, paid by expatriate American heiress Winnaretta Singer, Princess Edmond de Polignac. At the same sale a painting by Renoir sells for 47,000 francs.[20]

June 13 Monet asks Durand-Ruel to pay Vollard 2,500 francs for a Cézanne that he has bought. Around this time, Denis notes in his diary, as if it were hearsay, that Monet's wife takes pains to hide the Cézannes in his collection when he becomes discouraged with his own work.[21]

September 28 Monet writes to Durand-Ruel that he has had a wonderful summer of work.[22]

October 22 Death of Cézanne.

October 25 Maintaining his role as Minister of the Interior, Clemenceau is appointed Prime Minister by President Fallières.

October 25–26 Monet goes to Paris with Alice to see the Salon d'Automne (October 6–November 15), attend the theater, and pose for Renoir, who has been commissioned by Vollard to do a sketch of Monet.[23]

Late December In Paris, Monet agrees to a May 8, 1907, opening date for his Durand-Ruel exhibition of *Water Lilies* paintings.[24]

1907

January 26–February 14 Exhibition at the Durand-Ruel Gallery, New York, of twenty-seven works by Monet (see cat. nos. 55 and 69).

February 1 Monet attends the inaugural exhibition at the Museum of Decorative Arts, Paris, of the thirty-four works donated by Etienne Moreau-Nélaton in 1903 and accepted by the French National Museums for eventual transfer (in 1934) to the Louvre. In addition to seven early paintings by Monet, this bequest contains Manet's *Luncheon on the Grass* (Musée d'Orsay, Paris). Later that Friday Monet calls on Clemenceau to request that Manet's *Olympia* (fig. no. 9) now be transferred from the Luxembourg Museum to the Louvre. Clemenceau accomplishes this by the following Monday.[25]

February 9 A letter written by Joseph Durand-Ruel indicates that his family's gallery has been buying up "old studies by Monet" for fifteen years in order to return them to the painter, who has already destroyed a considerable number of his own canvases.[26]

February 23 Durand-Ruel comes to Giverny and buys six paintings for 77,000 francs. Monet charges more for three floral still lifes apparently left over from his 1882–85 decorative projects for Durand-Ruel's sitting-room doors (see fig. no. 42) than for the paintings of London bridges.[27]

February–March Interrupting final preparations for his projected May *Water Lilies* exhibition, Monet struggles with a brand-new and very Cézannesque still-life subject: a glass pitcher, a basket, a napkin, and eggs in a basket on a table (see cat. no. 132).[28]

March 12–30 Sixteen paintings by Monet from the Durand-Ruel collection are exhibited at the Walter Kimball Gallery, Boston. Working closely with Durand-Ruel, this gallery, where five Monets had been included in a 1905 group show, will exhibit more Monet works each year through 1911 (cat. nos. 105 and 128 will be exhibited in 1910).

Late March–April 8 Monet works in his studio to finish more *Water Lilies* paintings for the upcoming exhibition at Durand-Ruel's. Preferring to exhibit these works together, he asks that the dealer leave the gallery "as it is, with one exhibition room" for the projected May show. By April 8, dissatisfied and realizing that some paintings can be finished only at the water garden site, Monet postpones the exhibition until the following year.[29]

April–July Eight paintings by Monet are included in the Fifth International Art Exhibition, Barcelona (see cat. no. 116).

April 27 Durand-Ruel asks Monet if he can purchase two or three finished *Water Lilies* paintings as consolation for the postponed exhibition, but Monet insists that they can only be presented as an ensemble. Moreover, he announces with satisfaction that he has just destroyed at least thirty canvases, and adds that if he could buy back the *Water Lilies* (cat. no. 125) that he sold to Sutton in 1904, he would destroy it as well.[30]

May 18 Deeply discouraged with his work and upset by the damage done to his garden by torrential rains, Monet at first refuses to receive Georges Durand-Ruel and the Newport, Rhode Island, collector Arthur B. Emmons. Realizing that Monet will change his mind, however, Alice Monet begins to clean his second studio (where housekeepers are not allowed).[31]

May 28–July 21 Seven works by Monet are shown in the Modern French Art exhibition at the Kaiser Wilhelm Museum, Krefeld, which now buys one of Monet's *Houses of Parliament* paintings (cat. no. 121).

Late May Monet has his waterproof shipping case, canvases, and easel brought to the water lily pond and begins this year's campaign there.[32]

June Hoping to cut down on the amount of dust settling on the water garden, Monet pays half the expense of paving two Giverny roads.[33]

June–September Monet asks Durand-Ruel to send Vollard 5,500 francs to buy a painting by Cézanne for his growing collection. He complains of unfavorable weather for painting. When the weather improves in July, he asks Alice to stay by his side while he paints. He works at the water lily pond through September.[34]

89. Interior of Monet's second studio at Giverny, photographed by Joseph Durand-Ruel, March 15, 1908.

September 20 Monet writes to Durand-Ruel that he continues to work a great deal on *Water Lilies* paintings and tells the dealer that he can soon come and see his latest (vertical format) works (see cat. nos. 131, 133, 134, and 136).[35]

October 1–22 Monet lends to the Salon d'Automne four of his five works by Morisot and Cézanne's *Negro Scipion* of 1867 (Museu de Arte de São Paulo Assis Chateaubriand). The exhibition catalogue omits the Cézanne and erroneously credits Monet with the loan of five works by Morisot.[36]

Late October Influenced by Clemenceau, the French National Museums purchase a *Rouen Cathedral* painting from Monet for 10,500 francs. Monet had bought this painting back when it appeared at auction on November 29, 1901. It is exhibited with other 1907 acquisitions at the Ecole des Beaux-Arts in December 1907. Monet's art income for 1907 will total 87,500 francs.[37]

November American painter Walter Pach visits Giverny. He had been given a letter of introduction by a French politician who had recently visited the United States and conceived the idea that Monet should paint New York harbor or Pittsburgh factories. Pach's account of his visit, published in *Scribner's Magazine* in June 1908, indicates that Monet admired Winslow Homer's *Nocturne*, in the Luxembourg Museum since 1900, and was well informed about other American painters, although he wondered why so many of them painted foreign scenes rather than their own homeland.[38]

November 14–30 Monet lends two of his early 1880s floral still lifes as well as a Cézanne still life to the "Flowers and Still Lifes" exhibition at the Bernheim-Jeune Gallery in Paris.[39]

90. Monet and Alice in the Piazza San Marco, Venice, October 1908.

Winter 1907–08 Fourteen paintings by Monet are included in the Modern French Paintings exhibition in Manchester.

1908

March 15 In the second studio at Giverny, Joseph Durand-Ruel takes snapshots of paintings (including several soon to be destroyed) being readied for the *Water Lilies* exhibition

91. Paul Signac, *Venice*, 1908. Watercolor; 19 × 25 cm, 7½ × 9¹³⁄₁₆ in. Musée Marmottan, Paris (5074).

92. Claude Monet, *Grand Canal, Venice*, 1908. Oil on canvas; 73.7 × 92.5 cm, 29 × 36⅜ in. Museum of Fine Arts, Boston, Bequest of Alexander Cochrane (19.171) [W 1738].

scheduled for late April (see fig. no. 89). Unconvinced of the success of the most recent works in the series, Paul Durand-Ruel balks at Monet's insistence that he purchase sixteen paintings outright for this exhibition at 13,000 to 15,000 francs each, half payable in advance. The dealer contacts the Bernheim brothers to discuss a partnership in the project, and their hesitancy provokes a confrontation with the artist, who now begins to complain about blurred vision and dizziness.[40]

Late March Monet purchases a Vuillard pastel, *Interior at Amfréville,* for his collection.[41]

April 12 Alice writes to Germaine Salerou that Monet, having again decided to cancel his upcoming *Water Lilies* exhibition, is tearing up unsatisfactory paintings daily.[42]

April 16 The Bernheim brothers come to Giverny to see the *Water Lilies* paintings, minus the three that Monet had destroyed the day before. They suggest a ride in their hot-air balloon as a distraction, and the Monets respond enthusiastically.[43]

April 21–May Eleven paintings by Monet are included in an exhibition of Impressionist still-life paintings at the Durand-Ruel Gallery, Paris. Monet is concerned about the possible unfavorable comparisons that might be drawn between his works and those by Cézanne in the same exhibition.[44]

May 15 The international press circulates news that Monet has destroyed $100,000 worth (ten to twenty canvases) of *Water Lilies* paintings realized during the last three years. Characterizing other accounts as exaggerated, the *London Standard* explains on May 20: "Early in spring

M. Monet had about thirty canvases in a more or less finished state, and it was arranged that he should exhibit two dozen, or as many as he could finish, in Paris, at the end of last month. Some little time before the exhibition, however, M. Durand-Ruel, with whom the exhibition was to be held, was asked to postpone it for three weeks. . . . Only a day or two beforehand, and when all arrangements had been made . . . Monet [canceled] the exhibition. I understand that all those who saw the pictures in February and March considered them 'overworked,' that is, they showed too plainly how long they had stood on the easel. One of M. Monet's friends even went so far as to say that there were four or five different pictures on each canvas. . . . Persuaded by his friends, M. Monet has decided to turn them to the wall . . . and go away for change and rest. Possibly the remaining pictures will be exhibited next year."[45]

May 18–June 6 The Durand-Ruel Gallery, Paris, presents an exhibition of "Landscapes by Monet and Renoir," with forty-two works by Monet (see cat. nos. 65 and 116).[46]

June 12 Monet attends the funeral in Paris of Auguste Rémy, the murdered husband of Alice's younger sister. Monet also sends payment for Bonnard's *Bathing Children,* purchased from the Bernheim-Jeune Gallery.[47]

June 22 Monet writes to Durand-Ruel about taking steps against a forger of his works.[48]

June 25 Monet finally returns to work on his *Water Lilies* after a two-month break. By mid-July protracted overcast weather obliges Monet to start new *Water Lilies* variations with muted light effects; however, windy weather impedes his efforts.[49]

July 8 Geffroy, who in March was appointed by Clemenceau as director of the Gobelins factory and immediately extended commissions to Chéret and Redon, now proposes that the Fine Arts Ministry commission a tapestry based on one of Monet's recent *Water Lilies* paintings.[50]

August 11 Monet writes to Geffroy: "You should know that I am absorbed by work. The landscapes of water and reflections have become an obsession. It is beyond my old man's powers, but nevertheless I want to render what I sense. I have destroyed some . . . and I began some again . . . and I hope that something will come from so many efforts." During late August and early September, Monet works on his *Water Lilies* paintings (see cat. nos. 137, 138, 140, 141, and 142) from 7 to 11 A.M. and from 1 to 3 P.M., receiving friends in the afternoons and working again at 5 or 6 P.M., when the water lilies start to close with the sunset.[51]

September 30 The Monets leave from Paris by train to Venice. There they stay, along with Mary Hunter, with whom Monet socialized in London, as guests of Mrs. Daniel Curtis at the Palazzo Barbaro on the north bank of the Grand Canal. Mrs. Curtis is the widow of a relative of Sargent. Monet will give Hunter one of his Venice paintings as a gift. Sightseeing during his first week in Venice, Monet is most impressed with murals by Tintoretto then under restoration.[52]

Around October 6 Monet begins work on the island of San Giorgio Maggiore, painting views of the Palazzo Ducale across the lagoon. The Florentine writer Carlo Placci arranges for Monet to work from a private balcony, but no paintings are known to have been made from this site. Monet quickly adopts a routine of working on four different motifs, each one addressed for two hours every day (8 to 10 A.M. and 10 to noon; 2 to 4 and 4 to 6 P.M.), the last session from a window at the Palazzo Barbaro.[53]

Before October 19 The Monets move to the Grand Hotel Britannia, not far from the Palazzo Barbaro. The hotel has a view toward San Giorgio (similar to one painted by Renoir in 1881) that Monet now adds to his motifs (see cat. no. 143). He intends to return the following year for a prolonged working campaign.[54]

November 4 Monet replies to Durand-Ruel, as he already had to the Bernheim brothers, that he cannot yet agree to reserve Venice paintings for him.[55]

November 16 Alice Monet writes to Geffroy that she stays by Monet's side continuously while he is painting in Venice.[56]

December 7 Monet writes to Geffroy: "What a shame not to have come [to Venice] when I was younger and fully daring. But I have spent delicious moments here, practically forgetting how old I am." That evening the Monets leave Venice, reaching Genoa the next morning, and passing through Bordighera en route to Cagnes, where they visit the Salerous, the Renoirs, and presumably Deconchy, who resides in a villa designed by Bonnier.[57]

December 19 The Monets have by now arrived in Giverny with three dozen paintings of Venice.[58]

December 29 Inviting Durand-Ruel to visit, Monet explains that the Bernheim brothers have already come to Giverny to see and reserve all the Venice paintings. Monet does not record this sale or any other for 1908 in his personal account ledger.[59]

1909

January 2 Mirbeau comes to Giverny to admire the Venice paintings. Monet expresses his wish to paint the snow-covered Giverny landscape, but the cold prevents him from doing so.[60]

January 11 Monet writes to Geffroy that he has been suffering from vertigo and that Alice has been very ill.[61]

January 28 Monet writes to Durand-Ruel that the trip to Venice has enabled him to see his *Water Lilies* paintings differently and that now the dealer can schedule an exhibition for early May.[62]

February 6 Durand-Ruel comes to Giverny. Despite his envy of the Bernheim brothers' reserve on Monet's Venice paintings, he still counts upon their partnership in the advance purchase of *Water Lilies* paintings, and he initiates a round of correspondence about which works will be reserved by whom.[63]

February The Brooklyn Museum, New York, purchases eighty-three Sargent watercolors, including many made in Venice from 1905 to 1908, from an exhibition at the Knoedler Gallery, New York.

March 3 Monet writes to Durand-Ruel that he has consulted Dr. Trousseau about his eyes, and that he has now completed and signed thirty *Water Lilies* paintings.[64]

March 8–20 Exhibition of works by Butler at the Bernheim-Jeune Gallery, Paris.

March 30 Monet goes to Paris to see the Courbet exhibition at the Bernheim-Jeune Gallery. Alice's health has finally improved.[65]

April 8 Monet explains to Georges Durand-Ruel that, as usual, he wants all of his frames returned after the upcoming exhibition.[66]

April 20 Monet, bothered by headaches, is again destroying many works. The Bernheim brothers have agreed to send a house painter to Giverny and to order replacement yellow Liberty fabric for the Monets.[67]

Around April 25–26 The Bernheim brothers are invited to Giverny to select sixteen *Water Lilies* paintings for purchase, so that the catalogue can be printed. But evidently the dealers do not choose until after the opening, informing Monet on May 15 that they prefer the earlier works to the 1908 paintings and those in tondo format. Monet charges 15,000 francs each for these works. His art sales this year will amount to 272,000 francs.[68]

May 6–June 5 Monet is in Paris May 3–7 to install his *Water Lilies* exhibition and to preside at its opening. Forty-eight paintings (eleven nearly square in format and four circular; see cat. nos. 126, 127, 128, 129, 130, 131, 133, 134, 135, 136, 137, 138, 139, 140, 141, and 142), grouped in the catalogue according to date, are exhibited in three rooms at the Durand-Ruel Gallery. The title Monet suggests for the exhibition, "Les Nymphéas: Series de paysages d'eau," must have been inspired by Courbet's decision in 1867 to call his seascapes "Paysages de mer." Also, in 1883 Geffroy had referred to Boudin's works as "Paysages de mer."

The exhibition is an enormous public and critical success, with many journalists comparing Monet's achievement to poetry or music, stressing the superimposition of near-at-hand and faraway, of below and above, in the interplay of reality and reflection. Several journalists regret that the ensemble of works will be dispersed instead of remaining intact as a great decorative triumph. Degas, who runs into Monet at Vollard's gallery, tells him, "I only stayed at your exhibition for a second. Your paintings gave me vertigo." According to Alexandre in *Comœdia* on May 8, "The painter would have wished to decorate a small circular room of

93. Monet in his second studio, probably 1911.

carefully calculated dimensions. All around, waist-high, would have reigned . . . a painting of water and flowers. . . . No furniture. Nothing but the table in the center of the room, which would have been a dining room." Durand-Ruel wishes to send the exhibition to London and Berlin; Monet is unwilling, but he does agree to extend the Paris exhibition until June 12.[69]

Late May–Early June Monet is upset by bad weather and roadwork in Giverny. The weather and a constant stream of visitors prevent him from working throughout May and June.[70]

June 1 An astounding and well-informed text by Roger Marx about the *Water Lilies* paintings appears in the June issue of *Gazette des Beaux-Arts*. Although their accuracy may be challenged, long and eloquent quotations seem to express the artist's thinking: "People who hold forth on my painting conclude that I have arrived at the ultimate degree of abstraction and imagination that can be found in reality. I should much prefer to have them acknowledge the gift, my total absorption in my work. I applied paint to these canvases in the same way that monks of old illuminated their books of hours; they owe everything to the close union of solitude and silence, to a passionate and exclusive attention akin to hypnosis. . . . Perhaps my originality boils down to being a hypersensitive receptor, and to the expediency of a shorthand by means of which I project on a canvas, as if on a screen, impressions registered on my retina. If you absolutely must find an affiliation for me, select the Japanese of old times . . . their esthetic that evokes a presence by means of a shadow and the whole by means of a fragment.

. . . I was once briefly tempted to use water lilies as a sole decorative theme in a room. Along the walls . . . this theme was to have created the illusion of an endless whole, of water without horizon or shore. Here nerves taut from over-work could have relaxed . . . [in] a refuge for peaceful meditation at the center of a flowering aquarium." This last concept echoes a passage in Matisse's "Notes of a Painter," published in *La Grande Revue* in December 1908: "What I dream of is an art of equilibrium, purity, tranquility, without disquieting or pressing subject matter that for every mental worker, the businessman as much as the writer, would be a soothing mental calmative, something like a good easy chair to refresh physical fatigues." Matisse, who was Rodin's neighbor at the Hôtel Biron, begins his famous music and dance decoration this year and signs a contract with the Bernheim-Jeune Gallery in September.[71]

July 2 Monet asks the Bernheim brothers to find out quietly whether the Princess de Polignac might be willing to sell *The Turkeys (Decorative Panel)* (cat. no. 46).[72]

Mid-July The Monets take an automobile trip to the vicinity of Cherbourg. Near the end of the month, they return to Landemer in Basse-Normandie, where Monet hopes to paint coast motifs that had appealed to him earlier in the trip, but he is unable to work.[73]

October 21 Monet complains to the Bernheim brothers of recurrent headaches that have plagued him for a year.[74]

December 3 Visiting Giverny with Bonnard, Vuillard is impressed by the abiding "newness" of Monet's work.[75]

December 7 Monet writes to Geffroy that he has been unable to paint for a year, thanks to poor health (which also prevented a return trip to Venice), bad weather, and the excitement resulting from his *Water Lilies* exhibition.[76]

December 13–18 Exhibition of works by Butler at the Bernheim-Jeune Gallery, Paris.

1910

January 10–22 Cézanne exhibition at the Bernheim-Jeune Gallery, Paris, includes a painting lent by Monet, which, owing to floods, has to be returned to him by boat. During the next several weeks, flood waters submerge the water lily pond and reach halfway up the central garden path leading to the house. Afterward, Monet makes important modifications to the water garden, curving the contours of the banks.[1]

Late February Alice Monet falls gravely ill with spinal leukemia. She will need radiation therapy, but is in remission from late May through July.[2]

94. Edouard Vuillard, *Gaston Bernheim de Villers and Joseph (Josse) Bernheim-Jeune*, 1912. Oil on canvas; 157 × 159 cm, 61¹³⁄₁₆ × 62⅝ in. Courtesy Galerie Bernheim-Jeune, Paris. The Bernheim brothers (Gaston is shown standing) are depicted in the office of their rue Richeplanche, Paris, gallery.

May Monet–Manet exhibition at the Miethke Gallery, Vienna, includes seventeen Monet paintings (see cat. no. 32).

May 5 Lottery at the Georges Petit Gallery, Paris, to raise funds for flood victims. Monet donates a *Charing Cross Bridge* painting.[3]

June 1–25 Seventeen Monet paintings are included in the Monet, Pissarro, Renoir, and Sisley group exhibition at the Durand-Ruel Gallery, Paris.

June 22 Monet goes to Paris for medical consultation about his headaches.[4]

July The Worcester Art Museum, Massachusetts, buys two Monet paintings, becoming the first museum to acquire a *Water Lilies* painting (cat. no. 140).[5]

Autumn Nine Monet paintings are shown in an exhibition entitled "Paintings from the Collection of Mrs. Potter Palmer" at The Art Institute of Chicago (see cat. nos. 15, 77, and 96).

Early November Geffroy comes to Giverny with his friend Dr. Vasquez, who examines Alice.[6]

November Monet begins to pose for the sculptor Paul Paulin, who had already made busts of Degas and Renoir in 1883 and 1902, respectively. Paulin sends Monet a bronze cast on October 25, 1911.[7]

November 11 Geffroy chooses two *Water Lilies* paintings (see cat. no. 129) to use as models for the Gobelins commission proposed in 1908. Monet sends a third painting the following April.[8]

Early December Alice Monet's health deteriorates further.[9]

December Monet donates three paintings, including a *Water Lilies* (cat. no. 127), to the Le Havre Museum, asking for a token payment of only 3,000 francs.[10]

1911

February 8–25 The Durand-Ruel Gallery, New York, presents seventeen paintings in a show entitled "Exhibition of Paintings of Different Periods by Monet."[11]

March 26 Durand-Ruel comes to Giverny and buys eight *Water Lilies* paintings for 113,000 francs (the 1909 price). Monet retouches two before sending them to Paris on March 28.[12]

May 19 Alice Monet dies at 4 A.M. She is buried next to her first husband, Ernest Hoschedé, and her daughter Suzanne on May 22. Degas attends the funeral. After rereading Alice's letters, Monet burns them.[13]

July 12 Clemenceau writes to the grieving Monet: "Remember the old Rembrandt in the Louvre. . . . He clutches his palette, determined to stand fast to the end through terrible trials. That is the model."[14]

95. Monet in his garden, probably taken by Sacha Guitry in 1913.

96. Claude Monet, *Weeping Willow*, preliminary drawing for the *Water Lilies* decorations, probably 1913–14. Pencil on paper, bound in a sketchbook; two sheets, each sheet 25.5 × 34 cm, 10 × 13⅜ in. Musée Marmottan, Paris (carnet I, folios 21 verso– 22 recto) (5128) [WD 123].

Late July G. Jean-Aubry comes to Giverny to obtain information for his biography of Boudin. His interview with Monet about his early experiences as an artist is published in *Havre-Eclair* on August 1.[15]

August Forty-five paintings by Monet (see cat. nos. 43, 57, 103, and 128) are exhibited at the Museum of Fine Arts, Boston, in the first American museum exhibition devoted to the artist.

September Many of Monet's closest friends, including Clemenceau, Geffroy, Mirbeau, and Renoir, visit Giverny this month, clearly to distract the bereaved painter from his lingering grief.[16]

October 14 Durand-Ruel comes to Giverny and buys seven paintings for 95,000 francs, bringing Monet's art sales for 1911 to 208,000 francs.[17]

October–December Monet finishes some Venice paintings.[18]

October 1911–January 1912 Six paintings by Monet (see cat. no. 130) are in a Durand-Ruel exhibition that travels to St. Louis, Chicago, and Cincinnati. Durand-Ruel arranges exhibitions in midwestern cities again in 1912 and yearly from 1914 to 1918. In Chicago these take place in lobby galleries at the Auditorium, Stratford, and Blackstone hotels.

December 2–23 Exhibition of twelve Monet paintings (see cat. nos. 28, 50, and 126) at the Durand-Ruel Gallery, New York.

December 20 Monet writes to Rodin's close friend and biographer Judith Cladel that he approves of a projected Rodin museum at the Hôtel Biron, Paris, where the sculptor had rented rooms since September 1908.[19]

1912

January 28 Nine paintings by Monet are included in the centennial exhibition of French art at the French Institute, St. Petersburg, Russia.[20]

February 12 Monet writes to the Bernheim brothers that he is ready to exhibit his Venice paintings and asks them to come to Giverny on February 19.[21]

February 18 Monet asks Clemenceau to help Albert Salerou obtain a vacant deputy sheriff's post in Mantes so that Germaine and her children can be close to Giverny, but Clemenceau is unable to help.[22]

February 24 Monet acquires an 1867 portrait of himself by Charles-Emile-Auguste Durand, known as Carolus-Duran (Musée Marmottan, Paris). Meanwhile, Jacques Hoschedé is threatening to sue Monet for items he believes to be part of his mother's estate, including a portrait by Manet. This suit will provoke Monet to break off relations with Jacques in July.[23]

February 29 Monet lunches with Vuillard and Mirbeau. On June 13 Monet will see Vuillard again at the Bernheims'.[24]

March 29 Monet sends off fifteen Venice paintings (one still wet), which had been purchased by the Bernheim-Jeune Gallery, Paris, for 166,000 francs. Durand-Ruel arranges with the Bernheim brothers to buy half of them two weeks later. "You know that I am attached to my frames and recommend them to you," Monet reminds them. A Vuillard portrait of the brothers in their office with a Venice painting on the wall (fig. no. 94) indicates that they did use Monet's frames for the exhibition.[25]

April 15 Monet now packs fourteen additional Venice paintings to send to Paris, but he evidently unpacks them and undertakes another month's refinements, driving himself to despair with fears that they are not up to his standards.[26]

May 3 The Metropolitan Museum of Art, New York, opens its Rodin Gallery with forty sculptures—including *The Thinker*—donated by the French State, millionaire Thomas F. Ryan, and Rodin himself. The walls are lined with Rodin drawings and watercolors.[27]

May 12 Durand-Ruel comes to Giverny to calm Monet, who has been considering calling off his Venice exhibition.[28]

May 15 Monet sends off the final fourteen Venice paintings, reserving the right to remove any works when he sees them together in Paris. Among the group are three large ones, just finished, that will cost between 14,000 and 15,000 francs each. This year his art income will be 369,000 francs.[29]

May 22 Monet writes to the Bernheim brothers that he will leave the installation of the Venice exhibition to them. "But I would be relieved to know, if having tried the other frames, you took care to mark mine in order that each of the canvases might be framed as I wished, which would be a satisfaction for me."[30]

May 28–June 8 Exhibition of twenty-nine paintings (see cat. no. 143) under the title "Monet Venise" at the Bernheim-Jeune Gallery, Paris. The catalogue preface is written by Mirbeau, who had studied the works at Giverny on April 7. Monet's usual supporters respond with enthusiasm, as do some other critics, among them Guillaume Apollinaire. Signac writes to Monet that the Venice paintings are his best in three decades.[31]

June 5–July 6 Twenty-one Monet paintings are included in an *Art moderne* exhibition organized by Joyant and Manzi at the newspaper's gallery at 15, rue de la Ville-l'Evêque, Paris.[32]

July 6 Monet learns that his son Jean has had a serious stroke.[33]

97. This photograph of Monet in his first studio was taken in mid-November 1913 and published in *Je sais tout* magazine, January 14, 1914. Hanging on the walls behind the artist are two early *Water Lilies* paintings (cat. no. 111 can be seen at the far left) and *The Red Kerchief: Portrait of Camille Monet* (cat. no. 25). Paul Paulin's bust of Monet is visible on the painter's desk.

July 18–September 30 Eight paintings by Monet are included in an exhibition of nineteenth-century French art at the Kunstverein, Frankfurt, which acquires two of the works.[34]

July 26 Monet reports to Geffroy that a Dr. Valude has diagnosed him with a cataract problem—"the right eye no longer sees anything, the other is also slightly affected"—and has prescribed treatment to retard the inevitable aggravation of the condition.

Clemenceau, a medical doctor himself (he received his degree in 1865), assures Monet on July 28: "You are in no danger whatsoever of losing your eyesight. . . . The cataract on the bad eye will certainly soon ripen and then one could operate. But that is nothing, and the continuity of your eyesight is assured."[35]

August 5 Monet reports that a bad storm has damaged the garden, breaking one of the weeping willows planted beside the water lily pond, drastically altering the shadow patterns fundamental to Monet's most important motifs.[36]

August Bonnard, who has exhibited at the Bernheim-Jeune Gallery, Paris, since 1906, buys a house called Ma Roulette at Vernonnet, outside Vernon. Like Monet, who is a frequent visitor, Bonnard paints out-of-doors on his property; unlike Monet, he does not cultivate a garden.[37]

September 17 Durand-Ruel sends two unsigned paintings of the Palazzo Ducale back to Giverny at Monet's request; the artist needs to refer to them in order to finish a third version.[38]

Late October Seven of Monet's Venice paintings are exhibited at the Brooks Reed Gallery, Boston. Working with Durand-Ruel, this gallery will present works by Monet, in group or one-artist exhibitions, every year from 1911 to 1923.

November At the sale of Alice Monet's belongings on November 8 organized by Jacques Hoschedé, Monet buys nearly everything back to give to the children. Probably around this same time, Jacques sells eight unsigned Monet paintings (perhaps gifts to Alice) to Georges Bernheim, cousin of Josse and Gaston Bernheim, who sells them back to Monet. Meanwhile, Jean Monet's condition worsens, and Monet buys a house for Jean and Blanche in Giverny, selling the trout farm they had started in Beaumont-Le-Roger (Eure) two years earlier. Monet asks Durand-Ruel to put aside a small Cézanne until further notice.[39]

November 29 Monet sends three figure paintings to Durand-Ruel to be relined. In 1913 he will send a still larger canvas to the dealer for the same reason.[40]

1913

January A group of Monet's Venice paintings are exhibited at the Durand-Ruel Gallery, New York.[41]

February 9 Durand-Ruel comes to Giverny and apparently buys ten paintings, which Monet sends to Paris in early March; the exact circumstances of the transaction are uncertain because

the whereabouts of any account ledgers Monet might have kept after 1912 are unknown.[42]

February 15–March 15 Five paintings by Monet are included in the controversial International Exhibition of Modern Art at the 69th Regiment Armory, New York. The exhibition travels to The Art Institute of Chicago (March 24–April 16), and Copley Hall, Boston (April 28–May 19).

Mid-February Monet takes a trip to Switzerland in his new car with Michel and the Butlers, stopping at Lucerne and St. Moritz and taking a scenic train trip. Monet wants to return to Switzerland to paint the following year.[43]

April 23 Monet goes to see Geffroy at the Gobelins factory, Paris, where the *Water Lilies* tapestries are finished.

In Paris, Dr. Vasquez accompanies Monet to another eye examination. This year Monet seeks many medical opinions in the hope that some specialist may provide non-surgical relief for his cataracts.[44]

May An exhibition of thirty-eight works by Butler is presented by Durand-Ruel in Paris, although the artist had returned to America with his family earlier in the year to install a group of historical murals in White Plains, New York. The outbreak of war in 1914 keeps the Butler family in the United States.[45]

June 23–July 10 Fourteen paintings by Monet are included in an *Art moderne* exhibition at the Manzi–Joyant Gallery, Paris.

July Celebrated horticulturalist Georges Truffaut visits Giverny and writes a preface for an article about Monet's irises (published in the October 1913 issue of *Jardinage*) written by his chief gardener, Félix Breuil. Over the next dozen years, Truffaut will use photographs of Monet's garden to illustrate *Jardinage* articles on topical horticultural issues.[46]

Around August 16–24 With Mirbeau, Monet visits the country home in Yainville, near Jumièges, of playwright/filmmaker Sacha Guitry and actress Charlotte Lysès to give them gardening advice.[47]

Summer Monet paints *Flowering Arches.* American opera singer Marguerite Namara visits the artist at the same time as Sacha Guitry and gives a recital at the water lily pond, where the Butlers' piano has been transported for the occasion. According to Namara, she often gave impromptu tea-time concerts at Monet's: "Once [Monet] came over to me at the piano and drew up his famous armchair and sat down. He asked me if I knew the soprano–baritone duet from *Le nozze di Figaro* of Mozart. Of course, I did, and we went right into it. We sang the entire thing, including the recitative; he knew all the words. His voice was not a very beautiful sound, but it was on pitch and full of vitality and energy just like himself."[48]

September 6–17 After a week-long visit with Guitry and Lysès, Monet has lunch with Vuillard at the Bernheims' Villers-sur-Mer country house, now being decorated with murals by the younger artist.[49]

Mid-November André Arnyvelde comes to Giverny to interview Monet for an article published on January 14, 1914, in *Je sais tout.* He notices three cars parked in the garage. Chain-smoking, Monet tells Arnyvelde that, with the exception of the past two or three months, he has hardly worked at all since his wife's death in 1911. A photograph of Monet in the first studio (fig. no. 97), taken to accompany the article, shows two early *Water Lilies* paintings (see cat. no. 111), one framed, of the sort Monet had shown to the reporter Guillemot in 1897. Their presence in the studio suggests Monet's interest in returning to a mural project.[50]

December 10 Monet goes with Geffroy to the 1913 National Museums Acquisitions exhibition at the Ecole des Beaux-Arts, Paris, to see the Gobelins tapestries based on his *Water Lilies* paintings.[51]

1914

January Monet, himself bedridden with flu, is preoccupied with the worsening condition of Jean Monet, who cannot be moved from the first studio. On February 9 Jean dies.[52]

February 1–16 Exhibition of twenty Monet paintings (see cat. nos. 11, 34, 105, and possibly 100) at the Durand-Ruel Gallery, New York.

98. Monet at work in the water lily garden on a large canvas (cat. no. 147) in July 1915. Nitia Salerou and Blanche Monet appear in the foreground.

99. Monet at work in the water lily garden during the summer of 1915. This photograph is a still from Sacha Guitry's silent movie *Ceux de chez nous.*

March 10 Monet goes to Paris, where his son Michel is convalescing in the Hôtel Terminus after an operation.[53]

March 2–21 Fifty paintings by Monet (see cat. no. 116) comprise a retrospective at the Durand-Ruel Gallery, Paris.[54]

April 30 Monet writes to Geffroy that he intends to do large works, taking up an old idea, referring to the water lily mural decorations that he had shown to Guillemot in 1897. Monet will later explain his momentous decision to undertake a culminating project departing in style from anything he had achieved previously: "A day finally came, a blessed day, when I seemed to feel that my [cataract] malady was provisionally checked. I tried a series of experiments destined to give me an account of the special limits and possibilities of my vision, and with great joy I found that although I was still insensitive to the finer shades and tonalities of colors seen close up, nevertheless my eyes did not betray me when I stepped back and took in the motif in large masses. . . . While working on my sketches, I said to myself that a series of impressions of the ensemble [of the water lily pond] done at the times of day when my eyesight was more likely to be precise, would be of some interest. I waited until the idea took shape, until the arrangement and the composition of the motifs gradually became inscribed in my brain, and then when the day came that I felt I had sufficient trumps in my hand to try my luck with some real hope of success, I made up my mind to act, and I acted."[55]

100. Claude Monet, *Water Lilies*, 1916. Oil on canvas; 200.5 × 201 cm, 78¹⁵⁄₁₆ × 79⅛ in. The National Museum of Western Art, Matsukata Collection, Tokyo (P.1959.151) [W 1800].

101. Interior of the third studio before a ventilator was installed in the southeast corner in late April 1916.

June 4 Because he is so absorbed in his new mural project, Monet does not attend the opening at the Louvre of the inaugural exhibition of the Camondo bequest, which includes fourteen of his paintings (see cat. no. 123), despite the museum's policy never to show works by living artists. He writes to Durand-Ruel on June 29 that he gets up at 4 A.M. and works all day. His eyesight does not trouble him.[56]

July 6 Monet invites Geffroy to come see the results of two months' ceaseless work. Around this time, writer Michel Georges-Michel and Clemenceau observe two enormous *Water Lilies* panels.[57]

August 1 When Germany declares war on Russia, France mobilizes its military forces. Germany declares war on France on August 3 and invades Belgium the next day, provoking Britain to declare war. Six days later Jean-Pierre Hoschedé leaves for the front. On August 24 one million German troops invade France.[58]

August 31 Concerned about the possible advance of enemy forces, Germaine Salerou (whose husband has been called up) and her children leave Giverny for Blois, where her aunt lives. Monet considers sending many of his paintings to be stored in Paris, but he will stay in Giverny.[59]

September 5 Allied forces halt the German advance toward Paris on the river Marne, roughly forty kilometers from the capital.

September–October Mary and Frederick MacMonnies, American artists residing in Giverny, establish a makeshift fourteen-bed hospital on their property for war wounded.

Monet provides vegetables for the hospital from his garden.[60]

December 1 Monet writes to Geffroy: "I am back at work; it is still the best way not to think too much about current woes, even though I should be a bit ashamed to think about little investigations into forms and colors while so many people suffer and die for us."[61]

1915

January 15 Monet writes to Raymond Koechlin —a collector and leader in arts organizations who served as the president of the Société des amis du Louvre—that, having recovered from an illness, he is again at work on his murals, developing studies begun at the water lily pond the previous summer. Given the difficulty of moving canvases of this scale in and out of the second studio—which is entered by a staircase—it is unclear where Monet works during these winter months. Also unknown is how the seventy-five-year-old painter manages to paint the bottom portions of such large canvases, which rest at floor level in his studio.[1]

February 1–16 Exhibition of eighteen works by Monet (see cat. nos. 109 and 114) at the Durand-Ruel Gallery, New York.

February 25 Monet asks Joyant to provide the dimensions of his gallery in Paris, presumably investigating possible exhibition sites for his murals.[2]

March The St. Louis Art Museum acquires Monet's *Charing Cross Bridge*.[3]

Mid-March Michel Monet goes to Rouen to begin infantry service as a volunteer. His

unit is deployed to Orbel on April 2. Now only Blanche Monet remains with Monet at Giverny, although Germaine Salerou and her children visit.[4]

June 17 Mirbeau, Geffroy, Lucien Descaves, Léon Hennique, and J.-H. Rosny—writers who are members of the Académie Goncourt, which holds monthly lunches in Paris to which Monet is invited—visit Giverny to see the murals in progress. Descaves later recalls seeing works of great size (2 × 3 and even 2 × 5 meters) in a studio space and that a special studio for these works is being built. Monet estimates that he will need five years to finish his project. He has already prepared 170 square meters of canvas, the amount required for about twenty large panels.[5]

June 21 Monet has lunch with Vuillard, who writes in his diary: "[Monet's] large canvases, like the ceiling of [the Sistine Chapel], suggest rhythm and color, all works linked by a majestic lyricism. After lunch alone with B[onnard] in the small studio . . . we went down to the water lily garden."[6]

Summer Two works by Monet (see cat. no. 11) are included in the Panama–Pacific International Exposition, San Francisco. Three works by Butler are also exhibited.

July 5 Monet is granted a work permit to construct a new studio on the northeast corner of his property, which he had recently extended by buying an adjacent plot of land. Maurice Lanctuit, a Vernon contractor, oversees the demolition of existing structures on the site and the subsequent building, initially estimating that the studio will cost roughly 30,000 francs to build, not including the installation

102. Monet in his third studio, late 1915/early 1916.

103. Blanche Hoschedé, Michel Monet, Claude Monet, and Jean-Pierre Hoschedé, September 1, 1916.

of central heating. The finished studio will be one huge skylighted space—fifteen meters high, with a floor area of 23 × 12 meters. But in August Monet will confess that he finds the exterior of the new studio hideously ugly.[7]

October 24 Monet writes to Geffroy that he is moving into the new studio and will soon finally get a good idea of the large-scale works that have been under way for more than a year already. By the end of the year, the cost of the building project rises to roughly 50,000 francs.[8]

November 22–December 5 Remarkable footage of Monet painting at the pond this summer is included in Sacha Guitry's film *Ceux de chez nous* (see fig. no. 99), presented at the Variétés Theater, Paris, with commentary provided by the filmmaker. Monet attends one of the screenings of this historic silent movie documenting France's greatest living artists, including Degas, Renoir, and Rodin. Unfortunately, the filmmaker's heirs have restricted the availability of this valuable film for decades.[9]

December 22 Monet writes to the Bernheim brothers: "I am working hard and wasting masses of color. Happily the days are short, otherwise I would need to stop, from being unable any longer to afford the paints I am using."[10]

1916

January–February Monet sends paintings, the signature on at least one of them still wet, to an exhibition at the Paris gallery of Georges Bernheim to benefit prisoners of war. Throughout the war, Monet will donate works to many such benefits.[11]

February German troops attack Verdun, where Michel Monet is deployed. This four-month-long battle leaves 650,000 dead. Michel takes a few days leave at Giverny in late February.[12]

April 1 Urged by Etienne Clémentel, wartime Minister of Commerce and Industry, Rodin signs the document donating his works to France on condition that the State transform the Hôtel Biron into a Rodin museum. Formal acceptance will follow on September 16, initiating debate in the Chamber of Deputies and then the Senate, which will give its approval at year's end.[13]

April 26 Monet asks Bonnard to come to Giverny to see his murals in progress, warning him that the following day workers will upset everything in his third studio while installing a ventilator. In the earliest snapshots of the murals in progress—still unframed, but mounted on chassis for easy movement—the ventilator is absent. Perhaps taken by Geffroy's friend Moreau, these snapshots show four panels dovetailed together to form a 17-meter-wide composition, dominated by two willow trees (see fig. nos. 101 and 102).[14]

April 29 Monet agrees to donate a pastel or an oil sketch to a sale organized by Clémentel's wife to benefit war orphans.[15]

May 9 Monet has been to Paris and left two *Thames* pastels for glazing, one of which he will donate to a benefit sale for French seamen. It does not sell. In December he will agree to donate another pastel to a war benefit.[16]

May 22 Hard at work, Monet orders from his art supplier six stretched canvases measuring 2 × 1.5 meters and six measuring 2 × 1.3 meters (see cat. no. 148).[17]

November 4 Durand-Ruel's sons come to Giverny, purchasing works that Monet, who is preoccupied with his decorations, does not send off until the end of March 1917.[18]

Around November 12 Clemenceau sees the murals in progress at Giverny.[19]

November 28 Monet writes to the Bernheim brothers that Matisse is welcome to come to Giverny in two weeks, since by that time Monet will have put the final touches on several large "machines," i.e., his murals. But by December 12 Monet has changed his mind, writing to the Bernheims that they should send no visitors for the time being: "Just now I have thrown myself into transformations on my large canvases . . . and my mood is foul." He explains to Guitry on December 14: "I lost things that had gone well that I wanted to improve, and I must recover them by whatever means."[20]

December 9–23 Exhibition at the Durand-Ruel Gallery, New York, of fifteen paintings by Monet (see cat. no. 108).

1917

January 16–17 Record-setting auction at the Plaza Hotel, New York, of James Sutton's art collection, including twenty-four Monet paintings. Of these, his 1903 *Water Lilies* (cat. no. 125) "caused a sensation when hung, for by

104. Monet's work table in the third studio, photographed by Georges or Joseph Durand-Ruel, November 11, 1917.

reason of the mirage and reflection of the water it appeared as if it were upside-down."[21]

February 9 Joseph Durand-Ruel writes to Monet that his brother Georges would like photographs of the large panels in progress: "He has talked about them with several of our clients who are interested in buying them for their city's museum, and he believes that he would have opportunities to sell them if he had photographs of the decorations and the prices that you would wish to have." Monet replies to Georges Durand-Ruel on February 12: "I have no photographs of the decorations and will make none until the work—which, by the way, does not always proceed as I would wish—is a little closer to being finished, at least in part. . . . So for now it is useless to talk of sales and prices."[22]

February 16 Death of Mirbeau. Monet, who had visited Mirbeau on his sickbed in late November 1916, is overcome with grief at the funeral in Paris on February 19.[23]

April 1 Monet agrees to donate a work to a sale arranged by Arthur Meyer to benefit war victims.[24]

April 13–29 Monet donates a 1913 painting to an exhibition at the Georges Petit Gallery, Paris, of works to be sold to benefit the Fraternity of Artists.[25]

April 16–May 5 An Etretat pastel by Monet is included in a benefit exhibition at the French Naval League, Paris.[26]

April 26 In response to a request from Clémentel and Albert Dalimier, the Deputy-Secretary for the Ministry of Fine Arts, Blanche suggests that Monet produce a design for a car-

pet that might be woven at the Gobelins factory to complement his mural decorations.[27]

April 30 Clémentel and Dalimier come to Giverny to discuss the project for a carpet. Monet agrees to their request to paint Rheims Cathedral, which had first been bombarded in September 1914, after the current shelling subsides. In return, they offer to help Monet keep his car and obtain gas for it. Monet also needs their help to obtain coal. Monet receives an official commission for the Rheims project on November 1, but it goes unrealized.[28]

May 1 Monet, who has just bought a painting by Albert Marquet of the bay of Naples from Georges Petit (apparently at a benefit sale), invites Marquet and Matisse to come to Giverny on May 10.[29]

August 7 Death of eighty-two-year-old Léon Monet in Maromme.[30]

August 28 Monet writes to Joseph Durand-Ruel that, since late May 1917, he has been working harder than ever; he will continue to do so through early October, when he moves his operations from the water garden site back to the third studio.[31]

September 27 Death of Degas. Monet attends the funeral in Paris on September 28.[32]

Mid-October Monet buys two paintings by Butler's son, James, from Durand-Ruel. James is serving in France with American forces.

The Bernheim brothers ask Monet to write to Degas's brother encouraging him to discuss the estate sale with them.[33]

Last Half of October After postponing their departure for nearly a week, Monet and Blanche take a rest trip to the Normandy coast.[34]

November 5 Clemenceau becomes Prime Minister, retaining his position as Minister of War.[35]

November 11 Georges and Joseph Durand-Ruel visit Giverny and take snapshots showing Monet's work table and eight or nine of the dozen 2 × 4.25-meter panels under way in the third studio (see fig. no. 104). Most of the large panels now have thin frame moldings along their top edges. The dealers reserve five old easel-size paintings, pending some finishing touches; eventually Monet destroys two of the five as unsatisfactory.[36]

November 17 Death of Rodin.[37]

November 26 Monet sends seven pastels to the Bernheim brothers for glazing. Monet intends the best four as a gift for someone unidentified, and the others are for future benefit sales.[38]

1918

January 11 Monet urgently needs more flat brushes and stretched canvases from his art supplier. In order to transport the large canvases to Giverny, Monet asks Clémentel to exempt him from wartime civilian rail freight restrictions.[39]

Early February Thiébault-Sisson apparently visits Giverny; his detailed account of the visit will be published in 1927. Monet has now finished eight of a projected twelve 2 × 4.5-meter works for an ensemble, and has already begun the remaining four, which he estimates might take another year to complete if his eyesight holds out. Monet also has some 6-meter- and 8-meter-wide canvases under way by now. "If I have regained my sense of color in the large canvases I've just shown you, it is because I have adapted my working methods to my eyesight and because most of the time I have laid down the color haphazardly, on the one hand trusting solely to the labels on my tubes of paint and, on the other, to force of habit, to the way in which I have always laid out my materials on my palette. I soon grew used to it, and I've never made a mistake. I should add that my infirmity has sometimes gone into remittance and that on more than one occasion my color vision has come back as it was before, and I have profited from those moments to make the necessary adjustments."[40]

February 20–21 Benefit sale organized by Countess Marquiset in Paris for a hospital for wounded soldiers at Janson-de-Sailly. Monet donates an important 1907 *Water Lilies* painting, which is bought by Durand-Ruel in partnership with the Bernheim brothers.[41]

March–July German forces shell Paris as they make their final westward advance. In June Monet considers abandoning Giverny in the face of this threat.[42]

105. Claude Monet, *Water Lilies*, 1917–19. Oil on canvas; 100 × 300 cm, 39⅜ × 118⅛ in. Musée Marmottan, Paris (5118) [W 1902].

March 17 The Bernheim brothers visit Giverny and choose several paintings to purchase jointly with Durand-Ruel, whose Paris gallery narrowly escapes bombing.[43]

April 30 Monet orders twenty stretched canvases, 1 × 2 meters each, from his art supplier (see cat. no. 153).[44]

May Fraternity of Artists benefit sale at the Georges Petit Gallery, Paris. Monet donates a 1908 *Water Lilies* tondo (cat. no. 141).[45]

Spring–Summer Monet begins three new series at his water garden: a group of *Japanese Bridge* paintings rendered on a few of the 1 × 2-meter canvases ordered from his art supplier on April 30; a dozen easel-scale *Weeping Willow* paintings, so darkly rendered that their twisting branches suggest anguish and grief, as if in response to the war (see cat. no. 152); and four easel-scale views of one end of the water garden (see cat. no. 151).[46]

June 21 Monet thanks Gaston Bernheim for offering to place his paintings in safekeeping at the Rouen Museum, but he declines. In the event of a enemy advance, he says, he would want to perish amidst what he had done at Giverny.[47]

June 28 *La Bulletin de la vie artistique* reports an official decision to maintain the gardens surrounding the Hôtel Biron as part of the Rodin Museum.

August 19 Bicycling from Vernon to Giverny, René Gimpel and Georges Bernheim visit Monet. Gimpel notes in his diary: "A dozen canvases arranged in a circle on the floor, one next to another, all about 2 meters wide and 1.2 meters high." The fourteen surviving 1 × 2-meter format *Water Lilies* paintings all show a single motif (as if Monet had adapted his single-theme series methods to decorative horizontal formats); in other words, they could not be ar-ranged end-to-end to provide a continuous panorama (see cat. no. 153). The dealers notice a total of about thirty canvases under way, all of which they would happily have bought, even though their size and the fact that they were conceived for installation at ground level would make them hard to market. Monet explains: "I work on the paintings all day. They bring them to me one after the other. In the atmosphere a color reappears that I had found and sketched on one of the canvases yesterday. Quickly I am passed the painting and I try my best to put down this vision definitively, but usually it disappears as quickly as it came into view to make room for another color already rendered several days before on another study which is almost instantly placed before me . . . and so on all the day." Gimpel comments upon the artist's youthful demeanor: "I have never seen a man of that age look so young. . . . He looked like a young father, who, on December 25th, put on a false white beard so that his children would believe in Santa Claus."[48]

October After a summer of constant work out-of-doors, Monet writes to Gaston Bernheim that he is now back in his third studio to work indoors for the winter. Monet asks Clémentel to help his paint supplier, who has run out of oil to make paints.

Shchukin's private art collection opens in Moscow as the First Museum of Modern Western Painting, with six works by Monet.[49]

November 11 Armistice.

November 12 Monet writes to Clemenceau, offering a new *Weeping Willow* painting and a large decorative *Water Lilies* panel, both nearly finished, to the State to celebrate the Allied victory. Monet specifies that they should go to the Museum of Decorative Arts, Paris, presumably since the Moreau-Nélaton collection is there. This offer is unrealized, perhaps because Cle-menceau and Geffroy propose a much more ambitious donation of twelve decorative panels as a monument to peace, when they come to Giverny on November 18 with two automobiles and four chauffeurs. "You saved France," Monet tells Clemenceau, who replies, "No, it was the infantry."[50]

November 23 Monet blacks out while working in the third studio.[51]

November 28 Georges Bernheim and Gimpel return to Giverny. Bernheim brings along a portrait of Monet by Renoir. Monet claims to have a quite similar one that is fake (possibly fig. no. 25). They also bring an early landscape for Monet to sign. Dissatisfied with the trees at left, Monet signs the canvas in the middle to indicate where he thinks it should be cut down. Bernheim buys two floral still lifes and a painting of apple trees for 48,000 francs. Gimpel's diary details the art supplies on Monet's low work table in the third studio.[52]

November 30 Joseph and Georges Durand-Ruel evidently visit Giverny and purchase six more paintings, including two brand-new *Water Lily Pond* compositions. Around this time, the Bernheim brothers also come to buy two *Weeping Willow* paintings. For his 1918 easel-scale works, Monet charges 20,000 francs each.

Monet's bank records indicate that his accounts at the Vernon bank bring him roughly 40,000 francs in annual interest.[53]

1919

January 18–End of January Monet–Rodin exhibition at the Bernheim-Jeune Gallery, Paris, includes four 1918 paintings that Monet had sent to Paris the week before the opening.[54]

February 19 Clemenceau is wounded in an assassination attempt.

May Exhibition of sixteen recent works by Monet (see cat. no. 126) at the Durand-Ruel Gallery, New York.[55]

June 24 Monet reports to Josse Bernheim that all the gardeners who have worked for him for the past twenty years have quit. Later this year the household staff quits.[56]

August 25 Monet is working on a series of landscapes, setting aside the *Water Lilies* murals until the winter. One dated *Japanese Bridge* painting (cat. no. 154) probably belongs to this new group of works; it is perhaps the first in a series Monet devotes to that theme over the next years. The smaller scale of these works poses some challenges for the artist. The following February, Monet explains to Gimpel, "I can't [paint on easel-scale canvases] anymore because I've become used to painting broadly and with big brushes."[57]

October or November The Bernheim brothers buy four 1 × 2-meter *Water Lilies* paintings (negotiating a half-share partnership in the purchase with Durand-Ruel in 1921).[58]

November 9 Clemenceau, who now visits Giverny frequently, recommends that Monet undergo an operation for his cataracts, but Monet hesitates because he is concerned that total blindness might result. He plans to contact Mary Cassatt, who recently underwent this operation.

Monet writes to Geffroy on November 19 that his worsening eyesight has forced him to stop painting before he could bring his decorations to satisfactory conclusion.[59]

November 29 Joyant has sent Monet the floor plan of his gallery in Paris, which might be a suitable exhibition space for the panels. Monet invites Joyant to Giverny to discuss the prospects, but he warns: "Even though my friends want me to exhibit, it is hard at my age, especially since it involves important things, at least in terms of scale."[60]

December 3 Death of Renoir in Cagnes.[61]

1920

January 14–15 Auction of the collection of Arthur B. Emmons, an early Newport, Rhode Island, collector, at the Plaza Hotel, New York, includes twenty Monet paintings.[1]

January 17 Awaiting the results in Giverny, Clemenceau is defeated in the French presidential election; he consequently resigns the premiership.[2]

January 20 Hampered by worsening vision and confessing complete discouragement with his work, Monet promises to help Geffroy with research for a biography commissioned by the Bernheim brothers. When Geffroy decides against participating in the project, Thiébault-Sisson and Alexandre compete to replace him as author.[3]

February 1 Gimpel visits Giverny with Georges Bernheim, who manages to buy three paintings for 18,000 francs each. Complaining again about his eyesight, Monet also tells them that Clemenceau visits him most Sundays.[4]

February 19 Monet thanks Koechlin for his support of the proposed purchase of *Women in the Garden* (fig. no. 14) by the Société des amis du Louvre. Monet will make this purchase a prerequisite for his donation of the *Water Lilies* decorations to the State.[5]

March 25 Representing the Nantes Museum, novelist Marc Elder visits Giverny, and Monet agrees to donate two pastels. Elder publishes an account of the visit in the April 6 issue of *Excelsior*. Around this time, constant appeals from buyers are disturbing to Monet. Among them is Léonce Bénédite, acting on behalf of Baron Matsukata, Kojiro, who is amassing works for a museum to be built in Japan.[6]

June 4 In the morning, Monet receives painter Albert André and his wife and agrees to donate a *Water Lilies* painting to the Léon Alègre Museum in Bagnols-sur-Cèze. After lunch Monet receives Joseph Durand-Ruel, accompanied by Mrs. Charles (Sara) Hutchinson (wife of the president of the Board of Trustees of The Art Institute of Chicago) and Chicago collectors Mr. and Mrs. Martin Ryerson, who are contemplating the purchase of Monet's *Water Lilies* decorations for their museum. One slightly later account of the visit contends that an architect accompanies the Chicago group. According to the Monet obituary published by the *Chicago Daily Tribune* on December 6, 1926, this three-million-dollar American offer was for thirty large paintings.[7]

Summer Less aggravated by poor eyesight, Monet takes up painting out-of-doors during the mornings. Despite the heat inside the third studio, he continues there in the afternoons.[8]

June–July Thiébault-Sisson unofficially negotiates with his close friend the Council of Ministers president Alexandre Millerand, the Fine Arts Ministry director Paul Léon, and Monet in an attempt to expedite the donation of the *Water Lilies* decorations to the State. By July 8 Monet warns Thiébault-Sisson to desist and to keep private any information shared with him. During at least some of this time, the writer is staying across the street from Monet, at the Hôtel Baudy. In August Alexandre also takes up unofficial negotiations.[9]

July 12 Presuming eventual agreement with the State about his donation of the *Water Lilies* decorations, Monet writes to Clémentel asking for ten tons of coal for his studio: "If the State

106. Georges Clemenceau, Monet, and Lily Butler on the wisteria-covered Japanese bridge, photographed at the time of the visit of Count Sanji Kuroki and Princess Matsukata in June 1921.

wants me to work for it, they must provide the means."[10]

September 23 Monet reschedules a lunch with Thiébault-Sisson, who is staying at the Hôtel Baudy, and then the same day postpones it to the following week: "Now, let me tell you that I absolutely refuse to have any more of these conversations that are more like interviews. . . . After you leave, I regret having said so much."[11]

September 27 Arrangements having been made by Alexandre, Paul Léon visits Giverny, accompanied at Monet's request by Koechlin, and they reach agreement in principle about the donation.[12]

September 28 Léon telephones Bonnier (now acclaimed as an Art Nouveau architect), requesting on behalf of Monet that he design a pavilion to house the artist's murals in the gardens of the new Rodin Museum in Paris.[13]

October 3 Bonnier visits Giverny to discuss the proposed pavilion for the *Water Lilies*. Two days later he sends a preliminary plan for a sky-lighted elliptical rotunda in line with Monet's intentions, as well as an alternative circular groundplan. At this stage, four multi-panel compositions are part of the twelve-panel ensemble: *Three Willows* (four panels running 17 meters wide, visible in fig. nos. 101, 102, and 104), *The Clouds*, *Green Reflections*, and *Agapanthus*. In the space between the water lily decorations and the ceiling, Monet plans to add a decorative frieze (cat. no. 156). Coordinating the radii of an ellipse encompassing compositions of different sizes raises complex architectural problems that require expensive solutions. Throughout October, November, and December, Bonnier works closely with Monet, whose concept for the building project evolves constantly.[14]

October 10 or 11 Georges Bernheim drives Gimpel to Giverny in his Panhard. A white-liveried butler serves an elaborate lunch in the yellow-on-yellow dining room (see fig. no. 65), reached via a blue-on-blue anteroom, both installed with Japanese prints. Monet had obtained the two sideboards near Fécamp, and he had painted them—as well as the three side tables and the chairs—in tones of yellow. Monet confirms to Bernheim that he will donate twelve of his recent decorative paintings for installation in the gardens on the boulevard des Invalides side of the new Rodin Museum, if a structure is constructed to his specifications. Monet also shows them *Women in the Garden* (fig. no. 14) and confides, "Today the State has agreed to buy it from me for 200,000 francs and has asked for two years to pay for it; it's to compensate me for the canvases that I am giving to the Rodin Museum."[15]

October 14–25 Press coverage of the negotiations under way between Monet and the State begins. Both Thiébault-Sisson and Alexandre publish insiders' accounts. Monet objects to their claims that the State has already agreed to purchase *Women in the Garden* and stresses that the agreement is contingent upon funding, pending parliamentary approval. Another article reports that Monet has offered his Giverny home and all remaining works to the State as a museum, reportedly even proposing a curator.[16]

November 14 Monet's eightieth birthday. Invited for the occasion, the Duke de Trévise writes an extensive account of this and another visit, which Monet will review prior to its publication in *La Revue de l'art ancien et moderne* in January and February 1927, supplemented by photographs taken by Claude Choumoff at a later date. Thiébault-Sisson had unsuccessfully proposed that Monet use his birthday for political gain by inviting high-ranking officials.[17]

November 16 First reference in the press to the possibility that Monet should be offered the Académie des Beaux-Arts seat now vacant after the death of Luc-Olivier Merson. By January 1921 Monet has declined the honor, to the dismay of his supporters, who are aware that the ongoing negotiations with the State can only be hampered by his easily misunderstood contempt for such official recognition.[18]

1921

January 21–February 2 Forty-five paintings by Monet (see cat. nos. 83, 138, 154, and possi-

107. Claude Monet, *The Japanese Bridge*, 1922. Oil on canvas; 89 × 116 cm, 35 × 45 11/16 in. Courtesy of Sotheby's [W 1921].

bly 133) are exhibited in a retrospective at the Bernheim-Jeune Gallery, Paris.[19]

January 26 Monet complains to the Bernheim brothers about an article commissioned by them from Marcel Pays that appears this day in *Excelsior*: "If you ever want to send a journalist to me, let me know in advance please, or better, never do it: these gentlemen have a way of making me talk which is hardly to my taste and moreover they are inclined to change totally what I tell them." Pays quotes the artist: "Alas, I see less and less. . . . I used to paint out-of-doors facing the sun. Today I need to avoid lateral light, which darkens my colors. Nevertheless, I always paint at the times of day most propitious for me, as long as my paint tubes and brushes are not mixed up. . . . I will paint almost blind as Beethoven composed completely deaf." Such an admission is perhaps imprudent during the current debate over State funding for Monet's project.[20]

January–March Bonnier, whom Monet has evidently requested to try another elliptical plan rather than a circular one, reports back that the difficulties are insurmountable. Unhappy with a circular scheme, Monet then proposes to Léon that the problem be solved by reducing the number of works in his intended donation from twelve to eight or ten. In response, the Ministry of Fine Arts proposes renovating an existing building under its auspices.[21]

February 2 Monet sends *Women in the Garden* to Paris, now that the State has agreed to

purchase it for 200,000 francs, which Monet will receive in May.[22]

February 21 Geffroy has begun to write a biography of Monet.[23]

March 20 Monet complains to Gaston Bernheim that the illustrations chosen for Alexandre's monograph are mostly works that have already been reproduced many times and that there are no figure paintings. Arrangements are made to photograph some figure paintings.[24]

April 1 Inspection by Bonnier, Clemenceau, Geffroy, and Léon of the Jeu de Paume and Orangerie buildings on the Place de la Concorde, possible structures to be renovated for Monet's decorative ensemble. Clemenceau rejects the Jeu de Paume but urges Monet to agree to the Orangerie, which had the previous December been placed under the administration of the Luxembourg Museum.

Monet inspects the Orangerie with Léon Bérard (Minister of Public Instruction and Fine Arts), architect Victor Blavette, Bonnier, Clemenceau, Geffroy, and Léon on April 6. Presumably on a visit to the Louvre this day, Monet tells Clemenceau that his favorite painting is Watteau's *Embarkation for the Island of Cythera*.[25]

April 17 Monet writes to Léon that he should cooperate with Bonnier to speed along the renovations at the Orangerie, warning that his donation will be nullified should he die before the space is ready. But by April 25 Monet again writes to Léon that he wishes to renounce his

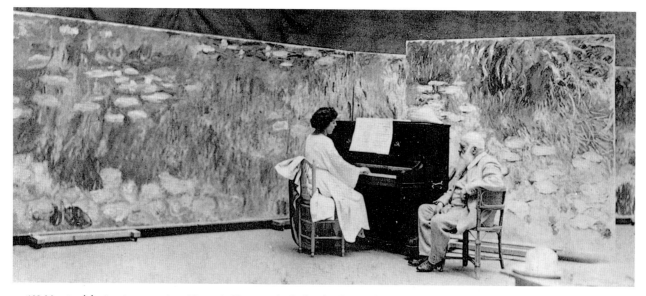

108. Monet and the American opera singer Marguerite Namara in the third studio, photographed by Harry B. Lachman in July 1922.

donation rather than compromise his original intentions by installing his decorations in the narrow Orangerie space.[26]

April 30 André comes to Giverny with a group of American friends, possibly from The Art Institute of Chicago, which around now commissions André (through Durand-Ruel) to paint Monet's portrait (one version in a private collection, one in The Art Institute of Chicago).[27]

Mid-May The Butlers return to Giverny from America, although by winter Alice (Lily) Butler will return to New York.[28]

June Probably early in the month, Clemenceau visits Giverny with Count Sanji Kuroki and his wife, Princess Matsukata (the baron's daughter); the Japanese collectors buy a 1907 *Water Lilies* painting (cat. no. 136). The guests later send Monet a group of snapshots taken during the visit (see fig. no. 106). Monet has many visitors now, including Elder, who is gathering material for a book about the artist.[29]

June 1 In a spirit of compromise, Monet asks Alexandre to inform Léon and Bérard that he will reconsider and even enlarge his donation if the Orangerie space can be extended three or four meters, thus allowing him to create ensembles in two rooms instead of one.

On June 19, replying to Alexandre that Bonnier could be replaced as architect if need be, Monet reports that he still has not heard anything from Léon about his last proposal and now has a serious offer for some of his *Water Lilies* panels and will need to sell. Bonnier is replaced by year's end.[30]

September 30 Publication by Éditions Bernheim-Jeune of *Claude Monet* by Alexandre.[31]

Before October 12 Monet takes a ten-day trip to the seashore with Blanche and Michel; they visit Clemenceau at Bernouville for several days beginning October 3 or 4 and stop at the Nantes Museum on their way home. The next month, Monet promises to donate a painting to the museum.[32]

Mid-October–Early November While receiving many visitors, Monet rearranges the installation of works in his first and second studios, which have been depleted by recent sales. Presumably among these recent sales are a group of as many as ten works bought for or by Baron Matsukata.[33]

October 30 A day after Clemenceau visits Giverny, Monet writes to him outlining in detail his proposal for the *Water Lilies* donation. Resigned to the Orangerie site, Monet has this summer "reduced several motifs." Instead of twelve panels, Monet now conceives of a suite of eighteen to be arranged in two rooms, a (lost) draft for which he encloses: in the second room his *Three Willows* composition would face *Green Reflections*, and to each side would be a 6-meter-wide panel (possibly cat. no. 159). Clemenceau immediately discusses this possibility with Léon, who agrees to Monet's new two-room proposal, putting the donation back on track by November 2, although the news needs to remain confidential until an official order can be issued. Clemenceau also proposes that Léon consider accepting for the Louvre the unfinished *Self-Portrait* (cat. no. 144) that he had rescued from Monet in 1917 when the artist threatened to destroy it.[34]

November 8 Clemenceau brings Léon and Bonnier to Giverny to discuss revived donation plans. The following day Monet provides Léon with a list of works for each room. Although Monet refers to eighteen panels in the text

of this letter, the accompanying list includes twenty panels grouped into four compositions for each room: *Green Reflections* (two panels), *Agapanthus* (now two panels), *The Clouds* (three panels, considerably reworked since December 1920 but eventually dropped from the project), *Morning* (three panels not included in the December 1920 ensemble, and eventually reworked by Monet, who replaces one of the panels with two half panels), *Three Willows* (four panels, eventually reworked into two compositions), *Reflections of Trees* (two panels not included in the December 1920 ensemble), and two 6-meter-wide panels to be determined (see cat. no. 158). Léon tells Monet to expect the renovation work to be completed by spring 1922, which will allow him another three to four months' work on the paintings and a final chance to compare the paintings with the motifs at his garden pond.[35]

December 14 Léon assures Clemenceau that a working budget will be approved in a few days. He has selected a new architect, Camille Lefèvre, recently appointed as architect to the Louvre.[36]

1922

January Lefèvre makes plans for the Orangerie rooms that correspond to the panels specified by Monet in his November 9, 1921, letter to Léon, except that in the second room there will now be four 6-meter-wide panels installed as two facing diptychs. The total number of panels at issue is now twenty-two. Meanwhile, Monet is hard at work.[37]

January 4–21 Exhibition at the Durand-Ruel Gallery, New York, of nineteen paintings by Monet (see cat. no. 154).

109. Monet in the third studio, photographed by Henri Manuel, late 1923/early 1924.

110. Monet seated in the first studio, probably 1923 or 1924. Note the artist's dark corrective glasses on his desk.

February 5 Death of Paul Durand-Ruel. Monet does not attend the funeral in Paris on February 7.[38]

February–March A flurry of last-minute revisions takes place as all parties strive to put the *Water Lilies* donation under contract.[39]

April 12 Monet and Léon notarize a provisional act of donation in Vernon, referring to the January 20, 1920, groundplan by Lefèvre, modified only insofar as the *Agapanthus* diptych is now replaced by a single 6-meter-wide panel (*Setting Sun*—possibly cat. no. 159). The paintings are to be finished by April 1924. The estimated cost to the State for renovations is 600,000 francs. The contract will receive final State approval on December 4.[40]

May 4 Monet asks Bénédite to arrange for the paintings (see cat. no. 93) sold to Matsukata in mid-October to be picked up. Monet writes to Clemenceau that his eyesight is gone, and, as a result, he stops working.

Clemenceau replies that Monet's eye problems could be solved with a simple operation. Around this time Clemenceau composes "Philosophical reflections from the very high concerning the very low," in which God visits Monet, reminding him that "Over a year ago, a wizard [Clemenceau] invited you to the cure. You put it off like those weak people who await everything tomorrow. Today's crisis results. To get out of it, the same wizard shouts to you, 'It's time.' And you still reply, 'Tomorrow.' The clock will not stop for you."[41]

May 8 Monet writes to Elder that he ruined his decorations over the winter in a final effort to perfect them, that he is almost blind and unable to work, and that he has destroyed several of his large panels.[42]

June 25 Clemenceau comes to Giverny. Monet thanks Geffroy for sending his newly published biography of the artist, but he feels that the quality of the color plates obliges them to halt distribution.[43]

July Even though Monet is temporarily back at work on his large panels, he agrees that Marguerite Namara can return to Giverny, where she will give a recital in the third studio. American painter/photographer Harry B. Lachman takes photographs of the visit (see fig. no. 108). These show 1-meter-wide and 2-meter-wide panels (including one used for *Morning*, as installed at the Orangerie), evidently painted as extensions for longer panels to provide a variety of flexible new configurations for Monet's constantly revised ensemble.[44]

September 8 Monet goes to Paris for a consultation with Dr. Charles Coutela, an eminent opthamologist: his better left eye sees only 1/10. With drops prescribed for this eye, Monet can see two or three times better and thus wants to finish his decorations before any operation. Monet's disappointment that no construction work is yet under way at the Orangerie prompts the removal of some forty-five orange trees from the site only days afterward.[45]

October 15 Joseph Durand-Ruel comes to Giverny. In recent weeks, Monet had been painting a large number of works in his garden with motifs familiar to the dealer, who claims that the paintings are so "black and sad" that they could hardly be marketed.[46]

Probably Late October Elder and his wife visit Giverny and are shocked by the disarray in the large studio: "I saw the frames in the back of the workshop against the wall, those big frames on which Claude Monet fixed those ephemeral confessions of his water lily pond. Shreds of torn canvas hung on the edges. The trace of the knife is still vivid, and the painting bleeds like a wound. The nails are in place; the canvas is still stretched. A raging hand . . . lacerated the panels without bothering to take the canvas off patiently as one would with a precious rug being put away. . . . Under the table is the pile of canvases that the servants have been ordered to burn."[47]

November 9 Monet, complaining of nightmares, asks Clemenceau to have Coutela postpone the operation scheduled for November 18.[48]

December 14 Monet reminds Georges Durand-Ruel that he has honored Durand-Ruel's and the Bernheims' request (made two years earlier) that he charge other dealers double. The artist wonders why they have made no purchases since then, and he now considers himself free of any obligation.[49]

1923

January–February At the Neuilly clinic of Dr. Coutela, Monet undergoes surgery for the removal of the cataract on his right eye, probably on January 8 or 10. He reacts badly to the local anesthetic and recuperates in Paris until January 14.

111. Monet in his garden, probably 1924.

112. Monet in the central pathway of his garden, probably 1925.

He returns to Coutela's clinic on January 31 for a second operation on his right eye and remains there, a very difficult patient, to recuperate. Visitors include the Kojiro Matsukatas.

Monet is allowed to leave the clinic to visit the Orangerie with Clemenceau and Léon on February 17. He returns to Giverny the next day.[50]

March–April Clemenceau and Coutela make visits to Giverny, delivering dark corrective eyeglasses and urging a third operation, on Monet's left eye.[51]

March Exhibition at the Durand-Ruel Gallery, New York, of eighteen works by Monet (see cat. no. 52).

May 18 Monet donates one of his World War I garden paintings (cat. no. 151) to the Grenoble Museum.

July 16 Monet informs the Bernheim brothers that he has now signed canvases that they bought from him recently: some dozen works, including five *Water Lilies* paintings, all to be sold by the dealers to pharmaceuticals magnate Henri Canonne, who amasses a collection of over forty works by Monet (see cat. nos. 133 and 135) almost all at once. Monet misdates at least one of the earlier works that he now signs with difficulty. In late August, the Bernheim brothers visit Giverny to acquire still more canvases for their client Canonne, including additional *Water Lilies* variations.[52]

July 18 Dr. Coutela, assisted by Dr. Jean Rebière, performs a third operation on Monet's right eye at Giverny. Monet's nervousness makes the procedure under local anesthetic extremely difficult, and Coutela is apprehensive, but when he examines Monet on July 20, he is satisfied. Perhaps during this recuperation,

Georges Bernheim sends to Monet two seascapes from the Salon of 1865 (see cat. no. 4) as a nostalgic diversion.[53]

August–November Monet has difficulty acclimating himself to new eyeglasses provided by Coutela. Because Monet now sees everything yellowed, Coutela provides tinted lenses to counter the problem and again suggests operating on the left eye. Monet wants to know whether any other painter has had such treatment with successful results. Thanks to yet another pair of corrective eyeglasses, received from Germany in October, Monet goes back to work on his decorations.[54]

October 20 The Durand-Ruel brothers visit Giverny and buy four paintings, but find the many recent garden paintings Monet hopes to sell "atrocious and violent." Considering that Monet had told Elder in 1922 that he wished to paint the Japanese bridge with wisteria, perhaps the dark versions of this motif (see cat. no. 155 and fig. no. 107) are at issue.[55]

November 11 Clemenceau again discusses with Léon the donation of Monet's *Self-Portrait* (cat. no. 144) to the Louvre.[56]

1924

January While Giverny is again flooded, Monet works on his decorations "as if he had an eternity before himself," according to Clemenceau, who wants the project finished on schedule.[57]

January 4–18 More than sixty paintings (see cat. nos. 32, 73, 87, and 152) by Monet are exhibited at the Georges Petit Gallery, Paris, to benefit victims of the devastating September 1, 1923, earthquake in Tokyo. Twenty-four of these works belong to the Matsukata collection, including two late works. Unwilling to exhibit

at this time a large panel like those promised to the State (see fig. no. 100), Monet has Clemenceau urge Léon to force Bénédite not to include it.[58]

January 18 Monet writes to Coutela that he has received new glasses, although with them he sees even less. He also asks for a bill, which comes to 10,000 francs.[59]

February Exhibition at the Durand-Ruel Gallery, New York, of ten *Water Lilies* paintings (see cat. nos. 125 and 139).

March 1 Concerned that work at the Orangerie is nearly complete, Clemenceau writes to Monet: "You decided that your work, interrupted when you were at the end of the race, would be taken up again with half vision. And you found a way to produce a realized masterpiece (I am talking of the *Cloud* panel) and some marvelous preparations. Thereupon, Monet told himself: there is nothing to do but continue. But the good Lord himself will tell you that one cannot make · miracles all the time. You are only a man, my friend, and I am greatly glad of that, for if you were the good Lord you would be quite annoying." Whether the *Cloud* panel referred to is the revised version of a triptych photographed in December 1920 or the four-panel-wide composition (see fig. no. 116) showing two thin willow trees silhouetted against clouds reflected on the pond's surface, is not known.[60]

April–June Although Clemenceau dissuades Coutela from seeing his patient at this time, Coutela prescribes new Zeiss glasses, apparently on the recommendation of Denis. Denis's friend, painter André Barbier, delivers these eyeglasses to Monet on June 6 and acts as a liaison between Monet and Denis's oculist, Dr. Jacques Mawas, a research scientist, who comes to Giverny. In June or July, while working out-of-doors, Monet

114. The water lily garden, probably photographed in 1924 and published in *L'Illustration*, January 15, 1927.

113. Monet seated in his garden, photographed by Nickolas Muray, probably July 1926. The Museum of Modern Art, New York, Gift of Mrs. Nickolas Muray.

complains that he sees only blue and thus chooses colors on the basis of tube labels. In response, Barbier has Monet's eyeglasses tinted pale yellow. Monet also asks Barbier to get special paintbrushes for him.[61]

June 29 The deadline for delivery long past, Clemenceau, Léon, and apparently Lefèvre come to Giverny and learn that Monet is still unwilling to release his ensemble. Monet now works toward a January 1925 deadline.[62]

October The Durand-Ruel Gallery moves to the avenue Friedland. Around this same time, the Bernheim-Jeune Gallery also moves, to the avenue Matignon.[63]

October 8 Angered by Monet's never-ending refinements on his panels, Clemenceau writes: "First you wanted to finish the incomplete parts. That was hardly necessary, but understandable. Then you had the absurd idea to improve the others. Who knows better than yourself that a painter's ideas are constantly changing. If you went back to your *Rouen Cathedral* paintings you would change them. You made new works, the majority of which were and still are masterpieces, if you have not ruined them. Then you wanted to make super-masterpieces—and with an impaired visual faculty that you yourself refused to have corrected. . . . At your request a contract was

completed between yourself and France. The State has kept its part. You asked for a postponement of your deadline and with my intervention you got it. I acted in good faith and now you make me appear like a conspirator who does a disservice both to art and to France to accommodate a friend's foibles. . . . You must finish this honorably."[64]

October 30 Monet and Blanche go to Paris for lunch with Chéret, who is now blind.[65]

November In an article published in *Jardinage* this month, Georges Truffaut proclaims the gardens as Monet's greatest work.[66]

November 8 *Art News* publishes a first-hand account of Monet's final months at work.[67]

November–December Barbier brings the paintbrushes that Monet ordered in late July. Monet shows him and Mawas two versions of a *Japanese Bridge* composition, one with inaccurate, dark colors done before the operation (see cat. no. 155) and another with more accurate tones done afterward in forty-four work sessions (see fig. no. 107). Monet's eyesight improves with new Meyrowitz glasses prescribed by Mawas.[68]

November 28 The Municipal Museum of Art and Industry in Saint-Etienne buys a 1907

Water Lilies tondo from Monet for 30,000 francs (plus 200 francs for the frame).[69]

December 22 Clemenceau writes: "I know that you have begun the large panel again."[70]

1925

January–March Learning that Monet has written to Léon to revoke his donation, Clemenceau cancels his intended visit to Giverny and will have nothing further to do with someone who breaks his word of honor to France. Clemenceau writes to Blanche on February 12 that he no longer wishes to be involved with the donation and that, should Léon contact him, he will tell him to talk to Monet. Realizing that his strategy is pointless, however, on March 22 Clemenceau returns to Giverny to reestablish his friendship with the artist.

On March 25 Monet writes to Mawas, apologizing for not having tried his newest glasses. "When a singer has lost his voice he retires; the painter operated on for a cataract has to give up painting, and it is this which I could not do. Excuse my candor."[71]

May 7 Death of Marthe Butler at Giverny.[72]

July 17 Monet writes to Barbier: "I warn you in advance that I must be free at 10 A.M., being hard at work and with an unequaled joy, for, since your last visit [in April], my vision is completely improved. I am working as never before, satisfied with what I am doing, and if the new eyeglasses are still better, then I ask only that I live to be 100 years old."[73]

August Monet works on a group of easel-size paintings of his house and rose garden.[74]

115. The *Water Lilies* murals installed in the east room of the Orangerie, Paris.

September–November Monet writes to Geffroy that he worked hard all summer, despite variable weather, and now can get back to his large panels before finally sending them off. He now anticipates delivering the panels the following spring.[75]

1926

January 4 Monet promises Denis that, should he ever again go to Paris, he will see the ceiling fresco that his young colleague has painted above a staircase at the Petit Palais Museum. The history of French art is its subject, culminating with a group portrait of Cézanne, Courbet, Monet, Renoir, and Rodin.[76]

February 8 Clemenceau writes that he is happy to learn that the first shipment of panels to the Orangerie will occur as soon as the paint is dry.[77]

April 4 Clemenceau comes to Giverny to tell Monet that Geffroy died that morning. Afterward, Clemenceau writes: "The human machine is coming apart at the seams. He is stoic and even gay at moments. His panels are finished and will not be touched again. But it is beyond his powers to separate them from himself. . . . The poor Monet did not even find the strength to make a tour of his garden and the expense becomes such that he asked if it would not be best to give it up."[78]

June 14 Marriage at Giverny of Alice (Lily) Butler and Roger Toulgouat.[79]

June 30 Vuillard, Roussel, his daughter Annette, and her husband Jacques Saloman come to Giverny to find Monet briefly recovered. In the third studio, they ask why he has a large sheet of absorbent paper, and he replies that tube paints have too much oil for his needs.[80]

July 2 Gimpel comes to Giverny and buys two figure paintings for a total of 200,000 francs.[81]

Probably July Nickolas Muray photographs Monet at Giverny (fig. no. 113).[82]

July 17 Gimpel returns to Giverny with his wife and buys two more paintings for a total of 150,000 francs. Monet tells them that in the last two weeks he has destroyed some sixty paintings, although Blanche says that this is an exaggeration. Blanche cuts the paintings out of the frames with a knife and then Monet oversees incineration.[83]

Late August Dr. Rebière X-rays Monet and learns that he has an incurable tumor on his left lung. At Clemenceau's urging, specialists are consulted; they diagnose Monet as having pulmonary sclerosis.[84]

September 18 Monet writes to Clemenceau that he can eat and sleep again, thanks to medication: "You should know that if my powers do not return to the point where I can do what I want with the panels, I have decided to give them as they are, at least a part of them."[85]

October 4 Monet writes his last letter, to Léon, expressing his intention now to get back

to work slowly and to arrange for him and the architect to come to Giverny to discuss details.[86]

October 25 Marriage at Giverny of Simone Salerou and Robert Piguet.[87]

November–Early December Clemenceau visits on November 21. Monet talks about his garden and predicts that Clemenceau will see the flowers next spring without him. Clemenceau again visits the bedridden and suffering painter on December 2.[88]

December 5 Clemenceau returns to be at Monet's bedside when he dies around 1 P.M. According to one account, Monet's last gesture is to hold up two fingers as an indication of the width he intends for the frames of the *Water Lilies* murals to be installed in the Orangerie.[89]

December 8 Monet is buried in the family plot in the Giverny cemetery, with Clemenceau in attendance. What Monet had hoped would be a small family affair, without ceremony, instead draws a crowd and gets extensive press coverage. Artist Henri Vidal will recall that on a table in Monet's studio there was a volume of Baudelaire's poems open to "L'Etranger," a poem about a man who loves clouds more than anything else.[90]

December 12 Clemenceau gives Monet's *Self-Portrait* (cat. no. 144) to the Louvre, where it is installed a few days later next to Delacroix's *Self-Portrait*, in the same room as Manet's *Olympia* (fig. no. 9).[91]

116. The *Water Lilies* murals installed in the west room of the Orangerie, Paris.

Postscript

May 16, 1927 Private viewing of Monet's *Water Lilies* murals installed at the Orangerie, Paris, one day before the official inauguration on May 17. The public opening follows three days later. When someone notices a repaired tear in one of the Orangerie panels, Clemenceau laments that Monet frequently slashed works out of dissatisfaction and anger, estimating that he may have burned five hundred works.[92]

Because Monet left no will, Michel Monet inherits everything. He subsequently lives off sales of works from his father's collection as well as Monet works left unsold during the artist's lifetime. He builds a country house, where he resides with Gabrielle Bonaventure, a former model, whom he marries in 1931. Michel allows Blanche, who had been caring for Monet since the death of her husband, Jean Monet, in 1914, to stay on at Giverny. She dies on December 8, 1947, after which time the guardianship of the Giverny house passes to her brother Jean-Pierre Hoschedé, who dies on May 27, 1961. Michel dies in a car accident on February 3, 1966. He had willed the remainder of Monet's holdings to the Musée Marmottan, Paris.

June 1971 Renovated to accommodate Michel Monet's bequest, the Musée Marmottan presents its rich holdings of the late works by Monet.

May 1980 Magnificently restored by Director Gérald van der Kemp under the auspices of the Académie des Beaux-Arts, Monet's Giverny house and gardens open to the public.

Notes to Chronology

All works are fully listed in Works Cited (pages 267–70). Citations within each note are organized chronologically by their date of publication. W, the most frequent citation, stands for: Wildenstein, Daniel. *Claude Monet: Biographie et catalogue raisonné*. Lausanne, vol. I, 1974; vol. II, 1979; vol. III, 1979; vol. IV, 1985; vol. V, 1991.

This reference work includes all of Monet's surviving correspondence (here referred to as letters). Unfortunately, Wildenstein's plan to number the letters in chronological order was thwarted as new letters (or fuller versions of partially known ones) were discovered after the publication of the volumes where they ideally belonged. In these notes, letters that later appeared in more complete forms are recognizable by an asterisk (*) following the letter number. The letters that Wildenstein found after the publication of the volume in which they should have appeared are here chronologically integrated with the letters that were first published. The résumé below indicates in which volume the reader may find the letters as cited in these notes.

PJ stands for *pièces justificatives*, documents included by Wildenstein that were not written by Monet, but were written to or about him. Monet's drawings (indicated by D) are catalogued in Wildenstein volume V.

Volume I: letters 1–226; PJ 1–84

Volume II: letters 227–766; PJ 85–112

Volume III: letters 767–1433; PJ 113–50

Volume IV: letters 1434–2685; PJ 151–344; 2494* (page 292).

Volume V: letters 2686–3106 (pages 183–88); PJ 345–62; all * references (with the exception of 2494*).

1840–1859

1. W, I, 1 and letter 2390.

2. W, I, 1.

3. W, I, 1–2.

4. Jean-Aubry 1922, 20, 25, 27; W, I, 2–3.

5. Leslie, 29, and for French translations, see Leslie in the list of Works Cited.

6. Jean-Aubry 1922, 31.

7. Thiébault-Sisson 1900; Jean-Aubry 1911, 1; Elder, 15–16; Thiébault-Sisson 1926; House 1978b, 679; W, I, 4–5; W, V, 59ff., 133ff., 146.

8. W, I, 4.

9. Rewald 1961, 102; Bailly-Herzberg 1975, 48–49.

10. Le Roux, 20; W, I, 5.

11. Jean-Aubry 1922, 36; W, I, 6.

12. W, I, 4.

13. Elder, 62–64.

14. W, I, 6.

15. Courbet, 166–67, 629.

16. Jean-Aubry 1922, 36; W, I, 6.

17. Jean-Aubry 1922, 40–41; Baudelaire 1973 I, 573–80; Delouche 1980, 28.

18. W, I, 7–8 and letters 1–2.

19. Jean-Aubry 1922, 37–42; Baudelaire 1976, 665–66.

1860–1864

1860

1. W, I, 12.

2. Elder, 23–24; W, I, 8–10 and letters 3–4.

3. Geffroy 1922, 10–15; W, I, 10–11.

4. W, I, 9–10 and letters 3–4.

5. W, V, D511 and letter 5.

6. W, I, 12 and letter 4.

7. Moreau-Nélaton, 78–79; Bailly-Herzberg 1975, 50, 52.

1861

8. Jean-Aubry 1922, 48–51.

9. Le Roux, 2; Thiébault-Sisson 1900; Arnyvelde, 32–34; Geffroy 1922, 24; W, I, 12–14.

10. Baudelaire 1973 II, 196–97, 752–53; *Japonisme*, 72.

1862

11. W, I, 14.

12. Robinson July 3, 1892; Thiébault-Sisson 1900; Jean-Aubry 1922, 54–55; Elder, 16–18; W, I, 14–19; W, V, PJ 347.

13. W, I, 20.

14. Elder, 19–20; Renoir, Jean, 122–23; W, I, 20–24.

1863

15. W, I, 24 and letter 6; Bazille, 50–51.

16. W, I, 25.

1864

17. Clemenceau 1928, 58–59; W, I, 16, 26 and letters 7, 15.

18. W, I, 26.

19. Bailly-Herzberg 1975, 55.

20. W, I, 26; Bazille, 90–92.

21. Jean-Aubry 1922, 103–04; W, I, 26–27 and letters 8–14; Bazille, 97.

22. W, I, 27 and letter 12.

23. W, I, 27 and letter 13.

24. W, I, 28; Bazille, 97–98.

25. Bazille, 100.

1865–1869

1865

1. W, I, 28–29; Bazille, 104.

2. W, I, 29 and letters 17–18.

3. W, I, 29–30 and letters 16, 2391; Isaacson.

4. W, I, 30 and letters 19–21; Bazille, 109, 115.

5. Courbet, 273.

6. W, I, 30–31; Young, Andrew I, lx.

7. W, I, 31; Bazille, 115–16.

1866

8. W, I, 31–32; Bazille, 120.

9. Courbet, 277; Levine 1994, 8.

10. Bailly-Herzberg 1972, 211–16; *Aspects*, 74.

11. Geffroy 1922, 36–37; Trévise, 122; Gimpel, 87; Roskill; W, I, 32–35 and letters 25, 2686, 27, 44; Distel 1995, 314.

12. Zola 1866; Bailly-Herzberg 1972, 250–51; W, I, 31–35 and letters 23–26, PJ 12.

13. W, I, 35.

14. W, I, 35; Courbet, 298–300.

15. W, letters 29–30.

1867

16. Goncourt, chap. 83.

17. Billot; W, I, 35, PJ 13; Courbet, 303; *Origins*, 249–50.

18. W, I, 36, PJ 14; Bazille, 135.

19. *Aspects*, 55; *Japonisme*, 78.

20. W, I, 37.

21. W, I, 36 and letters 2687, 32–33; Bazille, 136–37.

22. W, I, 37 and letters 32–33.

23. W, I, 37 and letters 31–33; Levine 1994, 9.

24. W, I, 37 and letters 33–35, 36a–b; Stevens, 261.

25. W, I, 38 and letters 34, 36b.

26. W, I, 37 and letter 37.

27. W, I, 38 and letter 39; Bazille, 149.

1868

28. W, I, 38, PJ 17.

29. W, letter 2688.

30. Jean-Aubry 1922, 66; W, I, 38.

31. W, I, 41.

32. W, I, 39 and letter 40.

33. Zola 1868; W, I, 39, PJ 18–20, 23; Wagner, 619n18.

34. Flescher, 360; *Monet in Holland,* 74.

35. W, I, 40, PJ 21–22.

36. W, I, 40 and letters 41–42.

37. Geffroy 1922, 40–41; W, I, 40–41 and letter 42, PJ 22.

38. W, I, 40 and letter 43, PJ 22, 27.

39. W, I, 40–41 and letter 43.

40. W, letter 43.

41. W, I, 41 and letters 44–48, PJ 25; Stuckey 1981, 104–06.

1869

42. W, I, 42.

43. W, I, 42, PJ 23.

44. W, I, 42, PJ 25; Bazille, 172; *Origins,* 322.

45. Poulain, 121; W, I, 42 and letter 49; Fernier II, no. 326.

46. W, I, 45 and letters 50, 52–53; *Aspects,* 36–51; Herbert 1988, 210–19.

47. Kendall 1993, 85–107.

48. Maupassant, 87.

49. Rewald 1961, 212–13; House 1978b, 679; W, I, 45 and letter 54.

1870–1874

1870

1. W, I, 45.

2. Elder, 69; Gimpel, 155; W, I, 45–46, 186; W, letter 2587; Rewald 1986b, 299–300.

3. W, I, 46.

4. W, I, 51 and letter 61; P, I, 65–69.

5. W, I, 51.

6. *Renoir,* 296.

7. W, I, 51.

8. *Degas,* 58.

9. W, I, 51 and letter 55; *Monet in Holland,* 39.

10. W, I, 52; Flescher, 37.

11. W, I, 55n379.

12. W, I, 52; House 1978a, 636–38.

1871

13. W, I, 52.

14. W, I, 55.

15. Dewhurst, 40; W, I, 52–55; P, I, 175; P, V, 282–83.

16. W, I, 55 and letters 57–59; House 1978a, 637–38.

17. Rewald 1961, 263; W, I, 56; *Monet in Holland,* 19ff., 72–82.

18. W, I, 56; *Monet in Holland,* 39–43, 182; House 1978a, 638.

19. W, I, 56 and letter 59; *Monet in Holland,* 29–32, 40–41, 182.

20. *Monet in Holland,* 41–43, 182.

21. Jean-Aubry 1922, 79; W, I, 57.

22. Walter 1966, 333–35; W, I, 58 and letter 61; Tucker 1982, 10.

1872

23. Thiébault-Sisson 1927a, 3; W, I, 62–63, 87; P, I, 71; Tucker 1982, 10.

24. Jean-Aubry 1922, 80–81; W, I, 57–58; Courbet, 447–48.

25. Hôtel Drouot, lot 183.

26. W, I, 61 and letter 63; Pissarro, 8.

27. Rewald 1961, 288; W, I, 61–62; Delafond, 125–26.

1873

28. W, I, 63n435; W, letter 2587.

29. Whistler, 252–53.

30. W, I, 63.

31. W, I, 65 and letter 64.

32. Rewald 1961, 309; W, I, 66 and letter 65.

33. W, I, 64 and letters 66–67, 70–72, PJ 28 bis, 28 ter; P, I, 79, 85.

34. W, I, 66 and letter 69.

35. W, I, 64.

36. W, I, 66–69 and letters 74–75.

37. W, I, 63.

38. W, I, 65; Rewald 1986a, 383–93.

39. W, I, 69 and letters 75–76.

1874

40. Bodelsen, 332; *Aspects,* 54–58; W, I, 80–82 and letter 76.

41. W, I, 70–71; *Monet in Holland,* 43, 145–46; *Aspects,* 78; *Splendid Legacy,* 363.

42. Hôtel Drouot, lot 26.

43. Rewald 1961, 309–40; W, I, 69–71; *Impressionism; Schiff; Aspects,* 109–10; Moffett, 51–59, 92–142; Spate, 92–99; *Paris 1874.*

44. Tucker 1982, 50.

45. Walter 1966, 336; W, I, 71–72 and letter 78.

46. W, I, 72; *Manet,* 353–64.

47. Walter 1966, 336–40; W, I, 72; Tucker 1982, 47.

48. Rewald 1961, 336; Rewald 1986a, 394–95; Hôtel Drouot, lot 82.

1875–1879

1875

1. Bodelson, 333–36; W, I, 74.

2. W, letters 79–83.

3. W, I, 87n617.

4. W, letter 84; *Manet,* 347–49; Pickvance, 163.

1876

5. Rewald 1969, 39–42; W, I, 79 and letter 86; P, I, 145–46; Berhaut 1994, 6–7 and letter 1; Distel 1995, 312.

6. Rewald 1961, 366–74; W, I, 79–80; Moffett, 144–86; Stuckey 1987, 25–70; Spate, 112–18.

7. W, I, 80 and letters 88, 91–92, 97; *Aspects,* 61.

8. W, letters 87, 97.

9. W, I, 80.

10. W, I, 79, 82 and letter 89.

11. W, I, 82; *Aspects,* 60.

12. W, I, 82–83 and letter 97; *Aspects,* 58–61.

13. Berhaut 1994, 12.

1877

14. Renoir, Jean, 187; W, I, 83–84 and letters 100–01; Distel 1989, 100; Berhaut 1994, letter 3; Distel 1995, 313.

15. W, I, 84.

16. Rewald 1961, 390–94; W, I, 84 and letter 104; Moffett, 188–240; Spate, 121–25; P, I, 78n3.

17. Bodelson, 336–39.

18. W, I, 87 and letters 103, 106–07, 112.

19. W, I, 73n527.

20. W, I, 88 and letters 98–99.

21. W, I, 81n561, 83, 91.

22. W, I, 87n611, 88 and letter 109.

23. W, I, 87 and letters 110–11.

1878

24. Duret, 98; W, I, 89 and letters 98, 117, 124, PJ 30.

25. W, I, 89.

26. Distel 1995, 314.

27. W, I, 89 and letter 121.

28. P, I, 132; Moffett, 244–47; Distel 1989, 34.

29. W, I, 89.

30. *Japonisme,* 90.

31. W, I, 90; P, I, 112n1.

32. W, I, 91–92 and letters 135, 138; Bodelson, 339–40.

33. Gimpel, 178; W, I, 90.

34. W, I, 92–93 and letters 139–40, PJ 32.

35. W, I, 93–94, 96; Distel 1995, 314.

36. W, I, 93 and letters 141–45.

37. W, letter 148.

1879

38. W, I, 95 and letters 152–53.

39. W, I, 95 and letters 155–56.

40. Moffett, 247–48; Berhaut 1994, letter 15; Distel 1995, 314.

41. Rewald 1961, 421–24; W, I, 95–96 and letter 157; Moffett, 242–89; Spate, 136–37.

42. W, I, 96, PJ 36; Berhaut 1994, letter 19; Distel 1995, 315.

43. W, I, 96–99 and letters 158–59.

44. W, I, 96–97 and letter 3091; Gauguin, 338.

45. W, I, 97–98 and letter 161.

46. W, I, 98.

47. W, I, 98–99 and letters 162–63.

48. W, I, 99–100 and letters 166–67; Distel 1995, 315.

49. W, I, 100, PJ 37.

50. W, I, 100–05; *Aspects,* 65–66.

51. P, I, 131–32.

52. W, I, 105.

53. W, I, 105, PJ 38–39.

54. W, I, 105–06, 115 and letters 168–70.

1880–1884

1880

1. W, I, 106–07, PJ 41.

2. W, I, 107–08.

3. W, I, 109.

4. W, I, 109 and letter 173.

5. W, I, 116 and letter 225; P, I, 177.

6. W, I, 110–11 and letter 176.

7. Zola 1880; W, I, 110–11.

8. W, letters 179, 181–84, 2703.

9. W, I, 112 and letters 186, 191, PJ 45–46.

10. Taboureux, 380; W, I, 115.

11. W, I, 115 and letters 188, 198.

12. W, I, 115 and letters 196, 200.

13. W, I, 115.

14. W, letter 200.

15. W, letter 203.

16. W, I, 116.

1881

17. W, letter 208.

18. Berhaut 1994, letter 23; Distel 1995, 315.

19. W, I, 117 and letter 210.

20. W, I, 117 and letters 211–13; Herbert 1994, 38–43.

21. W, I, 118 and letter 214.

22. Distel 1995, 315.

23. W, I, 118 and letter 218.

24. W, I, 119.

25. W, letter 223.

26. W, I, 120.

27. *Renoir*, 300–01.

28. W, I, 120.

29. W, I, 120; W, II, 5–6.

1882

30. W, II, 1.

31. W, II, 2 and letters 233–38.

32. W, II, 2 and letters 237–38, 243.

33. W, II, 2–4 and letters 241–43.

34. W, II, 2–4 and letters 249–50; P, I, 154–57.

35. Jean-Aubry 1922, 88; Reutersvärd 1950; W, II, 4–5 and letter 263 bis; P, I, 162; Moffett, 378–79, 382–84; Levine 1994, 28–29.

36. W, II, 5 and letters 252*, 2708.

37. W, letters 260, 264, 266, 270; Herbert 1994, 46–54.

38. W, II, 6 and letters 268, 270–71; Distel 1995, 316.

39. W, II, 6.

40. W, II, PJ 85.

41. W, II, 6 and letters 275, 280, 2712, 287.

42. W, II, 9n102.

43. W, letter 287.

44. W, II, 9n102, 21n213; P, I, 249n4.

45. W, II, 9 and letter 295.

46. W, II, 9 and letters 299–300.

47. W, letters 305, 361–62; Distel 1989, 37–38.

1883

48. W, II, 10–12 and letters 307, 310; Herbert 1994, 61–89.

49. W, II, 10–12 and letters 312, 319–20.

50. W, II, 10–12 and letters 314–15, 328.

51. W, letter 321.

52. Pennell I, 310.

53. W, II, 12–13 and letters 306–07, 312–13, 317, 319, 324, 327, 333–34.

54. W, II, 13–14 and letters 336–38, 342; P, I, 184; Levine 1994, 34–38.

55. W, letter 339.

56. Cooper, cat. no. 11; W, II, 21n213 and letter 354.

57. W, II, 17–21 and letters 344–48.

58. W, II, 17 and letters 349–50.

59. W, II, 20 and letters 356, 369; W, III, 43n1052.

60. Huth, 229–31; W, II, 21n213 and letters 372–73, 377–78, 380–85; *Aspects*, 75.

61. Venturi 1939 I, 126–27; W, II, 21 and letter 386.

1884

62. W, letters 460, 462, 467; Morisot, 119, 121.

63. W, II, 21–22 and letters 388–91, 397.

64. Tabarant 1947, 426; W, II, 22–27 and letters 394, 397, 404–05, 430, 450, 502.

65. W, II, 24 and letters 393, 404, 442, PJ 58.

66. W, II, 22 and letter 395.

67. W, II, 37 and letters 397–98, 408, 419, 464, 548–49, 556, 564, 576–77.

68. W, II, 27 and letters 403–04, 415, 460.

69. W, II, 24 and letters 402, 405, 407–08; Baudot, 58.

70. W, II, 24–27 and letters 409–10, 414, 420, 432, 436, 446.

71. W, II, 24–27 and letters 412, 414, 418.

72. W, II, 27 and letters 421–22, 424, 465, 469–70.

73. W, II, 27–28 and letters 435, 438–39, 443, 468–69, 471.

74. W, letters 441–42.

75. W, II, 28–30 and letters 464–78.

76. W, II, 30–32 and letters 489–90, 497–98, 504.

77. Venturi 1939 I, 127–29; W, II, 30 and letters 490–96, 504–07, 510, 512–14, 519–21.

78. W, II, 32 and letters 508, 508 bis (p. 292); Distel 1995, 316.

79. W, II, 32 and letters 516–18.

80. W, II, 32.

81. W, II, 37 and letters 523, 547, 551, 562.

82. W, II, 33, 39 and letters 531, 534.

83. W, II, 33–34 and letters 515, 523, 529–32, 543, 684.

84. Mirbeau 1884; W, II, 33–34, PJ 87; Spate 168–69.

1885–1889

1885

1. W, II, 34–37 and letters 538, 542.

2. W, II, 37 and letters 543–44.

3. W, II, 37–38 and letters 557, 559–60.

4. W, II, 38–39; Spate, 169–70; Levine 1994, 44–46.

5. W, letter 566.

6. Cézanne, 176–80.

7. W, II, 39 and letter 578; P, I, 346.

8. W, letter 592.

9. Maupassant; Robinson Sept. 15, 1892; W, II, 40, 42 and letters 583–91, 602, 604, 635; Herbert 1994, 100–27.

10. W, II, 43 and letters 593–99, 602–08, 612, 614–15, 618–20, 622–34, 645a.

11. W, II, 44n454 and letters 616, 637–38.

12. W, II, 44 and letters 635–41, 647–48.

13. W, II, 44 and letters 642, 644.

1886

14. W, II, 44 and letters 650–52.

15. W, II, 42–43, 46 and letters 605, 611, 638–39, 646–47, 3092 bis.

16. W, II, 46 and letters 654–56, 658–59.

17. Huth, 239; W, II, 47 and letters 665–66, 668, 670, 673, 675.

18. W, III, 1, 4n644; Mirbeau 1990, 12.

19. Perry, 120; W, II, 49–50.

20. Walter 1963 and 1964; W, II, 47–48 and letters 664, 667; W, V, 2945.

21. Huth, 237–40; W, II, 47; P, II, 56, 61; *Aspects*, 75–78.

22. W, II, 48 and letters 669, 671–72; *Monet in Holland*, 43–44, 166–75.

23. Huth, 241–44; W, II, 47; *Aspects*, 77–82.

24. W, II, 48–49 and letters 674, 676–79, 681–82, 684, 694.

25. Stuckey 1987, 123.

26. W, II, 50 and letters 676–78, 690, 699; Delouche 1980, 34.

27. W, II, 50 and letters 684–85.

28. W, II, 50–52 and letters 686–87.

29. W, II, 52 and letters 688–89, 691–92, 696–97.

30. W, II, 52–55 and letters 691–92, 697–700.

31. Geffroy 1897; Geffroy 1922, 1–2, 274–75; Elder, 31–32; Le Braz; Hoschedé I, 33–35; W, II, 55–56 and letters 702, 726; Delouche 1980, 28.

32. W, II, 55–56 and letters 706–18.

33. W, letters 712, 715, 722, 726.

34. W, II, 57 and letter 721.

35. W, II, 57 and letters 729–30.

36. W, II, 57 and letters 731, 734–42, 744; Mirbeau 1990, 10–11, 35–42.

37. W, letter 743.

38. W, letter 746.

39. W, letters 749–51, 753, 755.

40. W, II, 55 and letters 747, 750.

41. W, II, 57–58 and letters 753–60, 762.

1887

42. P, II, 101.

43. W, III, 1–2 and letters 771, 773–79.

44. Robinson July 6, 1892; Rewald 1973 I, 4, 10, and II, 98; W, III, 2 and letters 568, 571, 781–83; P, III, 62; *Monet in Holland*, 84, 183.

45. W, III, 2, 4n647 and letter 784; *Monet in Holland*, 183.

46. Levine 1976, 78–89; W, III, 2–3 and letter 786; P, II, 161–67.

47. W, III, 3 and letters 789, 794.

48. W, III, 1n608.

49. Charteris, 97; W, III, 4.

50. Greta, 78; Breck, 13; Joyes 1975, 24–27; Bruce, 123–25; de Veer, 41, 44; Gerdts 1984, 57–61; *Lasting Impressions*, 45; Gerdts 1993, 23–32, 222ff.

51. W, III, 4 and letters 794–95, 1424; W, V, 2723–24; Mirbeau 1990, 48, 61.

52. Gerdts 1993, 222.

53. Venturi 1939 II, 217–19; W, letter 742.

54. W, III, 4 and letters 797–99, 2727; Mallarmé 1964, 6.

1888

55. W, III, 4–5 and letters 805–12, 815, 820, 824, 827, 829–30.

56. W, III, 6 and letters 810–11, 814, 821.

57. W, III, 8 and letters 2729, 815, 817–18, 822, 825, 841; *Lasting Impressions*, 48, 146–47; Gerdts 1993, 222.

58. W, III, 5 and letters 824, 827–28, 832–33.

59. W, letter 836.

60. W, III, 6 and letters 833, 835, 843–45, 847–48, 855; Rewald 1973 I, 21 and II, 98–99.

61. W, III, 8n683 and letter 846.

62. W, III, 8 and letters 811–12, 814, 819, 849–50, 856, 858, 862; Dixon, 124; *Lasting Impressions*, 50–51, 147.

63. W, III, 8–9 and letters 852–54, 856–57, 2734, 864–65.

64. Gerdts 1993, 222.

65. W, III, 8 and letters 868–69.

66. W, letters 869–71, 873–74, 878.

67. Mallarmé 1964, 14–15, 18–19; W, III, 8–9 and letters 865, 879, 881–82.

68. W, III, 9 and letters 886–88, 891–92; *Monet–Rodin*, 210; P, II, 251.

69. Gerdts 1993, 222.

70. W, letters 2738, 889, 892; *Monet–Rodin*, 24, 33–39.

71. W, letters 893–94.

72. Rewald 1973 I, 22–23, and II, 99; Levine 1976, 89–95; W, III, 9–10, 11n721 and letters 895–97; P, II, 239–42.

73. Pays 1921a; W, letter 1425*.

74. W, III, 10 and letter 905*; Spate, 193–94.

75. W, III, 11 and letters 898, 899, 902–03; P, 242.

76. W, letters 898 bis, 899, 2741, 907.

77. W, letter 901.

78. W, III, 12–13 and letters 2741, 901, 904.

79. W, III, 20n806 and letters 818, 822, 905*.

80. Rewald 1973 I, 34, and II, 99; W, III, 11; *Monet in Holland*, 86, 183.

1889

81. Morisot, 132–33, 137, 145; Mallarmé 1969 III, 212, 254–55, 290–91; W, III, 12 and letters 908, 911, 1007; Levine 1994, 125–36.

82. Le Roux; Rewald 1973 I, 38, and II, 100; Levine 1976, 96, 98, 102–12; W, III, 12n736, 14–17 and letters 909–10; Spate, 198–99; Levine 1994, 99–100.

83. *Monet–Rodin*, 25.

84. W, III, 14 and letter 912; Levine 1994, 103–06.

85. W, letters 912–13.

86. Geffroy 1922, 292–93; W, III, 14–17 and letters 913, 2747, 915, 923, 2748; *Monet in Holland*, 86–87, 183.

87. W, III, 17 and letters 916–17.

88. W, III, 18 and letters 920–30.

89. W, III, 18 and letter 937.

90. W, III, 18 and letters 938–40, 942–43.

91. W, I, PJ 64; W, III, 18 and letters 918, 921, 927, 929, 934, 936, 941, 944–45, 947–50, 952, 954–55, 957–59; *Monet–Rodin*, 212.

92. Rewald 1973 I, 38, 63n90; W, III, 17 and letters 926, 933, 959, 971; *Monet in Holland*, 87–88, 183; Flint, 310–12.

93. W, III, 18–20 and letters 950–51, 953–54, 956, 959–66, 968.

94. Geffroy 1922, 289; W, III, 20 and letters 971, 973–80.

95. W, III, 21, 23; *Monet–Rodin*, 27; Tucker 1989, 61–63.

96. Gerdts 1993, 222.

97. W, letters 979–80.

98. W, I, PJ 65–67; W, III, 21 and letters 969–70, 981–83, 2753–54, 988–91, 2757; *Monet in Holland*, 183.

99. Geffroy 1889; M. 1889; Fitzgerald, 184; W, III, 21 and letters 993–96; *Monet–Rodin*, 45.

100. W, III, 24–27; Gerdts 1993, 33–34, 222.

101. Levine 1976, 102–15; W, III, 22–23, 27 and letters 997–98, 2760; Tucker 1989, 51–55; Levine 1994, 116–24.

102. W, letters 2758, 2762–63, 999*; P, III, 367–68.

103. W, III, 23–24, 27–29 and letters 1000–02, 2764–65, 1004, 1006, 1008–18, 1030–31, 1033–36, 1426*, 2775–76, 1037–39, 1041, 1045, 2777–78.

104. Rewald 1973 I, 43, and II, 100; W, III, PJ 117; P, II, 294.

105. Perry, 123; W, letter 2767.

106. W, II, PJ 88–90; W, III, 34 and letter 1007.

107. W, III, PJ 91.

108. W, III, 28–30 and letters 1020–21, 1023*–28, 2774, 1029*.

1890–1894

1890

1. W, III, 30, 32–33 and letters 1032, 1042–43, 3093, 2780–81, 1046, 2783–84, 1048–51, 2785, 1052–54, 2786, 1061–62, 1072; Tucker 1989, 57–61.

2. Gerdts 1993, 223.

3. Gerdts 1993, 223.

4. W, letters 2785, 2785 bis.

5. Robinson July 21, 1892; W, III, 11n724 and letter 1428*.

6. Rewald 1973 I, 52.

7. W, III, 33–37 and letters 1060*, 1064, 1066–67, 1069; Mirbeau 1990, 101.

8. Morisot, 154; W, III, 34 and letters 1063–65.

9. Clemenceau 1895; Clemenceau 1928, 77, 85; W, letter 2788.

10. W, letter 2789.

11. W, letters 1075, 1077–79; *Monet in Holland*, 91, 184.

12. W, III, 1076; Mirbeau 1990, 111.

13. Trévise, 126; Barotte; Hoschedé I, 47; W, III, 37–38, 40 and letters 1076, 1082, 1085, 1088, 2798, 1096; Seiberling, 84–96.

14. W, letters 1080, 2791, 2794.

15. W, III, 37 and letters 1079, 2791, 1085.

16. W, III, 38 and letter 1085.

1891

17. Rewald 1973 II, 73, 101; W, III, 37; W, letters 2758, 2762, 2801–2802.

18. Robinson July 21, 1892; Manet, Julie, 88; W, letters 1097, 2804–05, 1100, 2810.

19. W, letters 2806, 2815.

20. W, III, 40 and letters 1082–83, 1085, 1088; Tucker 1989, 98.

21. W, III, 40–41 and letters 1102, 2808.

22. W, letters 2793, 1086–87, 1089, 2795–97, 1094–95, 2799, 2803, 2805–11.

23. W, III, 42n1042; P, III, 55, 60.

24. Gerdts 1993, 24.

25. W, letter 1104.

26. Byvanck, 175–78; W, III, 38, 42, 47n1086, and letters 1106–07, 1492*; Brettell; P, III, 72, 75; Seiberling, 99–106; Tucker 1989, 99–105.

27. Robinson Oct. 5, 1892; Lewisohn, 210; W, III, 42; Seiberling, 111–21.

28. W, letter 1111 bis.

29. W, III, 42n1042 and letters 1113–17, 2823.

30. W, letters 2823–27.

31. W, III, 47 and letter 1139; Stevens, 220–21; Gerdts 1993, 58, 224.

32. Gerdts 1993, 224.

33. W, letters 1107, 1119, 2831; P, III, 69–70, 105, 111, 114.

34. W, letter 1121.

35. Elder, 11–12; Perry, 120–21; Gimpel, 318–19; W, III, 42–43 and letters 1431*–32*.

36. Love, 415.

37. W, letter 1124; Spate, 220.

38. W, letters 2833, 2835–37, 2839.

39. W, III, 43 and letters 1103, 1125, 2841–42, 2812, 1126, 1129, 2844; P, III, 160, 162, 191, 217, 218n3.

40. W, III, 44; Pissarro, 15.

1892

41. Rewald 1973 II, 79, 102; W, III, 44 and letters 2845–46, 2848–49, 1131.

42. W, III, 44 and letters 1132–33, 2852; Pissarro, 15ff.

43. W, letters 1134–35, 2843–55; Mirbeau 1990, 133–34.

44. Groom, 20–21.

45. Robinson Nov. 1, 1892; Levine 1976, 141–49; W, III, 47 and letters 1135, 2854, 1136 bis*, 1138, PJ119; P, III, 206–207; Seiberling, 121–32; Tucker 1989, 132–41, 290–91; Spate, 221; Levine 1994, 148–57.

46. Perry, 122; W, III, 44–46 and letters 1136, 1137, 1140; Pissarro, 16–19.

47. W, III, 47 and letters 1139, 1141–42, 1156.

48. Gimpel, 180; Vaisse, 204.

49. Robinson Apr. 4, 1892; Levine 1976, 139.

50. Perry, 122; W, III, 46 and letters 1145–46.

51. Robinson July 3 and Dec. 14, 1892; Ross, 155; W, III, 46 and letters 2860, 1155–56, 1159; Butler, 399.

52. Robinson May 23, 1892; Young, Dorothy, 190; Joyes 1975, 25; W, letters 1143, 1145; Mirbeau 1990, 136–37.

53. Robinson June 3 and July 6, 1892; Love, 110.

54. Robinson June 10, 1892.

55. W, III, 48, 56, 74 and letters 1157–58, 2863–66, 1160–61, 1163, 1172, 2877, 2880, 2931–33, 2949, 1346–48, 3003; P, III, 236, 238–40, 242–43, 246–48, 252–55, 286, 296–97, 299, 300, 377, 403, 497; P, IV, 53, 60, 63, 164, 192, 205.

56. Robinson July 3, 1892.

57. Hallowell July 9, 1892.

58. Robinson July 12, 1892.

59. W, III, 47 and letter 2867.

60. Robinson July 20, 1892; Joyes 1975, 29–30; W, III, 47 and letters 2867–68; Love, 114–15, 160.

61. Robinson Aug. 10, 1892.

62. Robinson Sept. 5 and 14, 1892.

63. Robinson Oct. 3, 1892.

64. Robinson Sept. 14, Oct. 3, and Nov. 1, 1892; Perry, 125; W, III, 48.

65. Robinson Nov. 6, 1892; W, III, 48–49.

66. Levine 1976, 140–41; W, III, 44; Kendall 1993, 183–230.

67. Robinson Dec. 2, 1892.

68. W, letters 2878–80.

1893

69. W, III, 49–50 and letter 1174.

70. W, III, 50 and letter 1174, 2882; P, III, 307–09.

71. W, I, 72; W, III, 50.

72. W, III, 46, 50–52 and letters 1175–88; Pissarro, 16ff.; Love, 119.

73. W, III, 48–50 and letters 1191–93, 1195, 2885, 2889–90.

74. W, III, 52–53 and letters 1192, 1196, 1198, 1200–1201, 2886*, 1203, 1205–12.

75. W, III, 55.

76. W, III, 56 and letters 1219–21; Mirbeau 1990, 149–50.

77. W, III, 56 and letters 1222–25, 1228.

78. Manet, Julie, 23; Joyes 1989, 35.

1894

79. W, letters 2906, 2911.

80. W, III, 57 and letters 2907, 1232, 2908.

81. W, III, 57 and letter 1233.

82. W, III, 57–58 and letters 1231, 1233, 2908, 1233 bis, 2909–10; Manet, Julie, 30; Groom, 104–05.

83. W, III, 57n1182 and letter 1433*; Berhaut 1985, 224–25; Distel 1995, 318–20, 322–40.

84. Joyes 1975, 36; W, letters 1234–35, 1238.

85. W, III, 57n1187 and letters 1236, 1239, 1242, 2911–12, 1433*; Tucker 1989, 162–64.

86. W, III, 58 and letter 1239.

87. W, III, 58 and letters 1239–43, 2911–13, 1251.

88. W, letters 1433*, 1244, 2914.

89. P, III, 462–64.

90. Rewald 1973, 81; W, III, 58–59 and letters 1245–53, 1293, PJ 122; P, III, 381–82; P, IV, 189–90.

91. P, III, 496–97.

92. Elder, 47–48; Gasquet, 149; Cassatt, 278–79n10; Gerdts 1993, 226.

93. Geffroy 1922, 196; W, III, 60 and letters 2922, 1256*–57.

1895–1899

1895

1. W, III, 182.

2. Berhaut 1985, 231–32.

3. W, letters 2926–27.

4. Geffroy 1891, preface; Joyes 1975, 29; W, III, 62–63 and letters 1262–66.

5. W, III, 63 and letters 1267–69.

6. W, III, 63 and letters 1269–72.

7. W, III, 64 and letters 1273*–76.

8. W, III, 74; Berhaut 1985, 232–33.

9. W, III, 70 and letters 1279–80.

10. W, III, 64 and letters 1277–83.

11. W, III, 65 and letters 1288–89.

12. Reutersvärd 1948, 215–16; W, III, 65 and letters 1282–83, 1286–87, 1290.

13. W, III, 65 and letter 1290.

14. W, III, 65.

15. W, letters 2934–35; Rewald 1977, 385–86.

16. W, letters 1291 bis, 1292.

17. P, IV, 70–71.

18. Buisson; Gasquet, 149; Hamilton 1960; W, III, 65–68 and letters 1294–95, 1299, 1302; Seiberling 134–87; P, IV, 69, 71, 74–75, 77–78; Tucker 1989, 162, 175–87, 291–92; Pissarro; Mirbeau 1990, 162–66.

19. W, III, 67 and letters 1298, 2938; P, IV, 74–75.

20. W, letters 2938–40.

21. W, III, 69–70 and letters 1300–01, 1303, 1305, 1313–14; Mirbeau 1990, 169–71.

22. W, III, 69 and letters 2932, 1292, 2935, 2938, 1302, 1304, 1306–07, 2941.

23. W, letters 1317–18, PJ 122; Martindale, 44.

24. W, letters 2943, 1320.

25. Mack, 339–43; W, III, 70 and letters 2943, 1344; P, IV, 116.

26. W, III, 70 and letters 2943, 1320–21, PJ 122; Mirbeau 1990, 177–78.

27. Weisberg, 46–95; Marrey, 31–40.

1896

28. W, letter 1322; Delafond, nos. 68–70.

29. W, III, 73 and letters 1322–26, 1327*–28.

30. Distel 1995, 318.

31. Manet, Julie, 77–88; W, III, 70 and letters 1324, 1326, 1327*–28, 2948, 1331 bis, 1332, 1344.

32. W, III, 73 and letters 1329–34*, 1335*–36*, 1337*–45.

33. W, letters 1321, 1326, 1340, 2954.

34. Beaux, 201–22; W, III, 75 and letter 1353.

35. Manet, Julie, 102–07; P, IV, 249.

36. W, III, 75 and letter 1354.

37. W, III, 75; P, IV, 489.

38. W, III, 74–75 and letter 1355.

1897

39. W, III, 75 and letters 1356*, 1358, 1360*, 1362*.

40. W, III, 75 and letters 1360*, 1362*–64*, 2962, 1366.

41. W, III, 77 and letters 1362*, 2963–64.

42. W, III, 76 and letters 1364*,1368.

43. W, III, 76 and letters 1365*, 1367*, 1370*–71*, 1372–73*, 1374–75*, 1376*–77, 2965–66, 1378*–79*, 1380–81*, 1382–84*, 1385–86*, 1387*–88*.

44. W, III, 77; Groom, 45; Distel 1995, 318.

45. W, III, 75 and letters 1357, 1360*–61.

46. W, III, 78–79 and letter 1391.

47. W, III, 75 and letters 1353, 1355, 1357, 1368.

48. W, III, 78 and letters 1370*, 1373*, 1394 bis, 2971–72.

49. W, III, 79 and letter 2973.

50. Love, 182–84.

51. W, III, 80 and letter 1397.

1898

52. W, III, 83 and letters 1399, 1401*–04; P, IV, 434–35; Tucker 1989, 239–42.

53. W, letters 2979–80.

54. Morhardt; Tancock, 77; W, III, 84 and letters 1407, 1411.

55. W, III, 83–84; P, IV, 486–88.

56. W, I, 84–86 and letters 1406, 2981, 1408, PJ 129; Manet, Julie, 165–67; Seiberling, 188–92.

57. Tucker 1989, 234–35.

58. Fuller 1899, 15.

59. W, letter 2984.

60. W, IV, 10n60 and letters 1416–17, 2632a.

61. W, letters 1417, 1419, 1422.

1899

62. W, IV, 1.

63. W, IV, 1n7.

64. W, IV, 1n6; Stevens, 280–81.

65. W, IV, 2 and letters 1434–35, 2986; Stevens, 280–81.

66. Manet, Julie, 216; W, IV, 2n16 and letters 1436, 1442, 2987.

67. W, IV, 1n8.

68. W, IV, 3–4 and letters 2631, 1440–41.

69. W, IV, 4–6.

70. Manet, Julie, 228–29; W, letters 1445–49, 1451–62, 1464–65, 2632, 2988.

71. W, IV, 6 and letters 1463–64, 1481.

72. W, letter 1465.

73. Rewald 1969, 80–89; Manet, Julie, 236–39; Stuckey 1984, 56; W, IV, 6 and letter 1467.

74. W, letter 1468.

75. W, letter 1470.

76. W, IV, 5 (ill.), 9.

77. Joyes 1975, 32, 36; W, IV, 9 and letter 2632a.

78. W, IV, 10 and letters 1473, 2632b, 3094; Love, 206–10, pl. 47.

79. W, IV, 10 and letter 1473.

80. W, IV, 10.

81. W, IV, 10 and letters 1474, 1490, 1492.

82. W, letter 1477.

83. W, IV, 11 and letters 1476, 1479–80, 1482–85, 1488–89, 2633, 1499, 1556, 1568.

84. W, IV, 11 and letter 1485.

85. W, IV, 11 and letters 1482, 1486; Clemenceau 1993, 72.

86. W, IV, 12 and letters 1485, 1488, 2633, 1499.

1900–1904

1900

1. W, IV, 11–12 and letters 2633, 2989–91, 1491–94, 1496–97, 2993, 1509–10, 1512, 1538.

2. W, letters 1486, 1490, 1494.

3. W, letters 1495, 1497, 1502.

4. W, letters 1494a, 1549.

5. W, IV, 12 and letters 1495, 1501, 1502.

6. W, IV, 12, 15 and letters 1503–05.

7. W, IV, 12–14 and letters 1505–09, 1511, 1515–25, 1527–29.

8. W, IV, 16 and letters 1513, 1515; Geffroy 1922, 308–11; Clemenceau 1993, 42.

9. W, letters 2633, 1495, 1510, 1514–15, 1524; Love, 205–12.

10. W, IV, 14–19 and letters 1530–37, 1539, 1541–48.

11. W, IV, 19 and letters 1546, 1548.

12. W, letter 1550.

13. André, 474–77; W, IV, 19–21 and letters 1552–53.

14. W, IV, 20 and letters 1560–61.

15. Fitzgerald, 9; W, letters 1589, 1610a.

16. W, IV, 5 (ill.) and letter 1563.

17. W, IV, 21 and letters 1564–65.

18. W, IV, 22 and letters 1573–74.

19. P, V, 219.

20. W, IV, 22–23 and letters 1575–76.

21. W, IV, 23 and letters 1580–81, PJ 151–52.

22. W, IV, 23 and letters 1582a–b, 2998, 1591, 1621; for Monet's chauffeurs, see Joyes 1975, 32.

1901

23. W, IV, 23–24 and letters 1583, 1588, 1590, 1600, 1602, 2998.

24. W, IV, 23 and letters 1588–91; W, V, 155.

25. W, IV, 24 and letter 1592.

26. W, IV, 23–24 and letters 1593, 1595.

27. W, IV, 23–24 and letters 1587, 1595.

28. W, letters 1600, 1602, 1631, 1637, PJ 153–54.

29. W, letters 1608b–c, 1610.

30. Fuller, 24; W, IV, 24 and letters 1606a, 1608c, 1610, 1610a, 1611–12, 1616, 2999.

31. W, IV, 25 and letters 1616–29.

32. W, IV, 25 and letters 1630–32; P, V, 175.

33. Gordon; W, IV, 26.

34. W, letters 1637, 1640.

35. W, IV, 29.

36. Centre culturel, 264–65; W, IV, 30–31 and letter 1644.

37. W, IV, 26–29 and letter 1641.

38. W, IV, 25 and letters 3906, 1646–47, 1649a, PJ 155.

39. W, letters 1649a, 1653a.

1902

40. W, letters 2634a–b.

41. W, IV, 34n312.

42. Gordon; Centre culturel, 265.

43. W, IV, 31, PJ 157.

44. W, IV, 32–33 and letters 1649b–c, 1652, 1652a, 1653–53a, 1655, 1658a, 1661, 1663, 1665, 1668–69, PJ 156, 158; P, V, 219–20.

45. W, letters 1660, 1664.

46. W, letter 3002.

47. W, IV, 33–34 and letters 1640, 1671.

48. Joyes 1975, 29; W, IV, 33–34 and letters 1667, 1670, 1679.

49. W, IV, 35n324 and letters 1672, 1680, 1690, 1690a, PJ 161–62.

1903

50. W, letters 1687, 1689.

51. *Redon*, 318 (ill.), 319–20.

52. W, IV, 36 and letter 1690a; P, V, 327.

53. W, IV, 36 and letters 1691–95, 1699, 1702.

54. W, IV, 36 and letter 1699.

55. W, IV, 38n341 and letters 3003–04.

56. Joyes 1975, 29; W, IV, 36n339, 37 and letters 1700, 1704.

1904

57. W, IV, 39.

58. W, letters 1718, 1722.

59. Tancock, 112–20; W, letters 3105, 1730.

60. W, IV, 38 and letters 1706, 1720–21, 1723–24.

61. Seiberling, 192–98; W, IV, 38–41 and letters 1726, 1728–29, 1733, 1735, 1737, PJ 165–68.

62. W, IV, 41.

63. W, IV, 42 and letter 1736.

64. W, letters 1737–39, 1743.

65. W, IV, 42, PJ 169–71, 173–74.

66. Elder, 53; Centre culturel, 266–69; W, IV, 42 and letter 1742.

67. W, IV, 42–43 and letters 1748–52.

1905–09

1905

1. W, IV, 43 and letters 1757–58, 1760–61.

2. W, IV, 43 and letters 1758–60, 1762.

3. W, IV, 43–44 and letters 1764–65, 1767–68, 1779, PJ 180, 189.

4. W, IV, 44n412.

5. W, IV, 44n412.

6. W, IV, PJ 182–87.

7. W, IV, 47–48 and letters 3011, 2635a.

8. W, IV, 44 and letter 1780.

9. W, IV, 48n439 and letters 1784, 1787, 1789.

10. Centre culturel, 216–17; W, letters 1784–87, PJ 192, 238, 253.

11. W, IV, 47.

12. W, IV, 44n412.

13. W, IV, 48–49.

1906

14. W, IV, 48n441 and letter 1803.

15. Centre culturel, 277; W, letters 1796–96a.

16. *Redon*, 271, 324.

17. Centre culturel, 277; W, IV, 48n439 and letters 1796, 1796a–b, 1812.

18. W, IV, 48n440, 50.

19. Centre culturel, 277; W, letter 1797a.

20. W, IV, 50 and letters 1791, 1793, 1803a.

21. Denis II, 46; W, letter 1805.

22. W, IV, 49 and letter 1811.

23. Centre culturel, 281.

24. W, letter 1818.

1907

25. W, IV, 52–53 and letters 1686, 1766, 1822–25.

26. W, V, PJ 345.

27. W, letters 1826–27.

28. W, IV, 53 letters 1826, 1827a.

29. W, IV, 53 and letters 1828, 1830–31.

30. W, IV, 53 and letter 1832, PJ 198.

31. Centre culturel, 277; W, IV, 53.

32. Centre culturel, 278.

33. Centre culturel, 278; W, IV, 54 and letters 3014, 3017.

34. Centre culturel, 278; W, IV, 54 and letters 1835–36.

35. W, IV, 54 and letter 1837.

36. Centre culturel, 277–78; W, IV, 54 and letters 1833, 1837–38, 2239.

37. W, IV, 54.

38. W, IV, 56.

39. W, letter 1838a.

1908

40. Centre culturel, 270; W, IV, 55 and letters 1844–48.

41. W, IV, 135n1266 and letter 1845a.

42. Centre culturel, 271; W, letter 1848, 1850–51.

43. Centre culturel, 271; W, letter 2636.

44. W, IV, 55–56.

45. W, IV, 56.

46. W, IV, 56.

47. W, IV, 56–57.

48. W, IV, 55, 65n570 and letters 1853, 1865–66, 1872.

49. Centre culturel, 272.

50. W, IV, 57n530; W, V, 178, PJ 348–49, *Redon*, 325–36.

51. W, IV, 57 and letters 1854–55, 1857.

52. Elder, 53; W, IV, 60–61 and letters 1860, 1870.

53. Centre culturel, 139; W, IV, 61 and letter 1862.

54. W, IV, 61 and letter 1861.

55. W, IV, 61 and letters 1863a, 1864, 1864a.

56. W, IV, 62.

57. Joyes 1975, 68 (ill.); Centre culturel, 138–40; W, IV, 62 and letter 1869.

58. W, IV, 62 and letter 1871.

59. W, IV, 62, 65 and letters 1872, 1872a.

1909

60. Centre culturel, 278.

61. W, IV, 62 and letters 1873, 1875, 3018.

62. Centre culturel, 272; W, IV, 65 and letter 1875.

63. Centre culturel, 272; W, IV, 65 and letters 1876–79a.

64. W, letter 1880.

65. W, IV, 62 and letter 1882.

66. W, letters 1883, 1895, 1899, 1905–06, 1909.

67. Centre culturel, 273; W, letter 1884a.

68. W, IV, 69n627 and letters 1884a–87, 1891, 1897, PJ 213.

69. Centre culturel, 273; W, IV, 65–68 and letters 1889–90, 1892, 1895, 1896a, 1897; Levine 1994, 211–50.

70. Centre culturel, 279; W, IV, 68 and letter 1903.

71. W, IV, 67–68 and letter 1893; Levine 1994, 222, 230–38.

72. W, letters 1902a.

73. W, IV, 68–69 and letter 1904.

74. W, IV, 69 and letters 1904b, 1906, 1908.

75. Groom, 175.

76. W, IV, 69 and letter 1908.

1910–1914

1910

1. Joyes 1975, 73 (ill.), 98 (ill.); Gordon, 164; Centre culturel, 273–76; W, IV, 69–70 and letters 1911a–13.

2. W, IV, 72 and letters 1916–19a, 1924–26, 1930.

3. W, IV, 72 and letter 1915, PJ 222.

4. W, letter 1929.

5. W, IV, PJ 223, 227.

6. W, IV, 73 and letters 1941–42, 1947–48; Groom, 90–91.

7. W, IV, 73 and letters 1943, 1953, 2637a–b, 3020.

8. W, V, 178–79 (ill.) and letters 1944–50, 1952, 1960, 1968, PJ 350.

9. W, letters 1948–50.

10. W, IV, 73 and letters 1937, 1951, PJ 228, 230–31.

1911

11. W, IV, 73.

12. W, IV, 73 and letters 1954–56, 1958.

13. W, IV, 73–74 and letters 1966, 1977.

14. W, IV, 74; Clemenceau 1993, 75–76.

15. W, IV, 74 and letters 1973–74, 1991, 1994.

16. W, letters 1977, 1980, 3100–01.

17. W, IV, 75 and letters 1983, 1983a, 1985.

18. W, IV, 75 and letters 1984, 1986, 1988–90.

19. Tancock, 84; W, letter 1992; Butler, 459–63, 465.

1912

20. W, IV, 76.

21. W, IV, 75 and letters 1995–96a.

22. W, IV, 77n703 and letters 1997, 1999, 3023, 2027.

23. W, IV, 72, 77 and letters 1927, 1998, 2000, 2022.

24. Vuillard, MS.5397, carnets 5–6.

25. W, letters 2001a–c, PJ 239.

26. W, letters 2001d, 2002, 2003a–b, 2009–10.

27. Butler, 413–17.

28 W, letters 2007, 2010.

29. W, IV, 77 and letters 2012, 2012a, PJ 240.

30. W, letter 2012b.

31. W, IV, 75–76 and letters 2014–15.

32. W, IV, 76.

33. W, IV, 77 and letters 2018–20, 2022–23; Clemenceau 1993, 78.

34. W, IV, 76.

35. W, IV, 77 and letters 2023–24a; Clemenceau 1993, 78–79.

36. W, letter 2024a.

37. W, letter 2638.

38. W, letters 2028, 2031, PJ 246, 252, 257.

39. Gimpel, 66; W, IV, 72, 77 and letters 2033, 2050, 2061–62.

40. W, letters 2037–38, 2049–50.

1913

41. W, IV, 77n707.

42. W, letters 2050, 2058.

43. W, IV, 77 and letters 2051–57, 2060.

44. W, IV, 77–78 and letters 2064–65, 2069, 2072–73, 2180, PJ 261, 351.

45. Love, 369, 372.

46. Hoschedé I, 64–65; W, IV, 78.

47. W, IV, 78 and letters 2075–77.

48. Joyes 1975, 39, 93 (ill.); Ardoin, 80–81; W, IV, 78; Levine 1994, 252.

49. W, IV, 78n715 and letters 2079–82; Vuillard, loose sheet, carnet 7.

50. W, IV, 78 and letter 2089.

51. W, letter 2091.

1914

52. W, IV, 78–79 and letters 2094–98, 2100–09, 3027–28.

53. W, IV, 79 and letters 3028, 2110–11.

54. W, IV, 79.

55. Thiébault-Sisson 1927b, 46, 48; W, IV, 79 and letter 2116.

56. W, IV, 79 and letters 2119, 2123.

57. Georges-Michel, 1954; W, IV, 80 and letter 2124.

58. W, IV, 80 and letter 2126*.

59. W, IV, 80 and letters 2127–28, 3102, 2642.

60. W, IV, 83.

61. W, letter 2135.

1915–1919

1915

1. W, IV, 83 and letter 2142.

2. W, IV, 83 and letter 2148.

3. W, IV, PJ 272.

4. W, letter 2149.

5. Descaves; W, IV, 83–84 and letter 2153.

6. Vuillard, MS.5397, carnet 8.

7. Thiébault-Sisson 1927b, 48–49; Centre culturel, 235 (ill.); W, IV, 84 and letter 2155.

8. W, IV, 84 and letter 2160.

9. W, IV, 83 and letter 2162.

10. W, letter 2165.

1916

11. W, IV, 86n798 and letters 2169, 2191, PJ 352; perhaps related to an incident related by Gimpel, 66.

12. W, IV, 80 and letters 2164, 2172.

13. W, letter 2195; Butler, 503–05.

14. Joyes 1975, 110–12 (ill.); Gordon–Forge, 245 (ill.); Centre culturel, 236–37 (ill.); W, IV, 84 and letters 2179, 3033.

15. W, letters 2171, 2176.

16. W, letters 2181, 2188, 2209.

17. W, IV, 85 and letters 2180, 2183, 2186–87; for more about Monet's paint colors, see Tabarant 1923, 289.

18. W, IV, 85 and letters 2199, 2205–06, 2220, PJ 281.

19. Centre culturel, 241 (ill.), 243 (ill.); W, IV, 85 and letter 2200.

20. W, IV, 85 and letters 2205, 2205a, 2208, 2210.

1917

21. Anon. 1917; W, IV, 85n788 and letters 2212, 2216.

22. Venturi 1939 I, 445–46; W, letter 2216.

23. W, IV, 85–86 and letter 2202.

24. W, letter 2223.

25. W, letters 2212, 2214, 2220, PJ 279.

26. W, V, 86, PJ 353–54.

27. W, IV, 86 letter 2228.

28. W, IV, 86 letters 2230–31, 2232a, 2235a, 2243, 2249.

29. W, letters 2229, 3040.

30. W, IV, 85 and letter 2236.

31. W, IV, 86 and letters 2235, 2238.

32. W, IV, 86 and letters 2241, 2644.

33. W, letters 2243, 2244, 2245–46, 2248.

34. W, IV, 86 and letters 2241–42, 2247.

35. W, letter 2253.

36. W, IV, 88, 316–17 and letters 2247, 2254, 2266–67, 2269, PJ 286, 355.

37. W, letters 2252, 2644; Butler, 511–13.

38. W, letters 2253, 2256.

1918

39. W, IV, 88 and letters 2259–60.

40. Thiébault-Sisson 1927b, 41; W, IV, 88.

41. W, letters 2251, 2254, 2267, PJ284.

42. W, letter 2275.

43. W, letters 2265–66.

44. W, IV, 88 and letter 2271.

45. W, letters 2268, 2277, PJ 287.

46. W, IV, 89n823.

47. W, letter 2277.

48. Gimpel, 65–69; W, IV, 88.

49. W, IV, 89 and letters 2282, 2285.

50. Geffroy 1920, 80–81; Gimpel 89–90; W, IV, 89 and letters 2287, 2290, 3043.

51. Gimpel, 87; W, letters 2288–89.

52. Gimpel, 87–90.

53. W, IV, 90 and letters 2290–91, 2294, 2297–98, 2305.

1919

54. W, letter 2302.

55. W, IV, 90n835.

56. W, IV, 90n842 and letters 2316, 2319b, 2321, 2328.

57. Gimpel, 154; W, IV, 90 and letter 2319.

58. W, IV, 89–90n840.

59. W, IV, 90 and letters 2324, 2326.

60. W, IV, 90 and letter 2327.

61. W, IV, 90 and letters 2328–29, 2331.

1920–1926

1920

1. W, letters 2331, 2336–37, PJ 294, 296.

2. Gimpel, 154; W, IV, 90.

3. W, IV, 93, 103n950 and letters 2332, 2338*–39, 2349, 2360–61, 3050.

4. Gimpel 154–56; W, IV, 93.

5. W, IV, 93 and letter 2335.

6. W, IV, 93n855 and letters 2340–41a, 2343–44.

7. Thiébault-Sisson 1920; W, IV, 94 and letters 2350–53, 2356, PJ 297.

8. W, IV, 93–94 and letters 2349, 2355, 2357.

9. W, IV, 94 and letters 2358–2359*, 2364.

10. W, letters 2362.

11. W, letters 3051, 2371–72, 2386.

12. W, IV, 94 and letters 2367–70, 3053.

13. W, IV, 94–96.

14. Thiébault-Sisson 1920; W, IV, 96–98, PJ 297a.

15. Gimpel, 176–79; W, IV, 96.

16. Thiébault-Sisson 1920; Alexandre 1920; Anon. 1920a; W, IV, 96 and letter 2378.

17. W, IV, 97 and letters 2383*–84, 2386.

18. Anon. 1920b; W, IV, 97.

1921

19. W, IV, 98.

20. Pays 1921a; W, IV, 97, 145 (ill.) and letter 2399.

21. W, IV, 98–99 and letters 2409–11, 2413, PJ 297b, 298.

22. W, IV, 98 and letters 2400, 2402, 2403, 2404, 2427, 2429.

23. W, letters 2409, 2431, 2449, 2453, 2457, 2459, 2461–62, 2479.

24. W, letters 2415–17, 2430.

25. Pays 1921b; Clemenceau 1928, 68; W, IV, 99 and letters 2418–19, 2421.

26. W, IV, 99 and letters 2422, 2426.

27. Gimpel, 231; W, IV, 145 (ill.) and letters 2425, 2428, 2433, 2438–39.

28. W, letters 2428, 2433, 2444, 2467; Love, 400–01.

29. Elder, 10, 33–34; Joyes 1975, 100–01 (ill.); W, IV, 100n927 and letters 2436, 2440–41, 2443–45; Clemenceau 1993, 88–89.

30. W, IV, 99–100 and letters 2437, 2442.

31. W, IV, 103 and letters 2451, 2454–55.

32. Elder, 45–46; W, IV, 103 and letters 2448a, 2450, 3057, 2451, 2453, 2469; Clemenceau 1993, 90–91.

33. Anon. 1921, 581; Gimpel, 192; W, letter 2461.

34. W, letter 2458; Clemenceau 1993, 91.

35. W, IV, 100 and letters 2460–64, 2466–67, PJ 304; Clemenceau 1993, 91.

36. W, IV, 100 and letters 2468, 2470, 2474–75, 2480; Clemenceau 1993, 94.

1922

37. W, IV, 104 and letters 2477, 2480; Clemenceau 1993, 95.

38. W, IV, 104 and letter 2484.

39. W, IV, 104–05 and letters 2486, 2487–91; Clemenceau 1993, 95–98.

40. Hoschedé II, 25–26; Stuckey 1979; W, IV, 105 and letters 2492, 2501, 2512; Clemenceau 1993, 101–06.

41. Elder, 63; W, IV, 105 and letters 2493, 3061–62, 2495, 3063; Clemenceau 1993, 101–05.

42. Elder, 81; W, letter 2494*.

43. W, IV, 105 and letters 2479, 2500.

44. Ciolkowski, 1923; Ardoin; W, IV, 95 (ill.), 106 and letter 2503.

45. W, IV, 106–108 and letters 2505–07, 2649, 2509; Clemenceau 1993, 96, 109–11.

46. W, IV, 108 and letters 2510–11.

47. Elder, 81–82.

48. W, IV, 108 and letters 2650–51, 2515.

49. W, IV, 108n1002 and letters 2516, 2518.

1923

50. W, IV, 108–09 and letter 2521; Clemenceau 1993, 113.

51. W, IV, 109–10 and letters 2652–53; Clemenceau 1993, 113–16.

52. W, letters 2525–27, 2532, PJ 359.

53. Gimpel, 253; W, IV, 110–13 and letters 2657–58, 2525–26; Clemenceau 1993, 119–22.

54. W, IV, 113–16 and letters 2526–28, 2659–60, 2529–30, 2661, 2531, 2533, 2662, 2534–39, 2663–65; Clemenceau 1993, 123–39.

55. W, IV, 115–16 and letter 2543.

56. W, IV, PJ 315; Clemenceau 1993, 140.

1924

57. W, IV, 117–18 and letters 2546–47; Clemenceau 1993, 146.

58. W, IV, 116–17 and letters 2532, 2544–45, 2548, 3073, 2554; Clemenceau 1993, 144–45.

59. W, letters 2669–70.

60. W, IV, 118, PJ 317; Clemenceau 1993, 147–48.

61. Hoschedé I, 145ff.; W, IV, 118–20, 123 and letters 2672–74, 2566, 2570–71, 2675, 2572, 2676, 2577, 2677, 2580; Clemenceau 1993, 150–53.

62. W, IV, 119n1122, 120n1140 and letters 2567, 2570; Clemenceau 1993, 153.

63. W, IV, 124 and letter 2576.

64. W, IV, 123; Clemenceau 1993, 158–60.

65. W, letter 2582.

66. W, IV, 124.

67. W, IV, 123–24 and letter 2576.

68. W, IV, 124 and letters 2679, 2580–81, 2583–84, 3076.

69. W, IV, 126–28 and letters 2591, 2593, 2597, PJ 322–23.

70. W, IV, 125; Clemenceau 1993, 161–62.

1925

71. W, IV, 125, 128 and letters 2592, 2596; Clemenceau 1993, 161–65.

72. W, IV, 128.

73. W, IV, 125–29 and letters 3077–78, 2599–2602, 2609, 2682, 2610; Clemenceau 1993, 169.

74. W, IV, 129.

75. W, letters 2611, 2683, 2613–15.

1926

76. W, IV, 130n1228 and letter 2617.

77. W, IV, 133, PJ 326; Clemenceau 1993, 177.

78. W, IV, 133 and letter 2621; Clemenceau 1993, 178.

79. W, IV, 134.

80. W, IV, 135 and letters 2625, 2627.

81. Gimpel, 317–18; W, IV, 136.

82. W, IV, 138 and letter 2628.

83. Gimpel, 318–19.

84. W, IV, 136–37 and letter 2629; Walter 1986, 58–62; Clemenceau 1993, 183–85.

85. W, letter 2685.

86. W, IV, 138 and letters 2629–30.

87. W, IV, 139.

88. W, IV, 139–40.

89. Gillet, 112; W, IV, 140.

90. Vidal; W, IV, 142–44.

91. W, IV, PJ 328–29.

Postscript

92. Anon. 1927; W, IV, 146.

Works Cited

Alexandre 1920. Alexandre, Arsène. "L'Epopée des Nymphéas." *Le Figaro* (Oct. 21, 1920), 1.

André. André, Edouard. "Les Plantes aquatiques à l'Exposition universelle et les nymphéas nouvelles." *Revue horticole* (Sept. 1900), 474–77.

Anon. 1917. Anon. *New York Daily Tribune* (Jan. 18, 1917).

Anon. 1920a. Anon. "La Donation Claude Monet." *La Bulletin de l'art ancien et moderne.* (Oct. 25, 1920), 187.

Anon. 1920b. Anon. "A l'Institut Claude Monet." *Le Populaire* (Oct. 26, 1920).

Anon. 1921. Anon. "Monet dans les jardins de Paris et de Tokyo." *La Bulletin de la vie artistique* (Nov. 15, 1921), 581.

Anon. 1927. Anon. *New York Times* (June 12, 1927).

Ardoin. Ardoin, John. "Namara: A Remembrance." *Opera Quarterly* 1, no. 14 (Winter 1983), 80–81.

Arnyvelde. Arnyvelde, André. "Chez le peintre de la lumière." *Je sais tout* (Jan. 15, 1914), 29–38.

Aspects. Rewald, John, and Frances Weitzenhoffer, eds. *Aspects of Monet: A Symposium on the Artist's Life and Times.* New York, 1984.

Bailly-Herzberg 1972. Bailly-Herzberg, Janine. *L'Eau-forte de peintre au dix-neuvième siècle: La Société des aquafortistes, 1862–1867.* 2 vols. Paris, 1972.

Bailly-Herzberg 1975. Bailly-Herzberg, Janine, and Madeleine Fidell-Beaufort. *Daubigny.* Paris, 1975.

Barotte. Barotte, René. "Blanche Hoschedé nous parle de Claude Monet." *Comœdia* (Oct. 24, 1942), 1–2.

Baudelaire 1973. Baudelaire, Charles. *Baudelaire Correspondance.* Vols. I (1832–60) and II (1861–66). Edited by Claude Pichois. Paris, 1973.

Baudelaire 1976. ———. *Œuvres complètes.* Vol. II. Edited by Claude Pichois. Paris, 1976.

Baudot. Baudot, Jeanne. *Renoir: Ses amis, ses modèles.* Paris, 1949.

Bazille. Bazille, Frédéric. *Frédéric Bazille Correspondance.* Edited by Didier Vatuone. Montpellier, 1992.

Beaux. Beaux, Cecelia. *Background with Figures: Autobiography of Cecelia Beaux.* New York, 1930.

Berhaut 1985. Berhaut, Marie. "Le Legs Caillebotte: Vérités et contre-vérités." *Bulletin de la Société de l'histoire de l'art français* (1983 [1985]), 209–39.

Berhaut 1994. ———. *Gustave Caillebotte: Catalogue raisonné des peintures et pastels.* Rev. ed. Paris, 1994.

Billot. Billot, Léon. "Exposition des Beaux-Arts." *Journal du Havre* (Oct. 9 and Oct. 31, 1868), 2.

Bodelsen. Bodelsen, Merete. "Early Impressionist Sales, 1874–94." *Burlington Magazine* (June 1968), 331–49.

Breck. Breck, Edward. "Something More of Giverny." *Boston Evening Transcript* (Mar. 9, 1895).

Brettell. Brettell, Richard R. "Monet's Haystacks Reconsidered." *The Art Institute of Chicago Museum Studies* 11, no. 1 (Fall 1984), 5–21.

Bruce. Bruce, William Blair. *Letters Home, 1859–1906: The Letters of William Blair Bruce.* Edited by Joan Murray. Moonbeam, Ontario, 1982.

Buisson. Buisson, J. *La République française* (May 28, 1895).

Butler. Butler, Ruth. *Rodin: The Shape of Genius.* New Haven and London, 1993.

Byvanck. Byvanck, W. G. C. *Un Hollandais à Paris en 1891.* Preface by Anatole France. Paris, 1892.

Cahn. Cahn, Isabelle. *Cadres de peintres.* Paris, 1989.

Cassatt. Cassatt, Mary. *Cassatt and Her Circle: Selected Letters.* Edited by Nancy Mowll Mathews. New York, 1984.

Centre culturel. Guillaud, Jacqueline, and Maurice Guillaud, eds. *Claude Monet au temps du Giverny.* Exh. cat. Centre culturel du Marais, Paris, 1983. Also published as *Claude Monet at the Time of Giverny* (Paris, 1983).

Cézanne. Cézanne, Paul. *Paul Cézanne, Letters.* Edited by John Rewald and translated by Marguerite Kay. London, 1941.

Charteris. Charteris, Evan. *John Sargent.* New York, 1927.

Ciolkowska. Ciolkowska, Muriel. "Monet—His Garden, His World." *International Studio* 76, no. 309 (Feb. 1923), 371–78.

Clemenceau 1895. Clemenceau, Georges. "Révolution de cathédrales." *La Justice* (May 20, 1895), 1.

Clemenceau 1928. ———. *Claude Monet: Les Nymphéas.* Paris, 1928.

Clemenceau 1993. ———. *Georges Clemenceau à son ami Claude Monet: Correspondance.* Edited by André Wormser. Paris, 1993.

Cooper. Cooper, Douglas. *The Courtauld Collection: A Catalogue and Introduction, with a Memoir of Samuel Courtauld.* London, 1954.

Courbet. Courbet, Gustave. *Letters of Gustave Courbet.* Edited and translated by Petra ten-Doesschate Chu. Chicago, 1992.

Degas. Boggs, Jean Sutherland, et al. *Degas.* Exh. cat. The Metropolitan Museum of Art, New York, and the National Gallery of Canada, Ottawa, 1988.

Delafond. Delafond, Marianne, and Geneviève Aitken. *La Collection d'estampes japonaises de Claude Monet.* Giverny, 1983.

Delouche 1980. Delouche, Denise. "Monet et Belle-Ile en 1886." *Bulletin des amis du Musée de Rennes* (1980), 27–55.

Denis. Denis, Maurice. *Journal.* Vol. II (1905–20). Paris, 1957.

Descaves. Descaves, Lucien. "Chez Claude Monet." *Paris–Magazine* 2, no. 30 (Aug. 25, 1920), 354.

De Veer. De Veer, Elizabeth, and Richard J. Boyle. *Sunlight and Shadow: The Life and Art of Willard L. Metcalf, 1858–1925.* New York, 1987.

Dewhurst. Dewhurst, Wynford. *Impressionist Painting: Its Genesis and Development.* London, 1904.

Distel 1989. Distel, Anne. *Impressionism: The First Collectors.* Translated by Barbara Perroud-Benson. New York, 1989.

Distel 1995. ———. "Chronology." In Distel, et al. *Gustave Caillebotte: Urban Impressionist,* 311–18. Exh. cat. The Art Institute of Chicago, 1995.

Dixon. Meixner, Laura L., et al. *An International Episode: Millet, Monet, and Their North American Counterparts.* Exh. cat. Dixon Gallery and Gardens, Memphis, 1982.

Doran. Doran, P. M., ed. *Conversations avec Cézanne.* Paris, 1978.

Duret. Duret, Théodore. *Histoire d'Edouard Manet et de son œuvre.* Paris, 1902.

Elder. Elder, Marc [pseud. Marcel Tendron]. *A Giverny, chez Claude Monet.* Paris, 1924.

Fénéon. Fénéon, Félix. "Le Précieux don de Claude Monet." *La Bulletin de la vie artistique* 1 (Oct. 15, 1920), 623–24.

Fernier. Fernier, Robert. *La Vie et l'œuvre de Gustave Courbet: Catalogue raisonné.* Lausanne, vol. I, 1977; vol. II, 1978.

Fitzgerald. Fitzgerald, Desmond. "Claude Monet: Master of Impressionism." *Brush and Pencil* 15 (Mar. 1905), 181–95.

Flescher. Flescher, Sharon. *Zacherie Astruc, Critic, Artist, and Japoniste.* New York, 1978.

Flint. Flint, Kate, ed. *Impressionists in England: The Critical Reception.* London, 1984.

Frankenstein. Frankenstein, Alfred. *William Sidney Mount.* New York, 1975.

Fuller. Fuller, William H. *Claude Monet and His Paintings.* New York, 1899.

Gasquet. Gasquet, Joachim. *Cézanne.* Paris, 1926.

Gauguin. Gauguin, Paul. *Correspondance de Paul Gauguin.* Vol. I. Edited by Victor Merlhès. Paris, 1984.

Geffroy 1889. Geffroy, Gustave. "Chronique: L'Exposition Monet–Rodin." *La Justice* (June 21, 1889), 1.

Geffroy 1891. ———. *Exposition d'œuvres recentes de Claude Monet dans la galerie Durand-Ruel.* Exh. cat. Galerie Durand-Ruel, Paris, 1891.

Geffroy 1897. ———. *Pays d'Ouest.* Paris, 1897.

Geffroy 1920. ———. "Claude Monet." *L'Art et les artistes* 15, no. 11 (Nov. 1920), 51–81.

Geffroy 1922. ———. *Claude Monet, sa vie, son temps, son œuvre.* Paris, 1922.

Georges-Michel. Georges-Michel, Michel. *De Renoir à Picasso: Les peintres que j'ai connus.* Paris, 1954.

Gerdts 1984. Gerdts, William H. *American Impressionism.* New York, 1984.

Gerdts 1993. ———. *Monet's Giverny: An Impressionist Colony.* New York, 1993.

Gillet. Gillet, Louis. *Trois variations sur Claude Monet.* Paris, 1927.

Gimpel. Gimpel, René. *Journal d'un collectionneur, marchand de tableaux.* Paris, 1963.

Gogh. Gogh, Vincent van. *The Complete Letters of Vincent van Gogh.* Vol. III. Greenwich, Connecticut, [1958].

Goncourt. Goncourt, Edmond and Jules de. *Manette Salomon.* Paris, 1867.

Gordon. Gordon, Robert. "The Changing Inspiration of Monet: The Lily Pond at Giverny." *Connoisseur* (Nov. 1973), 154–65.

Gordon–Forge. Gordon, Robert, and Andrew Forge. *Monet.* New York, 1983.

Greta. Greta [pseud.]. "Boston Art and Artists." *Art Amateur* 17 (Oct. 1888), 78.

Groom. Groom, Gloria. *Edouard Vuillard: Painter–Decorator.* New Haven and London, 1993.

Hallowell. Hallowell, Sara. Letter to Potter Palmer, July 9 [1892]. Ryerson and Burnham Archives, The Art Institute of Chicago (00.7).

Hamilton 1956. Hamilton, George Heard. "Cézanne, Bergson, and the Imge of Time." *College Art Journal* 16, no. 1 (1956), 2–12.

Hamilton 1960. ———. *Monet's Paintings of Rouen Cathedral.* Charleton Lectures on Art [1959]. London, 1960.

Hefting. Hefting, Victorine. *Jongkind: Sa vie, son œuvre, son époque.* Paris, 1975.

Herbert 1988. Herbert, Robert L. *Impressionism: Art, Leisure, and Parisian Societ.y.* New Haven and London, 1988.

Herbert 1994. ———. *Monet on the Normandy Coast: Tourism and Painting, 1867–1886.* New Haven and London, 1994.

Hoschedé. Hoschedé, Jean-Pierre. *Claude Monet, ce mal connu.* 2 vols. Geneva, 1960.

House 1978a. House, John. "New Material on Monet and Pissarro in London, 1870–71." *Burlington Magazine* 120, no. 907 (Oct. 1978), 636–42.

House 1978b. ———. "The New Monet Catalogue," *Burlington Magazine* 120, no. 907 (Oct. 1978), 678–81.

Huth. Huth, Hans. "Impressionism Comes to America." *Gazette des Beaux-Arts*, 6th ser., 29 (April 1946), 225–52.

Hôtel Drouot. *Archives de Camille Pissarro.* Auction cat. Hôtel Drouot, Paris, Nov. 21, 1975.

Impressionism. Distel, Anne, et al. *Impressionism: A Centenary Exhibition.* Exh. cat. The Metropolitan Museum of Art, New York, and Galeries du Jeu de Paume et de l'Orangerie, Paris, 1974.

Isaacson. Isaacson, Joel. *Monet: Le Déjeuner sur l'herbe.* London, 1972.

Japonisme. *Le Japonisme.* Exh. cat. Galeries nationales du Grand Palais, Paris, 1988.

Jean-Aubry 1911. Jean-Aubry, Georges. "Une visite à Giverny, Eugene Boudin et Claude Monet." *Havre–Eclair* (Aug. 1, 1911), 1.

Jean-Aubry 1922. ———. *Eugène Boudin.* Paris, 1922.

Joyes 1975. Joyes, Claire, Robert Gordon, Jean-Marie Toulgouat, and Andrew Forge. *Monet at Giverny.* London, 1975.

Joyes 1989. Joyes, Claire. *Monet's Table: The Cooking Journals of Claude Monet.* New York, 1989.

Kendall 1993. Kendall, Richard. *Degas Landscapes.* Exh. cat. The Metropolitan Museum of Art, New York, and the Museum of Fine Arts, Houston, 1993.

Kysela. Kysela, John D. "Sara Hallowell Brings 'Modern Art' to the Midwest." *Art Quarterly* 27, no. 2 (1964), 150–67.

Lasting Impressions. Gerdts, William H., et al. *Lasting Impressions: American Painters in France, 1965–1915.* Exh. cat. Musée Américain, Giverny, 1992.

Le Braz. Le Braz, Anatole. *Les Iles Bretonnes.* Paris, 1935.

Le Roux. Le Roux, Hughes. "Silhouettes parisiennes: L'Exposition de Claude Monet." *Gil Blas* (Mar. 3, 1889), 2.

Leslie. Leslie, C. R. *Memoirs of the Life of Constable, Esq., R.A.* London, 1843. Excerpts from the second edition of 1845 translated into French as "Pensées d'un paysagiste," *Magasin pittoresque* 23 (Aug. and Oct. 1855), 266–71 and 342–43, from which L. Présurier [pseud. Edmond Duranty] derived "Idées de Constable, peintre anglais," *Réalisme* 2 (Dec. 15, 1856), 29–30.

Levine 1976. Levine, Stephen Z. *Monet and His Critics.* New York, 1976.

Levine 1994. ———. *Monet, Narcissus, and Self-Reflection: The Modernist Myth of the Self.* Chicago, 1994.

Lewisohn. Lewisohn, Florence. "Theodore Robinson and Claude Monet." *Apollo* 78, no. 19 (Sept. 1963), 208–11.

Love. Love, Richard. *Theodore Earl Butler: Emergence from Monet's Shadow.* Chicago, 1985.

M. M., E. de. "Exposition Monet–Rodin." *La Liberté* (June 26, 1889).

Mack. Mack, Gerstle. *Paul Cézanne.* New York, 1935.

Mallarmé 1964. Mallarmé, Stéphane. *Correspondance Mallarmé–Whistler.* Edited by Carl Paul Barbier. Paris, 1964.

Mallarmé 1969. ———. *Stéphane Mallarmé Correspondance.* Edited by Henri Mondor and Lloyd James Austin. Paris, vol. II (1871–85), 1965; vol. III (1886–89), 1969.

Manet. Cachin, Françoise, et al. *Manet, 1832–1883.* Exh. cat. The Metropolitan Museum of Art, New York, 1983.

Manet, Julie. Manet, Julie. *Julie Manet: Journal, 1893–1899.* Paris, 1979.

Marrey. Marrey, Bernard. *Louis Bonnier, 1856–1946.* Liège, 1988.

Martindale. Martindale, Meredith. *Lilla Cabot Perry: An American Impressionist.* Washington, D.C., 1990.

Maupassant. Maupassant, Guy de. "La Vie d'un paysagiste, Etretat, septembre." *Gil Blas* (Apr. 28, 1886), 6, 84–88.

Mirbeau 1884. Mirbeau, Octave. "Notes sur l'art, Claude Monet." *La France* (Nov. 21, 1884), 2.

Mirbeau 1990. ———. *Correspondance avec Claude Monet.* Edited by Pierre Michel and Jean-François Nivet. Tusson, Charente, 1990.

Moffett. Moffett, Charles, et al. *The New Painting: Impressionism, 1874–1886.* Exh. cat. The Fine Arts Museums of San Francisco and the National Gallery of Art, Washington, D.C., 1986.

Monet in Holland. *Monet in Holland.* Exh. cat. Rijksmuseum Vincent van Gogh, Amsterdam, 1986.

Monet–Rodin. *Claude Monet–Auguste Rodin: Centenaire de l'exposition de 1889.* Exh cat. Musée Rodin, Paris, 1989.

Moreau-Nélaton. Moreau-Nélaton, Etienne. *Daubigny raconté par lui-même.* Paris, 1925.

Morhardt. Morhardt, Mathias. "La Bataille du Balzac." *Mercure de France* (Dec. 15, 1934).

Morisot. Morisot, Berthe. *Correspondance de Berthe Morisot avec sa famille et ses amis Manet, Puvis de Chavannes, Degas, Monet, Renoir, et Mallarmé.* Edited by Denis Rouart. Paris, 1950.

Origins. Tinterow, Gary, Henri Loyrette, et al. *Origins of Impressionism.* Exh. cat. The Metropolitan Museum of Art, New York, 1994.

P. Pissarro, Camille. *Correspondance de Camille Pissarro.* Edited by Janine Bailly-Herzberg. Paris, vol. I (1865–85), 1980; vol. II (1886–90), 1986; vol. III (1891–94), 1988; vol. IV (1895–98), 1989; vol. V (1899–1903), 1991.

Paris 1874. *Paris en 1874: L'Année de l'impressionnisme.* Exh. cat. The National Museum of Western Art, Tokyo, 1994.

Pays 1921a. Pays, Marcel. "Une visite à Claude Monet dans son ermitage de Giverny." *L'Excelsior* (Jan. 26, 1921).

Pays 1921b. ———. "Un don précieux: Les Nymphéas de Claude Monet attendent un emplacement." *L'Excelsior* (May 16, 1921).

Pennell. Pennell, Elizabeth Robins, and Joseph Pennell. *The Life of James McNeill Whistler.* 2 vols. London and Philadelphia, 1909.

Perry. Perry, Lilla Cabot. "Reminiscences of Claude Monet from 1889 to 1909." *American Magazine of Art* (Mar. 1927), 117–25.

Pickvance. Pickvance, Ronald. "Monet and Renoir in the Mid-1870s." In *Japonisme in Art: An International Symposium*, edited by Yamada Chisaburo, 157–65. Tokyo, 1980.

Pissarro. Pissarro, Joachim. *Monet's Cathedral: Rouen, 1892–1894.* New York, 1990.

Poulain. Poulain, Gaston. *Bazille et ses amis.* Paris, 1932.

Redon. Druick, Douglas, et al. *Odilon Redon: Prince of Dreams, 1840–1916.* Exh. cat. The Art Institute of Chicago, 1994.

Renoir. House, John, Anne Distel, et al. *Renoir.* Exh. cat. Museum of Fine Arts, Boston, 1985.

Renoir, Jean. Renoir, Jean. *Pierre-Auguste Renoir, mon père.* Paris, 1981.

Reutersvärd 1948. Reutersvärd, Oscar. *Monet.* Stockholm, 1948.

Reutersvärd 1950. ———. "The 'Violetto-mania' of the Impressionists." *Journal of Aesthetics and Art Criticism* (Dec. 1950), 106–10.

Rewald 1961. Rewald, John. *The History of Impressionism.* Rev. ed. New York, 1961.

Rewald 1969. ———. "Chocquet and Cézanne." *Gazette des Beaux-Arts* 74 (July–Aug. 1969), 33–96.

Rewald 1973. ———. "Theo van Gogh, Goupil, and the Impressionists." *Gazette des Beaux-Arts* (Jan. and Feb. 1973), 2–64, 65–108.

Rewald 1977. ———. "Catalog." In *Cézanne: The Late Work,* edited by William Rubin, 385–416. Exh. cat. The Museum of Modern Art, New York, 1977.

Rewald 1985. Rewald, John, ed. *French Paintings: The Collection of Mr. and Mrs. Paul Mellon in the Virginia Museum of Fine Arts.* Richmond, 1985.

Rewald 1986a. Rewald, John. *Histoire de l'impressionnisme.* Rev. ed. Paris, 1986.

Rewald 1986b. ———. "Paintings by Paul Cézanne in the Mellon Collection." In *Essays in Honor of Paul Mellon, Collector and Benefactor,* edited by John Wilmerding, 289–320. Washington, D.C., 1986.

Robinson. Robinson, Theodore. Unpublished diaries, vol. I (Mar. 29, 1892–Feb. 4, 1893) and vol. II (Feb. 5, 1893–June 9, 1894). Collection of the Frick Art Reference Library, New York.

Roskill. Roskill, Mark. "Early Impressionism and the Fashion Print." *Burlington Magazine* 112, no. 807 (June 1970), 391–95.

Ross. Ross, Ishbel. *Silhouette in Diamonds: The Life of Mrs. Potter Palmer*. New York, 1960.

Schiff. Schiff, Richard. "The End of Impressionism: A Study in Theories of Artistic Expression." *Art Quarterly* 1, no. 4 (Autumn 1978), 338–78.

Seiberling. Seiberling, Grace. *Monet in London*. Exh. cat. High Museum of Art, Atlanta, 1988.

Silverman. Silverman, Debora. *Art Nouveau in Fin-de-Siècle France: Politics, Psychology, and Style*. Berkeley, 1989.

Spate. Spate, Virginia. *Claude Monet: Life and Work*. New York, 1992.

Splendid Legacy. Frelinghuysen, Alice Cooney, et al. *Splendid Legacy: The Havemeyer Collection*. Exh. cat. The Metropolitan Museum of Art, New York, 1993.

Stevens. Stevens, MaryAnne, ed. *Alfred Sisley*. Exh. cat. The Royal Academy of Arts, London, 1992.

Stuckey 1979. Stuckey, Charles F., and Robert Gordon. "Blossoms and Blunders: Monet and the State." *Art in America* 67, nos. 1 and 5 (Jan.–Feb. and Sept. 1979), 102, 117–25; 109–25.

Stuckey 1981. Stuckey, Charles F. "What's Wrong with This Picture?" *Art in America* 69 (Sept. 1981), 96–107.

Stuckey 1984. ———. "Degas as an Artist: Revised and Still Unfinished." In *Degas: Form and Space*, 13–64. Exh. cat. Centre culturel du Marais, Paris, 1984.

Stuckey 1987. ———. *Berthe Morisot, Impressionist*. New York, 1987.

Tabarant 1923. Tabarant, Adolphe. "Couleurs." *La Bulletin de la vie artistique* (July 15, 1923), 287–90.

Tabarant 1947. ———. *Manet et ses œuvres*. Paris, 1947.

Taboureux. Taboureux, Emile. "Claude Monet." *La Vie moderne* (June 12, 1880), 380–82.

Tancock. Tancock, John. *The Sculpture of Auguste Rodin*. Philadelphia, 1976.

Thiébault-Sisson 1900. Thiébault-Sisson, François. "Claude Monet: Les années d'épreuves." *Le Temps* (Nov. 26, 1900).

Thiébault-Sisson 1920. ———. "Art et curiosité: Un don de Claude Monet à l'Etat." *Le Temps* (Oct. 14, 1920), 2.

Thiébault-Sisson 1926. ———. "Claude Monet." *Le Temps* (Dec. 7, 1926).

Thiébault-Sisson 1927a. ———. "Autour de Claude Monet: Anecdotes et souvenirs." *Le Temps* (Jan. 8, 1927), 3.

Thiébault-Sisson 1927b. ———. "Les Nymphéas de Claude Monet." *La Revue de l'art ancien et moderne* 52 (June 1927), 6–25.

Trévise. Trévise, Duc de. "Le Pèlerinage de Giverny." *La Revue de l'art ancien et moderne* 51 (Jan. and Feb. 1927), 42–50, 121–34.

Tucker 1982. Tucker, Paul Hayes. *Monet at Argenteuil*. New Haven and London, 1982.

Tucker 1989. ———. *Monet in the '90s: The Series Paintings*. Exh. cat. Museum of Fine Arts, Boston, 1989.

Vaisse. Vaisse, Pierre. "Le Legs Caillebotte d'après les documents." *Bulletin de la Société de l'histoire de l'art français* (1983 [1985]), 201–08.

Venturi 1936. Venturi, Lionello. *Cézanne: Son art, son œuvre*. Paris, 1936.

Venturi 1939. Venturi, Lionello, ed. *Les Archives de l'impressionnisme*. 2 vols. Paris, 1939.

Vidal. Vidal, Henry. "Le Souvenir de Claude Monet." *La France de Marseille* (Feb. 19, 1947), 1–2.

Vuillard. Vuillard, Edouard. Unpublished journal (1880–1940). Institut de France, Paris. Courtesy Antoine Salomon.

W. Wildenstein, Daniel. *Claude Monet: Biographie et catalogue raisonné*. Lausanne, vol. I (1840–81), 1974; vol. II (1882–86), 1979; vol. III (1887–98), 1979; vol. IV (1899–1926), 1985; vol. V (additions to previous volumes, drawings, pastels, index), 1991.

Wagner. Wagner, Anne M. "Why Monet Gave Up Figure Painting." *Art Bulletin* 76, no. 4 (Dec. 1994), 613–29.

Walter 1963. Walter, Rodolphe. "Zola et Monet." *Les Lettres françaises* (Oct. 10–16, 1963), 1–12.

Walter 1964. ———. "Emile Zola et Claude Monet." *Les Cahiers nationalistes* 10, no. 26 (1964), 51–61.

Walter 1966. ———. "Les Maisons de Claude Monet à Argenteuil." *Gazette des Beaux-Arts* (Dec. 1966), 333–42.

Walter 1986. ———. *Le Médecin de Claude Monet: Jean Rebière*. Paris, 1986.

Ward. Ward, Martha. "Impressionist Installations and Private Exhibitions," *Art Bulletin* 73, no. 4 (Dec. 1991), 599–622.

Weisberg. Weisberg, Gabriel. *Art Nouveau Bing: Paris Style 1900*. New York, 1986.

Whistler. Whistler, James McNeill. "The Letters of James McNeill Whistler to George A. Lucas." Edited by John A. Mahey. *Art Bulletin* 49 (Sept. 1967), 247–57.

Young, Andrew. Young, Andrew McLaren, Margaret MacDonald, Hamish Miles, and Robin Spencer. *The Paintings of James McNeill Whistler*. 2 vols. New Haven and London, 1980.

Young, Dorothy. Young, Dorothy Weir. *The Life and Letters of J. Alden Weir*. New Haven, 1960.

Zola 1866. Zola, Emile. "Mon Salon: V, Les Réalistes au Salon." *L'Evénement illustré* (May 11, 1866), 3–4.

Zola 1868. ———. *L'Evénement illustré* (May 24, 1868).

Zola 1880. ———. "Le Naturalisme au Salon: I, II, III." *Le Voltaire* (June 18, 19, and 21, 1880).

Selected Bibliography

The following bibliography for general readers consists of selected works grouped into categories. For the most complete account of the enormous literature on Monet, see Daniel Wildenstein's catalogue raisonné (W, V, 228–65).

There is no up-to-date bibliography for Impressionist studies in general. Readers should start with the most recent English edition of John Rewald's *History of Impressionism* (New York, 1973).

Catalogue Raisonné and Complete Correspondence

Wildenstein, Daniel. *Claude Monet: Biographie et catalogue raisonné*. Lausanne, vol. I (1840–81), 1974; vol. II (1882–86), 1979; vol. III (1887–98), 1979; vol. IV (1899–1926), 1985; vol. V (additions to previous volumes, drawings, pastels, index), 1991.

Letters to Monet

Bazille, Frédéric. *Frédéric Bazille Correspondance*. Edited by Didier Vatuone. Montpellier, 1992.

Clemenceau, Georges. *Georges Clemenceau à son ami Claude Monet: Correspondance*. Edited by André Wormser. Paris, 1993.

Kendall, Richard. *Monet by Himself*. London, 1989.

Mirbeau, Octave. *Correspondance avec Claude Monet*. Edited by Pierre Michel and Jean-François Nivet. Tusson, Charente, 1990.

Pissarro, Camille. *Correspondance de Camille Pissarro*. Edited by Janine Bailly–Herzberg. Paris, vol. I (1865–85), 1980; vol. II (1886–90), 1986; vol. III (1891–94), 1988; vol. IV (1895–98), 1989; vol. V (1899–1903), 1991.

Interviews with Monet (in chronological order)

Taboureux, Emile. "Claude Monet." *La Vie moderne* (June 12, 1880), 380–82.

Maupassant, Guy de. "La Vie d'un paysagiste, Etretat, septembre." *Gil Blas* (Apr. 28, 1886), 6, 84–88.

Jeanniot, G. "Notes sur l'art—Claude Monet." *La Cravache parisienne* (June 23, 1888), 1–2.

Fuller, William H. *Claude Monet*. New York, 1891.

Byvanck, W. G. C. *Un Hollandais à Paris en 1891*. Preface by Anatole France. Paris, 1892.

Robinson, Theodore. "Claude Monet." *Century Magazine* (Sept. 1892), 696–701.

Manet, Julie. *Julie Manet: Journal, 1893–1899*. Paris, 1979.

Guillemot, Maurice. "Claude Monet." *Interview Revue illustrée* 13, no. 7 (Mar. 15, 1898).

Fuller, William H. *Claude Monet and His Paintings*. New York, 1899.

Dewhurst, Wynford. "Claude Monet—Impressionist." *Pall Mall Magazine* 21 (June 1900), 209–24.

Dewhurst, Wynford. "A Great French Landscapist: Claude Monet." *The Artist* 29 (Oct. 1900), 57–66.

Thiébault-Sisson, François. "Claude Monet: Les années d'épreuves." *Le Temps* (Nov. 26, 1900).

Fitzgerald, Desmond. "Claude Monet: Master of Impressionism." *Brush and Pencil* 15 (Mar. 1905), 181–95.

Vauxcelles, Louis [pseud. Louis Mayer]. "Un après-midi chez Claude Monet." *L'Art et les artistes* 2, no. 9 (Dec. 7, 1905), 85–90.

Pach, Walter. "At the Studio of Claude Monet." *Scribner's Magazine* (June 1908), 765–67.

Jean-Aubry, Georges. "Une visite à Giverny, Eugene Boudin et Claude Monet." *Havre–Eclair* (Aug. 1, 1911), 1.

Arnyvelde, André. "Chez le peintre de la lumière." *Je sais tout* (Jan. 15, 1914), 29–38.

Elder, Marc [pseud. Marcel Tendron]. "Une visite à Giverny chez Claude Monet." *Excelsior* (Apr. 6, 1920).

Thiébault-Sisson, François. "La Vie artistique: Claude Monet." *Le Temps* (Apr. 6, 1920), 3.

Elder, Marc [pseud. Marcel Tendron]. "Une visite à Claude Monet." *La Bulletin de la vie artistique* 1, no. 11 (May 1, 1920), 305.

Thiébault-Sisson, François. "Art et curiosité: Un don de Claude Monet à l'Etat." *Le Temps* (Oct. 14, 1920), 2.

Pays, Marcel. "Une visite à Claude Monet dans son ermitage de Giverny." *L'Excelsior* (Jan. 26, 1921).

Ciolkowska, Muriel. "Monet—His Garden, His World." *International Studio* 76, no. 309 (Feb. 1923), 371–78.

Thiébault-Sisson, François. "Claude Monet." *Le Temps* (Dec. 7 and 29, 1926).

Thiébault-Sisson, François. "Autour de Claude Monet: Anecdotes et souvenirs." *Le Temps* (Jan. 8, 1927), 3.

Trévise, Duc de. "Le Pèlerinage de Giverny." *La Revue de l'art ancien et moderne* 51 (Jan. and Feb. 1927), 42–50, 121–34.

Perry, Lilla Cabot. "Reminiscences of Claude Monet from 1889 to 1909." *American Magazine of Art* (Mar. 1927), 117–25.

Ciolkowska, Muriel. "Memories of Monet." *Canadian Forum* (Mar. 1927), 177–80.

Martet, Jean. *M. Clemenceau peint par lui-même*. Paris, 1930.

Saloman, Jacques. "Giverny, 8 juin 1926—Aujourd'hui déjeuner chez Claude Monet." *Les Arts* (Dec. 14, 1951), 10.

Gimpel, René. *Diary of an Art Dealer*. Translated by John Rosenberg. New York, 1966.

Howard-Johnson, Paulette. "Une visite à Giverny en 1924." *L'Œil*, no. 171 (Mar. 1969), 28–32, 76.

Saloman, Jacques. "Chez Monet, avec Vuillard et Roussel." *L'Œil*, no. 197 (May 1971), 20–25.

Critical Response

Flint, Kate, ed. *Impressionists in England: The Critical Reception*. London, 1984.

Geffroy, Gustave. *La Vie artistique*. 8 vols. Paris, 1892–1903.

Levine, Stephen Z. *Monet and His Critics*. New York, 1976.

Mirbeau, Octave. *Des artistes*. Paris, vol. I (1888–96), 1922; vol. II (1897–1912), 1924.

Reutersvärd, Oscar. "The 'Violettomania' of the Impressionists." *Journal of Aesthetics and Art Criticism* (Dec. 1950), 106–10.

Stuckey, Charles F., ed. *Monet: A Retrospective*. New York, 1985.

Zola, Emile. *Salons*. Edited by F. W. J. Hemmings and Robert J. Ness. Geneva and Paris, 1959.

Monographs (in chronological order)

Alexandre, Arsène. *Claude Monet*. Paris, 1921.

Geffroy, Gustave. *Claude Monet, sa vie, son temps, son œuvre*. Paris, 1922.

Elder, Marc [pseud. Marcel Tendron]. *A Giverny, chez Claude Monet*. Paris, 1924.

Hoschedé, Jean-Pierre. *Claude Monet, ce mal connu*. 2 vols. Geneva, 1960.

Seitz, William C. *Claude Monet*. New York, [1960].

Mount, Charles Merrill. *Monet*. New York, 1966.

House, John. *Claude Monet: His Aims and Methods*. Ph.D., University of London, 1976.

Isaacson, Joel. *Observation and Reflection: Claude Monet*. Oxford, 1978.

Gordon, Robert, and Andrew Forge. *Monet*. New York, 1983.

Rewald, John, and Frances Weitzenhoffer, eds. *Aspects of Monet: A Symposium on the Artist's Life and Times*. New York, 1984.

House, John. *Monet: Nature into Art*. New Haven and London, 1986.

Spate, Virginia. *Claude Monet: Life and Work*. New York, 1992.

Tucker, Paul Hayes. *Claude Monet*. New Haven and London, 1995.

Retrospective Exhibitions (in chronological order)

Claude Monet: Exposition Rétrospective. Exh. cat. Musée de l'Orangerie, Paris, 1931.

Claude Monet. Exh. cat. Edinburgh Festival and Tate Gallery, London, 1957.

Seitz, William C. *Claude Monet*. Exh. cat. City Art Museum, St. Louis, and the Minneapolis Institute of Art, 1957.

Seitz, William C. *Claude Monet: Seasons and Moments*. Exh. cat. The Museum of Modern Art, New York, 1960.

Wildenstein, Daniel. *Monet et la peinture de plein-air*. Exh. cat. Galerie Durand-Ruel, Paris, 1970.

Monet. Exh. cat. National Museum of Western Art, Tokyo, 1982.

Adhémar, Hélène, et al. *Hommage à Claude Monet*. Exh. cat. Galeries nationales du Grand Palais, Paris, 1982.

Claude Monet. Exh. cat. Museo español de arte contemporáneo, Madrid, 1986.

Claude Monet–Auguste Rodin: Centenaire de l'exposition de 1889. Exh. cat. Musée Rodin, Paris, 1989.

Monet: A Retrospective. Exh. cat. Bridgestone Museum of Art, Tokyo, 1994.

Monet's Technique

Bomford, David, Jo Kirby, John Leighton, and Ashok Roy. *Art in the Making: Impressionism*. Exh. cat. The National Gallery, London, 1990.

Callen, Anthea. *Techniques of the Impressionists*. London, 1987.

Callen, Anthea. "The Unvarnished Truth: Mattness, 'Primitivism' and Modernity in French Painting, c. 1870–1907." *Burlington Magazine* 86, no. 1100 (Nov. 1994), 738–46.

Herbert, Robert. "Method and Meaning in Monet." *Art in America* 67, no. 5 (Sept. 1979), 90–108.

Welton, Jude. *Monet*. London, 1992.

Periods and Painting Campaigns (in chronological order)

Caricatures

Edwards, Hugh. "The Caricatures of Claude Monet." *Bulletin of The Art Institute of Chicago* 37, no. 5 (Sept.–Oct. 1943), 71–72.

Georgel, Pierre. "Monet, Bruyas, Vacquerie et le Panthéon Nadar." *Gazette des Beaux-Arts* 72 (1968), 331–34.

Walter, Rodolphe. "Claude Monet as a Caricaturist." *Apollo* (June 1976), 488–93.

The 1860s

Isaacson, Joel. *The Early Paintings of Claude Monet*. Ph.D. University of California, Berkeley, 1967.

Isaacson, Joel. *Monet: Le Déjeuner sur l'herbe*. London, 1972.

Needham, Gerald. *The Paintings of Claude Monet, 1859–78*. Ph.D. New York University, 1970.

London

Bowness, Alan, and Anthea Callen. *The Impressionists in London*. Exh. cat. Hayward Gallery, London, 1973.

House, John. "The Impressionist Vision of London." In *Victorian Artists and the City*, edited by F. S. Schwarzbach and Ira Bruce Nadel, 78–90. New York, 1980.

House, John. "New Material on Monet and Pissarro in London, 1870–71." *Burlington Magazine* 120, no. 907 (Oct. 1978), 636–42.

Seiberling, Grace. *Monet in London*. Exh. cat. High Museum of Art, Atlanta, 1989.

Shanes, Eric. *Impressionist London*. New York, 1994.

Holland

Monet in Holland. Exh. cat. Rijksmuseum Vincent van Gogh, Amsterdam, 1986.

Argenteuil

Tucker, Paul Hayes. *Monet at Argenteuil*. New Haven and London, 1982.

Belle-Ile

Delouche, Denise. *Monet à Belle-Ile*. Rennes, 1991.

Normandy

Herbert, Robert. *Monet on the Normandy Coast: Tourism and Painting, 1867–1886*. New Haven, 1994.

Americans in Giverny

Gerdts, William H. *American Impressionism*. New York, 1984.

Gerdts, William H. *Monet's Giverny: An Impressionist Colony*. New York, 1993.

Gerdts, William H., et al. *Lasting Impressions: American Painters in France, 1865–1915*. Exh. cat. Musée Américain, Giverny, 1992.

Huth, Hans. "Impressionism Comes to America." *Gazette des Beaux-Arts*, 6th ser., 29 (April 1946), 225–52.

Meixner, Laura L., et al. *An International Episode: Millet, Monet, and Their North American Counterparts*. Exh. cat. Dixon Gallery and Gardens, Memphis, 1982.

Sellin, David. *Americans in Brittany and Normandy, 1860–1910*. Exh. cat. Phoenix Art Museum, 1982.

The 1890s Series Paintings

Brettell, Richard R. "Monet's Haystacks Reconsidered." *The Art Institute of Chicago Museum Studies* 11, no. 1 (Fall 1984), 5–21.

Hamilton, George Heard. *Monet's Paintings of Rouen Cathedral*. Charleton Lectures on Art [1959]. London, 1960.

Pissarro, Joachim. *Monet's Cathedral: Rouen, 1892–1894*. New York, 1990.

Rouen: Les Cathédrals de Monet. Exh. cat. Musée des Beaux-Arts, Rouen, 1994.

Seiberling, Grace. *Monet's Series*. New York, 1981.

Tucker, Paul Hayes. *Monet in the '90s: The Series Paintings*. Exh. cat. Museum of Fine Arts, Boston, 1989.

Norway

Hellandsjø, Karin. *Monet i Norge*. Exh. cat. Sonja Henies og Niels Onstads Stiftelser, Blommenholm, Norway, 1974.

Monet in Norway. Exh. cat. Rogaland Kunstmuseum, Stavanger, Norway, 1995.

Venice

Piguet, Philippe. *Monet et Venise*. Paris, 1986.

Giverny and the Water Lilies Paintings

Alexandre, Arsène. "Le Jardin de Monet." *Le Figaro* (Aug. 9, 1901).

Clemenceau, Georges. *Claude Monet: The Water Lilies*. New York, 1930. Originally published as *Claude Monet: Les Nymphéas*. Paris, 1928.

Geelhaar, Christian, et al. *Claude Monet: Nymphéas; Impression Vision*. Exh. cat. Kunstmuseum Basel, 1986.

Gordon, Robert. "The Changing Inspiration of Monet: The Lily Pond at Giverny." *Connoisseur* (Nov. 1973), 154–65.

Guillaud, Jacqueline, and Maurice Guillaud, eds. *Claude Monet au temps du Giverny*. Exh. cat. Centre culturel du Marais, Paris, 1983. Also published as *Claude Monet at the Time of Giverny* (Paris, 1983).

Hoog, Michel. *Les Nymphéas de Claude Monet au Musée de l'Orangerie*. Paris, 1984.

House, John. "Monet's Watergarden and the Second Waterlily Series (1903–9)." In *Claude Monet at the Time of Giverny*, edited by

Jacqueline and Maurice Guillaud, 150–96. Exh. cat. Centre culturel du Marais, Paris, 1983.

Joyes, Claire. *Monet's Table: The Cooking Journals of Claude Monet*. New York, 1989.

Joyes, Claire, Robert Gordon, Jean-Marie Toulgouat, and Andrew Forge. *Monet at Giverny*. London, 1975.

Joyes, Claire, and Jean-Marie Toulgouat. *Claude Monet: Life at Giverny*. New York, 1985.

Kahn, G. Maurice. "Le Jardin de Claude Monet." *Le Temps* (June 7, 1904).

Marx, Roger. "Les Nymphéas de M. Claude Monet." *Gazette des Beaux-Arts*, 4th ser., 1 (June 1909), 523–31.

Rouart, Denis, and Jean-Dominique Rey. *Monet Nymphéas ou les miroirs du temps*. Catalogue raisonné of the *Water Lilies* by Robert Maillard. Paris, 1972.

Stuckey, Charles F. *Monet: Water Lilies*. New York, 1988.

Stuckey, Charles F., and Robert Gordon. "Blossoms and Blunders: Monet and the State." *Art in America* 67, nos. 1 and 5 (Jan.–Feb. and Sept. 1979), 102, 117–25; 109–25.

Truffaut, Georges. "Le Jardin de Claude Monet." *Jardinage* (Nov. 1924), 55–59.

Wildenstein, Daniel. *Monet's Years at Giverny: Beyond Impressionism*. Exh. cat. The Metropolitan Museum of Art, New York, 1978.

Monet's Cataracts

Dittiere, Monique. "Comment Monet recouvra la vue après l'opération de la cataracte." *Sandorama*, no. 32 (Jan.–Feb. 1973), 26–32.

Ravin, James G. "Monet's Cataracts." *Journal of the American Medical Association* 254, no. 3 (July 19, 1985), 394–99.

Walter, Rodolphe. *Le Médecin de Claude Monet: Jean Rebière*. Paris, 1986.

Lenders to the Exhibition

Names of public institutions and private collectors
are followed by catalogue numbers.

Public Institutions

Brazil
Museo de Arte de São Paulo Assis
Chauteaubriand: 94

Canada
National Gallery of Canada, Ottawa: 66

Denmark
Ny Carlsberg Glyptotek, Copenhagen: 83

Ordrupsgaardsamlingen, Copenhagen: 9

France
Musée d'Orsay, Paris: 5, 17, 20, 40, 46, 123, 144

Musée des Beaux-Arts André Malraux, Le Havre: 127

Musée des Beaux-Arts de Caen: 129

Musée des Beaux-Arts, Grenoble: 151

Musée des Beaux-Arts de Nantes: 153

Musée Marmottan, Paris: 51, 124, 145, 146, 149, 150

Germany
Kaiser Wilhelm Museum, Krefeld: 121

Nationalgalerie, Berlin: 41

Niedersächsisches Landesmuseum, Hannover: 53

Staatsgalerie Stuttgart: 63

Great Britain
Courtauld Institute, London: 88

National Galleries of Scotland, Edinburgh: 7

National Gallery of Art, London: 21, 49

The National Museum of Wales, Cardiff: 143

Hungary
Szépmüvészeti Museum, Budapest: 22

Israel
The Israel Museum, Jerusalem: 134

Italy
Galleria Nazionale d'Arte Moderna e
Contemporanea, Rome: 111

Japan
Bridgestone Museum of Art, Ishibashi Foundation, Tokyo: 136

Kuboso Memorial Museum of Art, Osaka: 135

The National Museum of Western Art, Tokyo: 93

Tokyo Fuji Art Museum: 142

The Netherlands
Haags Gemeentemuseum, The Hague: 68

Norway
Nasjonalgalleriet, Oslo: 80

Switzerland
Kunsthaus Zürich: 122, 159

Kunstmuseum Basel: 154

Musée d'art et d'histoire, Neuchâtel: 47

United States
Allen Memorial Art Museum, Oberlin, Ohio: 10

The Brooklyn Museum: 67, 118

The Carnegie Museum of Art, Pittsburgh: 158

Sterling and Francine Clark Art Institute, Williamstown, Massachusetts: 79

The Cleveland Museum of Art: 25, 59

Columbus Museum of Art, Columbus, Ohio: 86, 152

The Currier Gallery of Art, Manchester, New Hampshire: 19

Dallas Museum of Art: 141

The Dayton Art Institute, Dayton, Ohio: 126

Denver Art Museum: 128

The Fogg Art Museum, Harvard University Art Museums, Cambridge, Massachusetts: 16

Joslyn Art Museum, Omaha, Nebraska: 54, 75

Kimbell Art Museum, Fort Worth, Texas: 4

The Metropolitan Museum of Art, New York: 3, 11, 13, 18, 31, 60, 71

The Minneapolis Institute of Arts: 102, 155

Museum of Fine Arts, St. Petersburg, Florida: 119

Museum of Fine Arts, Boston: 43, 45, 105

Museum of Fine Arts, Houston: 133

The Museum of Modern Art, New York: 157

National Gallery of Art, Washington, D.C.: 14, 37, 42

The Nelson-Atkins Museum, Kansas City: 39

North Carolina Museum of Art, Raleigh: 70

Norton Gallery of Art, West Palm Beach, Florida: 76

The Parrish Art Museum, Southhampton, New York: 8

Philadelphia Museum of Art: 36, 38, 90

The Phillips Collection, Washington, D.C.: 110

Portland Art Museum, Portland, Oregon: 147

Princeton University, The Art Museum, Princeton: 113

San Diego Museum of Art: 2

San Francisco Museum of Modern Art: 48

Shelburne Museum, Vermont: 56, 106

The Toledo Museum of Art, Ohio: 87

Wadsworth Atheneum, Hartford, Connecticut: 131

The Walters Art Gallery, Baltimore: 26

Worcester Art Museum, Worcester, Massachusetts: 140

Private Collectors

Her Majesty Queen Elizabeth The Queen Mother: 91

Fondation Rau pour le Tiers-Monde, Zurich: 29, 84

The Rothschild Art Foundation: 109

Sara Lee Corporation: 27

Gregory Callimanopulos: 138

Ralph T. Coe: 112

Mrs. Harvey Kaplan: 148

Mr. and Mrs. Herbert Klapper: 44, 64

Janice H. Levin: 32

Lucille Ellis Simon: 34

Mrs. John Hay Whitney: 33

Sallyan Windt: 58

Anonymous Lenders: 23, 24, 30, 35, 52, 57, 61, 62, 65, 69, 72, 73, 74, 78, 82, 85, 89, 103, 104, 125, 132, 137, 139, 156

Acknowledgments

James N. Wood proposed the idea for *Claude Monet: 1840–1926*, and he has played an enormous role in facilitating and advising every facet of the project. Douglas W. Druick, the Searle Curator of European Paintings and Prince Trust Curator of Prints and Drawings at the Art Institute, despite his own enormous interest in Impressionism and his departments' rich holdings in works by Monet, generously allowed me to guide this particular project and has been a source of support throughout its organization.

Acknowledging the contributions of all those involved in this project brings me to an especially satisfying pause from the relentless demands of such a large exhibition. This satisfaction is imperfect only from my inability to recall everyone who extended a helping hand along the way, from my awareness that condensed into this standard format the thanks is by definition insufficient, and from not knowing where to start.

It is fair to say that nearly every individual working at The Art Institute of Chicago has given considerable special effort to bring this catalogue and exhibition to realization. By fundraising, applying for federal indemnification, negotiating loans and shipping, overseeing conservation reports, handling the works, preparing for and serving visitors, and arranging for a wide variety of special educational programs, employees from every department of the museum have come together to present this important exhibition. It is a pleasure to acknowledge the following of my Art Institute colleagues for special thanks: Calvert W. Audrain, Reynold V. Bailey, Geraldine Banik, Judith A. Barter, Sally Bernard, D. Neil Bremer, John E. Bruyn, Michael Cayson, David Chandler, Blenda

T. Chinn, Jane H. Clarke, Jay Clarke, Tracie E. Nappi, Craig Cox, Robert T. Cozzolino, Lyn DelliQuadri, Courtney Graham Donnell, Brian Durand, Teri J. Edelstein, Victor Emeric, Robert W. Eskridge, Sanna L. Evans, Larry J. Feinberg, Donna Forrest, Katherine Houck Fredrickson, Edith B. Gaines, Gloria Groom, Madeleine Grynsztejn, Eileen Harakal, Faith Brabanec Hart, Todd Havel, John Foley Hindman, Richard Holland, Noriko Horie, Mary Kaiser, Robert B. Koverman, Mary H. Kuzniar, Maureen Lasko, Timothy J. Lennon, Stephen Little, Bryan Miller, Michael Mogilner, John A. Molini, Annie Morse, Mary Mulhern, Alan B. Newman, Jeffrey Nigro, Barbara A. Nobares, Molly S. Obourn, Christine O'Neill, Gregory J. Perry, Susan E. Perry, Alexis Petroff, George T. Preston, Ronald G. Pushka, Mollie Reiss, Susan F. Rossen, George P. Schneider, Dorothy M. Schroeder, Daniel Schulman, Kevin Sharp, Robert V. Sharp, Mary Solt, Steven D. Starling, Harriet K. Stratis, Pamela Stuedemann, Martha Tedeschi, Larry R. Ter Molen, Karin Victoria, Barbara J. Voss, Ann Wassmann, Faye Wrubel, and Frank Zuccari.

Without generous and supportive lenders, private and institutional, no exhibition is possible, and my thanks here can scarcely compensate them, both for the absence of their works for so many months and for the time involved with correspondence. I thank the directors, curators, registrars, photographers, art handlers, and shippers at the lending institutions, all of whom found time to handle the laborious essential details involved in every single loan arrangement; and I consider the efforts of private collectors, working without the assistance of these specialists, heroic. The extraordinary support, beginning at the inception of this project, of several particular lending institutions must be acknowledged as the foundation for our success: in Paris, the Musée d'Orsay and the Musée Marmottan; and in New York, The Metropolitan Museum of Art. I would like to emphasize, however, that the loans from the museums and collectors with fewer works by Monet often represent comparable or even greater sacrifices of their precious resources.

Besides the works themselves, information is the essential ingredient in a special exhibition. Where Monet is concerned, my own personal debts stretch back to the late 1970s and I wish first of all to thank the individuals who have supported my interest in the artist throughout these many years. Robert Gordon got me going when he showed me copies of family photographs that belonged to Monet's great-grandson, painter Jean-Marie Toulgouat and his wife, writer Claire Joyes, who have since become good friends. At that time I also received enormous help from the late Charles Durand-Ruel and his family, and from André Wormser, president of the Musée Clemenceau. These individuals continue to be an invaluable resource of archival information. Elizabeth C. Baker, editor of *Art in America*, encouraged Robert Gordon and me to publish new findings about Monet's final murals in that magazine, and as a result of those articles, the late John Rewald, who more than anyone brought Impressionism back to life for generations of readers, took me under his wing and introduced me to Barnabus McHenry, who guided Mrs. Lila Acheson Wallace's support of the restoration of Monet's house and gardens at Giverny, under the supervision of Gérald and Florence van der Kemp. Most importantly, John Rewald introduced me to Daniel Wildenstein, then compiling his monumental catalogue raisonné of Monet's work and the most thorough biography of the painter. Publisher Hugh H. Levin subsequently encouraged me to write texts for two beautifully produced books about Monet, projects that have brought me into dialogue with generous-minded Monet scholars such as Frances Weitzenhoffer and Hélène Adhémar, both now deceased; and others including Andrew Forge, George Heard Hamilton, Robert L. Herbert, John House, Joel Issacson, Charles S. Moffett, and Ronald Pickvance, all still fielding questions from me. In the last few years, while I have been compiling this catalogue, Paul Hayes Tucker and Joachim Pissarro have been especially helpful colleagues, taking calls sometimes day after day to help answer specialized questions.

Among the scholars, curators, dealers, and friends (many of them playing several of these roles at once), without whose understanding help this project would have been impossible, my heartfelt thanks go to: William R. Acquavella, Noriko Adachi, Rachel Adler, Alexander Apsis, Janine Bailly-Herzberg, Timothy Bathurst, William Beadleston, Frances Beatty, Robert Boardingham, J. Carter Brown, John Buchanan, Françoise Cachin, Dennis Cate, Desmond L. Corcoran, James Cuno, France Daquet, Donna De Salvo, Marianne Delafond, Philip Diotallevi, Maureen Duggan, Everett Fahy, James G. Faulkner, Richard L. Feigen, Walter Feilchenfeldt, Michael Findlay, Franck Giraud, Caroline Durand-Ruel Godfroy, Arnaud d'Hauterives, Tokushichi Hasegawa, Ay-Whang Hsia, Phillip M. Johnston, Sona Johnston, William R. Johnston, Steven Z. Levine, Margaret J. Lee, Christopher Lloyd, Henri Loyrette, Duncan MacGuigan, Neil McGregor, Patrice Marandel, Caroline Mathieu, Evan M. Maurer, Yutaka Mino, Philippe de Montebello, Mimi Muray, David Nash, Michèle Paret, Michael Pantazzi, Philippe Piguet, Edmund P. Pillsbury, Brenda Richardson, Joseph P. Rishel, William H. Robinson, Allen Rosenbaum, André Salomon, Margot Schab, George Schackleford, Manuel Schmit, Robert Schmit, Susan Seidel, David Setford, John W. Smith, Susan A. Stein, Cynthia Stowe, Michel Strauss, Martin Summers, Shuji Takashina, Mikinosuke Tanabe, Gary Tinterow, James Ulak, Kirk Varnedoe, John Vinci, Ian Wakeham, Gabriel Weisberg, Eric Zafran, and Alyssa Zeller.

Finally, it is with pride that I single out the cheerful and selfless professional help and gracious determination provided by members of my own department and exhibition staff, who did everything asked of them, including hours and weeks of extra work, for years, with little if any room for error or delay, and then themselves thought of still more to do to make this retrospective and publication as meaningful as possible. At the outset this team included Nina Gordon and Katharina Wolfe. Developing and working on the exhibition through its completion were Nicholas Barron, Kate Heston, Barbara Mirecki, Britt Salvesen, and Sophia Shaw, assisted by Jacqueline Henry, our Paris research correspondent.

Charles F. Stuckey
Frances and Thomas Dittmer Curator of Twentieth-Century Painting and Sculpture
The Art Institute of Chicago

Index

Photography Credits

Note: All photographs of works of art in the collections of The Art Institute of Chicago illustrated in this catalogue are © The Art Institute of Chicago. All other photography credits are listed below, including material supplied by other institutions, agencies, or individual photographers. Wherever possible photographs have been credited to the original photographers, regardless of the source of the photograph. Where no credit is given, photographs appear courtesy of the lender(s).

Front cover (cat. no. 128): Denver Museum of Art.

Frontispiece: © Agence photographique de la réunion des musées nationaux, Paris.

Plates

Cat. no. 2: San Diego Museum of Art. **3, 11, 13, 18, 31, 60, 71:** All rights reserved, The Metropolitan Museum of Art, New York. **4:** Michael Bodycomb. **5, 17, 20, 46, 123, 144:** © Agence photographique de la réunion des musées nationaux, Paris. **7:** Picture Library, National Galleries of Scotland. **8:** Noel Rowe. **9:** Ole Woldbye. **10:** Allen Memorial Art Museum, Oberlin College, Ohio. **14, 37, 42:** © 1994 Board of Trustees, National Gallery of Art, Washington, D.C. **16:** The Harvard University Art Museums. **19:** The Currier Gallery of Art, Manchester, New Hampshire. **21, 49:** Courtesy the Trustees of the National Gallery, London. **22:** Józsa Dénes. **24:** Acquavella Galleries, Inc. **25, 59:** © The Cleveland Museum of Art. **26:** The Walters Art Gallery. **29, 84:** Peter Schälchli, Zurich. **30:** Sarah Wells, New York. **32:** Richard Carafelli. **33:** Eric Pollitzer, New York. **35:** Los Angeles County Museum of Art. **36, 38:** Philadelphia Museum of Art. **39:** The Nelson-Atkins Museum of Art, Kansas City, Missouri. **40:** Rene Gabriel Ojéda. **41:** Jörg P. Anders, Berlin. **43, 45, 105:** Museum of Fine Arts, Boston. **44, 64, 65, 132:** Ali Elai, New York. **47:** Musée d'art et d'histoire, Neuchâtel, Switzerland. **48:** San Francisco Museum of Modern Art. **51, 124, 145, 146, 149, 150:** Musée Marmottan, Paris. **52, 57, 120, 137:** Galerie Nichido, Tokyo. **53:** Niedersächsisches Landesmuseum, Hannover. **54, 75:** Joslyn Art Museum, Omaha, Nebraska. **56, 106:** Shelburne Museum, Shelburne, Vermont, photograph by Ken Burris. **58, 148:** Michael Tropea, Chicago. **62, 66:** National Gallery of Canada, Ottawa. **63:** Staatsgalerie Stuttgart. **67, 118:** The Brooklyn Museum. **68:** Haags Gemeentemuseum, The Hague. **69:** Scott Hagar. **70:** North Carolina Museum of Art, Raleigh. **72:** Melville McClean. **73:** Est-Ouest S. A. R. L., Tokyo. **74:** M. Wörndl. **76:** Norton Gallery and School of Art, West Palm Beach, Florida. **79:** Sterling and Francine Clark Art Institute, Williamstown, Massachusetts. **80:** Nasjonalgalleriet, Oslo, photograph by J. Lathion. **82:** Skip Comer. **83:** Ny Carlsberg Glyptotek, Copenhagen. **85:** Sarah Lewis. **86, 152:** Columbus Museum of Art, Columbus, Ohio. **87:** The Toledo Museum of Art, Toledo, Ohio. **88:** Courtauld Institute Galleries, London. **89:** The Art Institute of Chicago. **90:** Graydon Wood. **91:** © 1995 Her Majesty Queen Elizabeth The Queen Mother. **93:** The National Museum of Western Art, Tokyo. **94:** Luis Hossaka. **102, 155:** The Minneapolis Institute of Arts. **103:** Jon Abbott. **104:** Greg Heins, Boston. **110:** The Phillips Collection, Washington, D.C. **111:** Alessandro Vasari, Rome. **112:** Courtesy Ralph T. Coe. **113:** Clem Fiori. **119:** Museum of Fine Arts, St. Petersburg, Florida. **121:** Volker Döhne. **122, 159:** © 1994 Copyright by Kunsthaus Zürich. All rights reserved. **125, 141:** Dallas Museum of Art. **126:** The Dayton Art Institute, Dayton, Ohio. **127:** Jean-Louis Coquerel. **129:** Martine Seyve. **131:** Wadsworth Atheneum, Hartford, Connecticut. **133:** The Museum of Fine Arts, Houston. **134:** © The Israel Museum, photograph by R. Terry. **135:** Kuboso Memorial Museum of Art, Osaka. **136:** Bridgestone Museum of Art, Ishibashi Foundation, Tokyo. **138:** Courtesy Gregory Callimanopulos, New York. **139:** Courtesy Sotheby's London. **140:** Worcester Art Museum, Worcester, Massachusetts. **142:** Tokyo Fuji Art Museum. **143:** The National Museum of Wales, Cardiff. **147:** The Portland Art Museum, Portland, Oregon. **151:** Musée de Grenoble. **153:** © P. Jean. **154:** Oeffentliche Kunstsammlung Basel, photograph by Martin Bühler. **156:** David Gulick. **157:** © 1995 The Museum of Modern Art, New York. **158:** Richard Stoner.

Chronology

Fig. no. 1: Courtesy the Board of Trustees of the Victoria and Albert Museum, London. **2, 3, 5, 9, 14, 17, 19, 21, 24, 27, 28, 30, 33, 37, 39, 44, 45, 49, 50, 54, 67, 115, 116:** © Agence photographique de la réunion des musées nationaux, Paris. **4, 22, 25, 26, 35, 56, 61, 77, 91, 96, 105:** Musée Marmottan, Paris. **6:** Phoenix Art Museum. **7, 40, 62, 86, 92:** Museum of Fine Arts, Boston. **8, 47, 48, 53, 74, 75, 79, 81, 83, 84, 103, 106, 111:** Collection Toulgouat. **10:** Pushkin State Museum of Fine Arts, Moscow. **11:** Rheinisches Bildarchiv, Cologne. **12:** From Virginia Spate, *The Colour of Time: Claude Monet* (London, 1992), 30. **13:** Kunsthalle Bremen. **15:** Artothek. **16:** Nationalmuseum, Stockholm. **18:** The Barber Institute of Fine Arts, The University of Birmingham, Great Britain. **23:** Shelburne Museum, Shelburne, Vermont, photograph by Ken Burris. **29:** Artothek, photograph by Joachim Blauel. **31:** © The Detroit Institute of Arts, City of Detroit Purchase. **32:** Musée du Petit Palais, Geneva. **34:** Musée des Beaux-Arts, Rouen. **38:** © Photothèque des musées de la ville de Paris, SPADEM. **41, 42, 78, 89, 104:** Document Archives Durand-Ruel, Paris. **43:** © Hunterian Art Gallery, University of Glasgow, Birnie Philip Bequest. **46:** Tate Gallery, London. **51:** From *Monet–Rodin*, 45. **52, 73, 88:** All rights reserved, Document Archives Durand-Ruel. **55:** Roger-Viollet, Paris. **57, 58:** © 1994 Courtesy Terra Museum of American Art, Chicago. **59:** Museum of Art, Rhode Island School of Design, Providence. **60:** © 1994 Board of Trustees, National Gallery of Art, Washington, D.C., photograph by Richard Carafelli. **63:** All rights reserved, The Metropolitan Museum of Art, New York. **64:** Courtesy Kirk Varnedoe. **65, 66, 82, 90, 98, 101, 102:** © Collection Philippe Piguet. **68, 71, 107:** © 1995 Sotheby's Inc. **69, 70, 72:** Lilla Cabot Perry Papers, Archives of American Art, Smithsonian Institution, Washington, D.C. **76:** National Gallery of Canada, Ottawa. **80:** Fotostudio Otto 1991. **85:** Rijksmuseum Twenthe, Enschede, The Netherlands. **87:** Artephot/Collection Sirot-Angel. **93:** Conservation des musées de la ville de Clermont-Ferrand. **94:** Courtesy Galerie Bernheim-Jeune, Paris. **95, 110:** Musée Clemenceau, Paris. **97:** From *L'Art et les artistes* (Oct. 1920–July 1921), 52. **99:** Bibliothèque nationale de France, Paris. **100:** The National Museum of Western Art, Tokyo. **108:** Photograph from Ciolkowska, 1923, p. 378. **109, 112:** Artephot/Musée Marmottan (Routhier). **113:** Copy print © 1994 The Museum of Modern Art, New York. **114:** L'Illustration/SYGMA.